THE PERIL OF
LOG BUILDING

THE PERIL OF LOG BUILDING

Raising a Voice for Log Building for Future Generations

ROB **PICKETT**

authorHOUSE®

AuthorHouse™
1663 Liberty Drive
Bloomington, IN 47403
www.authorhouse.com
Phone: 1-800-839-8640

Published by AuthorHouse   10/18/2012

ISBN: 978-1-4772-5545-2 (sc)
ISBN: 978-1-4772-5546-9 (e)

Library of Congress Control Number: 2012913981

Any people depicted in stock imagery provided by Thinkstock are models, and such images are being used for illustrative purposes only. Certain stock imagery © Thinkstock.

This book is printed on acid-free paper.

Because of the dynamic nature of the Internet, any web addresses or links contained in this book may have changed since publication and may no longer be valid. The views expressed in this work are solely those of the author and do not necessarily reflect the views of the publisher, and the publisher hereby disclaims any responsibility for them.

CONTENTS

ABSTRACT

Records show that log structures have been part of American heritage since colonization began. Log structures have historical relevance as homes, churches, schools, forts, ancient temples, hotels, resorts, and more. Whether simple, one-room structures of our pioneer past or complex hotels, log structures have remained a viable method of construction. Evolving from this heritage, the log home industry grew to over 400 handcrafters and manufacturers by the year 2000, providing homes and jobs to thousands who would have it no other way. With many different methods used to build log structures, it was an accomplishment when the industry came together with the International Code Council (ICC) to develop a consensus standard. Published by ICC in 2007, ICC400 *Standard on the Design and Construction of Log Structures* establishes criteria for evaluation of all methods of log home construction with consideration for structural and thermal performance, including settling allowance and fire resistance.

The log home industry serves a niche custom home market. Whether built to be a primary or second home, home owners relish the look and feel of their log homes. Log building systems rise from a foundation and subfloor with solid wood walls that support timber/log frame floor and roof structures. The common response from log home owners is that their home is warm, comfortable, and relaxing. For a log home owner, the on-going maintenance of a wood exposed to the environment is the only nuisance. Even in the cold climates of New England, homes built using log building systems experience lower energy consumption than their contemporary frame built homes.

This form of construction now faces many challenges—from accessibility of raw materials to obtaining the certificate of occupancy. The extent of these challenges is now threatening the livelihood of an entire network of individuals who work to make a new log home a reality. This network has enjoyed steady employment for the past several decades. Regulation and political platforms are well beyond the scope of this paper, but the recognition of a solid wood wall as an effective thermal envelope is a challenge that must be overcome. Current standards would tell us to use thicker log walls, but the expense of doing so will limit this form of construction to the upper end of the home buying market for reasons presented here. The questions are: How can this form of construction remain viable? How does the industry explain owner/occupant testimony to the performance of log homes over the past 50 years? And rather than looking for exceptions and exemptions to building energy codes, how does the world of building science and building standards explain the unpredictably low energy consumption of log homes in the cold climates of North America?

ACKNOWLEDGMENTS

It is extremely gratifying to be recognized for the work one does, especially by peers in the industry to which one is dedicated. I very much appreciate the recognition I have received and hope that this effort helps the log home industry now and in the future. I would like to thank those people and organizations that have specifically provided opportunities and supported my efforts. I am grateful to my friends and associates in the log home industry who, in one way or another, have contributed to my experience, and hence, this effort.

My professional association with the Log Homes Council began with my introduction by Steven Winter, Steven Winter Associates (SWA), which at the time was located in the Empire State Building, New York City. Among many interesting assignments, I was given the opportunity to advance the work that the SWA staff had already completed to establish a log grading standard. Many of my friends in the log home industry date back to contacts made while with SWA. While my efforts evolved further since, I am grateful to Mr. Winter and the others at SWA with whom I had the pleasure to work.

Further down the road, I am thankful to the two log home manufacturers that provided exceptional support for my activities on Log Homes Council (LHC) committees. The Real Log Homes family invited me to join them and allowed me to invest time as Chair of the LHC Grading Program, Chair of the Technical Committee, and 2 years on the LHC Steering Committee. With my move from Vermont to South Carolina, Southland Log Homes continued

that support for another 1-1/2 years. Southland was gracious in supporting my adventure into entrepreneurship as I established RobPickett &Associates, LLC on July 1, 2001.

There are many folks that I met through the LHC that became great friends with whom I have enjoyed many discussions and laughs. It was my pleasure to work with exceptional entrepreneurs and sales/marketing talents alongside experts in the fields of wood science, chemistry, and construction. The many years of collaborative committee work brought several rewarding experiences. Together, we developed tools for the Log Grading Program and several excellent technical documents that are widely spread through cyberspace! The contributions of subcommittee members to produce documents like *"Preservation & Maintenance of Log Structures"* and *"Prevention of Air & Water Infiltration"* were the key to these successful documents. And where would we have been without the stellar LHC support staff who provided invaluable support to the Technical Committee. We worked hard, balancing that with fun at President's Tour and BSC SHOWCASE events.

Back in Vermont after establishing RobPickett &Associates, my journey continued largely thanks to my family and my many friends and associates who make the industry the great one it is. To top the list are my partners in the Timber Technology Network, which spawned TimberLogic—Alex Charvat, PE, and Ed Burke, PhD. Our combined talents and interests give us a unique position for evaluating wood building systems. Together, we have done some

3

exceptional work on behalf of the LHC Log Grading Program, on the ICC400 log standard, and in the testing and analysis of innovative wood products and wood connections.

One of my most rewarding experiences came from the effort of the ICC IS-LOG Committee in creating ICC400. Originally coming from a wide divergence of opinions and perspectives, we eventually came together and recognized the commonality amidst the industry. Removing proprietary goals and interests, we realized that we all agreed on the end result. My compliments to the entire committee, friends of the committee and the ICC. The initial effort was so extensive that the effort for the 5-year update cycle involved a much smaller set of changes.

A constant positive influence from SWA days through his recruiting me to join Real Log Homes to his endless support to help me improve RP&A, Jerry Rouleau is missed. A mentor to many besides me, Jerry put his heart into everything he did. It is appropriate to end this section with a favorite closing of Jerry's . . .

Onward!

FOREWORD

I began my career in the log home industry in 1977 when I joined the design staff at Colorado Log Homes in Englewood, CO. After 35 years in and around the log home industry, I am still refreshed every time I stop for a grading inspection—by the dedication of the people, by the quality of the product, and by the smell and feel of the wood itself. The wonder of nature is recorded in every log that we visually inspect to determine the best use of the piece in a new home. While I have not yet had the opportunity to build my dream log home, I have spent much of my life working in log structures that housed my workplace. One day, I will build my own home and office with an appreciation for the rewarding career that I would like to enjoy until I retire.

It is unacceptable that the log home industry faces obsolescence because of building energy conservation codes.

The concept of this work is to present a factual review of a traditional building method void of bias toward any one philosophy or proprietary approach. There are many books written on log building, trees and forestry. Every day, there are more interesting pieces of information appearing—another old log home being restored for current use to a breakthrough in forest management to a new wood product that can help builders. If the information presented here can help another log structure be built to perform to high standards and last for many generations, my advocacy has been successful.

A thorough understanding of how log structures work and the methods that can be used will help insure that expected performance is achieved. Meeting expectations is every builder's goal, but many things can get in the way. In a small, niche market like this one, it takes a lot of successful projects to overcome the one that did not meet expectations. A key to building a custom log home (after all, most log homes are not in suburban planned unit developments) is in the planning, design and management of the project.

I share my passion for the log home industry with the many individuals who work in it or are otherwise associated with it. One friend of mine reminded me that one of the great things about log walls is that they are *WYSIWYG* (what you see is what you get). Another friend noted, "Isn't it amazing that this marvelous creation of Mother Nature called wood is such a mystery that after decades of study and testing, its thermal performance is still an unexplained phenomenon?"

This work is an effort to do just that—establish a quantifiable answer to how solid wood walls provide an energy efficient building. One objective is to explain why log home owners have repeatedly expressed gratitude for the energy efficiency, warmth and comfort of living in a log home. Another objective is to provide a platform for the industry to raise its voice and be heard where it otherwise may not.

THE PROBLEM . . .

The log home industry, as we know it today, is in jeopardy of being legislated out of business.

The primary problem with log building today is that the industry's voice is not loud enough. Overshadowed by the well-funded interests of competing building products and methods, not to mention Federal policy and mandates, the log building industry is comprised of hard-working folks who do not have the resources to campaign for their independent welfare.

> The **economy** continues to strangle the homebuilding industry (2008 through 2012), leaving the niche market of log homes with little resource for political action.

> The national effort to achieve a 2030 National Energy Independence generates increasing stress due to the need to demonstrate compliance with continually **changing building energy conservation codes** and standards that are geared toward insulation products and more common methods and materials of construction.

> Log walls do not readily conform to energy codes and require a different set of **evaluation criteria** that more accurately represents the testimonies of many log home owners who love the comfort and energy-efficient performance of their homes.

> The stress is amplified by political action of proponents who benefit in promoting the concept of **R-Value**. R-Value ratings provide fodder for emphatic presentations of the benefits of products. The problem is that R-Value is the basis for calculations that certify building energy performance, yet R-Values are based on static testing of heat transfer through a material. It does not account for real-world dynamic conditions affected by changes in temperature and air or vapor movement across and through the thermal envelope.

> And there is a concern for the many **existing log homes** that perform well today but may begin to have problems when "improved" in the name of "R-Value." What really happens when one adds insulation to a log wall?

DEFINING THE SCOPE

Log building is the theme, but the scope of the problem stems from the Federal R&D Agenda for Net-Zero Energy, High Performance Green Buildings Report, published by NIST in 2008[1]. Focused on commercial buildings, the impact carries over to residential construction as well. The report cites the 2007 DOE Building Energy Data Book for details of existing building energy usage and includes the following vision statement:

Buildings Technology Research and Development Vision

Enable designs of new buildings and retrofits of existing building that over the life cycle:

- Produce as much energy as they consume (net-zero energy) and significantly reduce GHGs.
- Double the service life of building materials, products, and systems and minimize life cycle impacts.
- Halve the use of domestic water (e.g., to 50 gal/day/person or less), maximize water recycling and rainwater harvesting, and minimize storm water runoff.
- Achieve breakthrough improvements in indoor occupant health, productivity, and comfort.

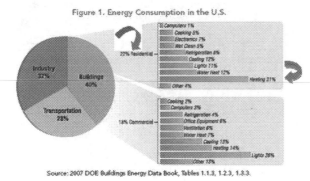

Figure 1. Energy Consumption in the U.S.

Source: 2007 DOE Buildings Energy Data Book, Tables 1.1.3, 1.2.3, 1.3.3.

Figure 1—Statistics point to home heating as a high priority for conserving energy. Source: 2007 DOE Building Energy Data Book

The characteristics of residential buildings reported from the 2005 American Housing Survey for the United States (HUD and DOC) provides a further breakdown—68% single-family housing, 25% multifamily, and 7% manufactured (HUD-code). If custom-built homes comprise 10% (perhaps 7% is more reasonable) in that statistic, then the percentage of custom homes would equal 1.5% of the national energy consumption. This would mean . . .

In the year 2000, if the log home market provided perhaps 2% of all custom homes, log homes were only 0.03% of the national energy consumption. This is why log homes are not on anyone's radar screen.

These statistics offer an indication of why log homes are not receiving attention in the drive to improve building energy conservation. The lack of attention and the economic distress of the industry combine to maintain the vacuum in standards development. However, building officials have asked for support so they are properly approving building permits. Based on their questions, the official Federal government response is provided on DOE's Energy Efficiency & Renewable Energy website (www.eren.gov) and repeated elsewhere (www.nwbuildnet. com/articles/loghomeeff.html).

It is imperative the log home industry establish evaluation methods that demonstrate the merits of log structures. This is the only way to convince building officials, state energy offices, and code development bodies that log buildings are beneficial to the building environment.

LOG BUILDING IN AMERICA

The log home industry supports the livelihood of many families across our nation. It is made up of traditional craftsmen and entrepreneurs who are proud custodians of forest environments that supply their single largest raw material.

This section covers

- The history and tradition of log building
- Relevance as an architectural style
- The log home market
- Products and services available
- Environmental impact
- Energy conservation
- Research on log homes that support the industry's claims of energy efficiency.

While the economy continues to strangle the homebuilding industry, the niche market of log homes is feeling the pain more than most. The stress is amplified by poor market conditions, issues with mortgage lending, and the national effort to achieve a 2030 National Energy Independence celebration. Mandating ever-changing building energy codes and standards, legislative action has become rampant due to political incentives. While today's log home industry is made up of many companies and families throughout the nation, these are typically not politically active people and their voice is not heard.

It is important to provide an approach to maintain an architectural emphasis to this traditional building system that is part of our national heritage. It is equally important to protect the economic viability of an industry that supports an extensive network of products and services. The log home industry supports more than builders and log home manufacturers, but includes the log supply network (e.g., private and national forest lands, loggers, haulers, sawmills), ancillary products (e.g., millwork, fasteners and connection hardware, sealants and adhesives, finishes), and services (e.g., independent sales representatives, design professionals, engineers, trucking companies).

HISTORICAL SIGNIFICANCE

Building with logs is an ancient form of construction dating back to 700 B.C. in Eastern Europe. Indigenous peoples of various continents have created a variety of log structures. Many log buildings are 300 years old and still functioning. Ranging from simple, often one-room pioneer structures to cathedrals, these log structures were built using renewable, readily available resources.

Native Americans used trees to build lean-tos, tepees, and other log pole structures with a variety of materials used to skin the structure for shelter from the weather. Log building in the western hemisphere benefitted from generations of European boat builders who learned how to stack full length logs that were supported by corner joinery. The horizontal seams between the logs were sealed with available materials, such as mud, straw, moss, etc. Some log buildings were built as temporary shelters, but where permanence was a goal, the logs were protected from weathering elements by roof overhangs, organic finishes from local ingredients, and other techniques.

Figure 2: Fort Christine, DE, restored. Circa 1650 Swedish settlement. Source: Steve Renzi, Delmarva Architecture, Spring 2006

Log structures have been a part of our American Heritage since settlers arrived in the 1600's. Craftsmen from the forests of Northern Europe, Northern Germany and Russia applied their knowledge to the woods of the New World. It has been reported that a Swedish settlement known as Fort Christina (in Delaware) was built about 1640 and consisted of a log palisade surrounding seven log buildings. During this same time, Dutch and English settlers were building structures with wood framing, brick and stone. In the Spring 2006 edition of *Delmarva Architecture*, Steve Renzi writes, "English and Dutch colonial reports almost always mentioned the great amount of sickness, especially pneumonia, amongst the settlers who lived in damp, drafty, and cold homes." In contrast, the Swedes did not experience the same fate.

The log cabin is an important political and cultural symbol of Americana—Where trees were available, log cabins became the typical frontier dwelling for waves of immigrants who built with the logs they had cleared from the land. Both Presidents Harrison and Lincoln are associated with log cabin heritage, although only Lincoln actually lived in one. Log construction was used for a variety of commercial and community buildings, including investments by railroads to attract riders west. Log structures built in the early 1900's continue to serve many Federal and State parks.

Figure 3: 1915 Harebell Cabin, back country Army cabin in Yellowstone National Park. Source: National Park Service

One of the best presentations of a log structure in the National Parks (home to more than 700 log structures[2]) is found at http://www.nps. gov/history/hps/tps/briefs/brief26.htm. Log construction was an easy choice for shelter because of the ease of construction and use of available materials. The Northeast Entrance Station of Yellowstone National Park was built in 1935 to the specifications of the Park Structures and Facilities. The native materials used in the Northeast Entrance Station are the logs and stone from the park, and the wood shingles of the roofs.

Figure 4: Theodore Roosevelt's Maltese Cross Cabin, ND ca 1884. Source: http://www.cr.nps. gov/logcabin/html/mc.html

A broad presentation of log building in the chronicals of the United States is available at http://www.cr.nps.gov/logcabin/. This site covers log cabin history as it relates to past U.S. Presidents. It includes the story of how Theodore Roosevelt built the Maltese Cross Cabin, a log home near Medora, ND in the 1880's. "Constructed of durable ponderosa pine logs that had been cut and floated down the Little Missouri River, the cabin was luxurious for its time, with wooden floors and three separate rooms (kitchen, living room, and Roosevelt's bedroom)." A testimony to the durability of log construction, "Although it is still in use as a cattle ranch, it is private property."[3]

Using Wikipedia for a quick reference, enter "log cabins" (http://en.wikipedia.org/wiki/ Log_cabin), and you will find an extensive discussion of the history, tradition, and symbolism of this form of construction. Enter "log homes" (http://en.wikipedia.org/wiki/ Log_home) and you will find a discussion of today's log home industry and relevant issues pertaining to log construction.

Comparing Log Building to Building Code & Regulation History

3500 BC—<u>Wikipedia</u> reports that the first log structures may date back to the Bronze Age in Northern Europe. Additional undated log structures were used by indigenous peoples of North America. Various Native American shelters (e.g., the wigwam, longhouse, tepee, grass house, or wattle and daub house) relied on pole structures on which they applied a variety of "skins"—early curtain walls.

2000 BC—Hammurabi, founder of the Babylonian Empire and known as an effective leader, wrote the earliest known code of law. Portions of the Hammurabi Code of Law dealt with building construction. Here are some translated examples of Hammurabi's Code of Law on Building Construction:

- No. 229: If a builder has built a house for a man and his work is not strong, and if the house he has built falls in and kills the householder, that builder shall be slain.
- No. 230: If the child of the householder is killed, the child of that builder shall be slain.
- No. 231: If the slave of the householder is killed, he shall give slave for slave to the householder.
- No. 232: If goods have been destroyed, he shall replace all that has been destroyed; and because the house was not made strong, and it has fallen in, he shall restore the fallen house out of his own material.
- No. 233: If a builder has built a house for a man, and his work is not done properly and a wall shifts, then that builder shall make that wall good with his own silver.

64 AD—When fire destroyed much of Rome, it was rebuilt in accordance with previously ignored principles of construction, sanitation and utility. Public and private building was closely controlled and monitored throughout the remainder of the realm of the Roman Empire.

1640 AD—Swedish settlement, known as Fort Christina (in Delaware), is founded.

1668—England's Parliament enacts the "London Building Act" in an attempt to prevent another devastating fire such as the 1666 fire that destroyed thousands of buildings in London.

1850—New York City adopts its first city building code.

1875—A building code and a fire prevention ordinance is enacted in Chicago, IL following the 1871 Chicago fire, the second most costly in American history.

1896—The <u>National Fire Protection Association</u> (NFPA) is founded and published its first code on sprinklers.

1902—National Lumber Manufacturers Association is founded.

1903-4—<u>Old Faithful Inn</u> constructed in Yellowstone National Park—a 7-story log wall and log frame structure.

1905—The National Board of Fire Underwriters publishes model building construction regulations.

1906—North American Construction, Bay City, MI, begins selling rail-shipped precut building out of a mail order plan book. The San Francisco Earthquake and Fire is the largest fire loss in U.S. history.

1914—Sears begins selling and financing rail-shipped precut buildings from a mail order plan book. Wisconsin adopts the first mandatory statewide building code.

1915—The Building Officials and Code Administrators International, Inc. (BOCA) is founded.

1920's—Royale A. Wright promotes a hollow log product that Art Clough actually invented. Two factories are built, one in Ontario, Canada and the other in Grayling, Michigan. In the 1930's, Canadian and U.S. patents are issued for the construction process using the hollow log called Air-Lock Logs.[4]

1922—The International Conference of Building Officials (ICBO) is founded.

1923—Bruce Ward, founder of Ward Cedar Log Homes, America's first manufactured log home company, pioneers modern log home construction techniques.

1927—ICBO's first edition of the Uniform Building Code (UBC) becomes the first model building code in the U.S. to include earthquake design criteria.

1932—Outside of Yellowstone National Park, a plat of Silver Gate, the small community just east of the entrance station, proposes that all of the structures in the community be of log construction.

1933—The first earthquake design legislation for schools (the Field Act) is enacted in California in 1933.

1940—The Southern Building Code Congress International, Inc. (SBCCI) is founded.

1945—SBCCI publishes the first edition of the Standard Building Code.

1946—National Log Construction establishes a milled log home company in the state of Montana. The company evolved from the Civilian Conservation Corps (CCC), established by the U.S. government to create jobs and teach skills.[5]

On Dec. 9, 1946, 119 people died in The Winecoff Hotel. It remains the deadliest hotel fire in U.S. history, the second worst hotel fire in world history, and prompted many changes in building codes.

1950—BOCA publishes the first edition of the BOCA National Building Code.

1965—National Forest Products Association (NFPA) is formed.

1966—BOCA publishes the BOCA Basic Fire Prevention Code.

1967—The National Conference of States on Building Codes and Standards, Inc. (NCSBCS) was established.

1971—ICBO publishes the first edition of the Uniform Fire Code.

1972—The Council of American Building Officials (CABO) is founded.

1976—In June 1976, Congress passes a building code to be administered by the US Department of Housing and Urban Development. The code ensured the construction of affordable housing on a federal level, superseding local building officials' authority to regulate mobile and manufactured homes in their communities. The US Weatherization Assistance Program (WAP) is created in 1976 to assist low-income families by reducing energy bills and decreasing dependency on foreign oil.

1977—The Log Homes Council (LHC) forms, holding its first meeting in Denver with 22 Charter Members represented. In Washington D.C., the U.S. Department of Energy is created to bring cabinet-level order to energy research and development.

1980—ASTM approves D3957 *Standard Practices for Establishing Stress Grades for Structural Members Used in Log Buildings.*

1981—National Evaluation Service publishes NES QA-154, accrediting the LHC Log Grading Program as a 3rd Party Inspection Agency. [Now accredited under the auspices of the International Accreditation Service—IAS.] CABO publishes the first *One- and Two-Family Dwelling Code.* NFPA forms the American Wood Council to address codes and engineering standards for wood construction.

1983—NBS thermal testing project is completed. CABO published the Model Energy Code (MEC). The 1998 edition of ICC's International Energy Conservation Code is the successor to the 1995 MEC.

1984—LHC mandates visual stress grading of log components as a requirement for membership.

1989—MEC is published with allowance for thermal mass wall construction.

1992—The European Community establishes the construction products and technologies initiative.

1994—The International Code Council (ICC) is established as a nonprofit organization dedicated to developing a single set of national mode construction codes.

1995—LHC submits a *Guideline for Construction Manuals* for log homes to US Dept. of Housing & Urban Development to support review of log buildings that are submitted for Federal financing.

1997—ICC publishes the International Urban Wildland Interface Code (IUWIC), recognizing log walls as a 1-hour fire-rated assembly when the minimum horizontal dimension is 6 inches.

2006—Completed the effort to integrate elements of ICC400 into REScheck, enhancing the ability of log home designers to evaluate the thermal performance of new home construction.

2007—ICC publishes ICC400 Standard on the Design & Construction of Log Structures.

2010—The ICC, ASHRAE, U.S. Green Building Council (USGBC), and Illuminating Engineering Society of North America (IES) launch the ANSI consensus process to develop the International Green Construction Code (IGCC). The American Wood Council (AWC) becomes independent of the American Forest & Paper Association.

2012—ICC publishes the first update of ICC400 Standard on the Design & Construction of Log Structures.

ARCHITECTURAL STYLE

"It recalls pioneers in the wilderness, felling trees and turning them into honest, simple shelters—the kind of place Abe Lincoln was born in," says architect Robert A.M. Stern. "Its spirit is irresistible to all of us. The beauty of log construction is that it provides its own structural logic—and even its own insulation," says Stern. "What you see is what you get, and this is why everyone loves logs."[6]

Log architecture is defined by features such as corner style, shape, size, and a uniform or hand-hewn finish. Common features in log home design include a log framing system for the second floor and roof. From historical uses and functional shelters to mountain retreats and tranquil rural dwellings, log architecture is craved by some. It is not only the link to our American Heritage, but a comfortable, peaceful lifestyle that attracts homebuyers. They love the natural elements.

The Entrance Station buildings designed and constructed at Yellowstone National Park exemplify why log buildings present a preferred architectural style. The following excerpt from "Architecture in the Parks" summarizes the attraction: [7]

> Rustic design is a style which, through the use of native materials in proper scale, and through the avoidance of rigid, straight lines, and over-sophistication, gives the feeling of having been executed by pioneer craftsmen with limited hand tools. It thus achieves sympathy with natural surroundings, and with the past. The native materials used in the Northeast Entrance Station are the logs and stone from the park, and the wood shingles of the roofs. The axe-cut log ends contribute to that frontier/pioneer feeling. The checking station in particular far exceeds those criteria by combining its solids (rooms) and voids (drive-throughs) with the sculptural quality of the concave log ends creating a highly mannered, expressive structure.

Northeast Entrance Station (detail)
Yellowstone National Park
Photo by L.S. Harrison. NPS 7/85

Figure 5: Northeast Entrance Station, Yellowstone National Park, 1985 [8] Source: National Park Service

Famous for its log architecture, the Adirondack region of upstate New York became the summer home of east coast urbanites during the industrial revolution. In the 1920's, pre-cut log home "kits" were introduced, featuring logs milled into shapes that were uniform along their entire length. Today, the design of log homes involve sophisticated design and engineering, often integrating computer aided design software that is capable of communicating with milling machinery to produce wall logs, joists, rafters, etc. that are ready to install without further modification on site.

Log homes can be quite simple and affordable when the exterior wall is of log while the rest of the home is built using common conventional methods (e.g., prefabricated wood roof trusses). Commonly, the cost of log building increases when timber frame roof systems are used. Over the framing is tongue and groove (T&G) lumber that provides both the structural roof deck and finish ceiling. Often called a double roof, lumber framing is added above the decking to provide a cavity for insulation. Increasingly, rigid foam insulation panels and structural insulated panels (SIPs) are replacing the double roof to get the necessary rated insulation value in less depth. Other cost factors include larger floor plans, more complicated designs (often reflected in the roof), and upgraded interior finish and fixture choices.

One premise of this discussion is that the requirement for increased log wall width will greatly reduce the affordability of a typical log home. While this is true, it is also recognized that log size is often selected because of the architectural scale of the project—again, the smaller affordable log home with economic log profiles versus a larger project with a sizable budget.

For those who are attracted to the log home motif, this style of design and construction is an important choice—often their dream home.

INDUSTRY & MARKET

What is the attraction? In a Q&A interview with Gastineau Log Homes President Lynn Gastineau (past Log Homes Council President and Building Systems Councils Board of Trustees Chair), Stacy Downs (sdowns@kcstar.com) reported in The Kansas City Star why people like log homes:

> "The thing I hear people say over and over is that they like the feeling they get when they go home. The adjectives I hear are nurturing, warm, homey, secure. They like that they're made of natural materials. The warmth comes from the wood."

Read more here: http://www.kansascity.com/2011/12/21/3330066/q-a-lynn-gastineau-new-bloomfield.html#storylink=cpy

No longer the one-room dwelling of settlers, today's log homes are identified as being higher-end, customized and widely desirable. In the mid-1980's, an average of 15,000 log packages were shipped annually. By 2003, that increased 73%, to more than 26,000 homes annually. In 2001, 30.5% or 388,265 of all new, single-family homes were custom built, according to the National Association of Home Builders and the Census Bureau. A niche market, the log home industry claims only 7% of 2001's custom home market which is only about 2% of the national new home market.

Appraisals of log homes can be tricky, as there may not be many log homes in a neighborhood, and if there are some, there is a good possibility that they may not have been resold. This means that appraisals may require comparables to a custom built home.

At the beginning of the 21st Century, the industry was estimated to generate $1.7 billion per year in revenue. This revenue represents a building materials package generally consisting of log components to build the walls, roof and loft/second floor of the structure as well as entrance doors, windows, and porch framing. Other ingredients provided in the material package typically included chinking materials, sealants, paint and finishes, fasteners, and adhesives. The log materials package was often said to be approximately one-third of the cost of building a log home, exclusive of land and land development. This would place the total economic impact of log homes built in the United States at over $5 billion annually.

The industry appears simple, but is actually an extensive family of participants that is illustrated in the carbon poster from The Forest Foundation (Figure 25). Sawmills develop long term network-type relationships with loggers, loggers with haulers, just as log builders rely on relationships with design and engineering firms. Access to raw materials and supplies are important elements of this industry, largely because of the increasing costs to transport logs and timbers and the fact that the use of native materials contributes to a form of regional branding that can increase a product's market value. A log home requires from 50 to several hundred logs, with an estimated average of about 200 logs per home. Log home producers use independent trucking companies with flatbed trailers to ship the material packages to the building site. Many log home companies sell through networks of independent dealers who arrange financing and may contract to erect the house. The trail from forest to building site involves well-established practices to maximize material use and minimize waste.

The log home industry is an integrated component of our national forestry industry. Some companies found that house logs were a byproduct (e.g., peeler operations creating plywood veneers leave a core that offers a uniform round house log), or a new product that would help their sawmill operations stay busy. It has a long history of working with the issues regarding available timber supply, from harvesting to a decline in sawmills. And for many years, log home producers have made use of standing dead timber (e.g., beetle or fire kill) that other wood industries declined to use.

PRODUCTS & SERVICES

With the growth in popularity of log homes in the 1960's and 70's, two periodicals evolved for and about the log home industry. For many years, *The Log Home Guide for Builders and Buyers* attempted to raise the standard for log building. Still going strong, Home Buyer Publication's *Log Home Living* works to provide a source of objective information in response to the questions that buyers were asking about the industry. Both gave a unique opportunity to market the products of log home companies and other companies that serve the industry or provide ancillary components from log furniture to antler chandeliers to specialty door hardware. A few other magazines have entered the picture to help producers market their products and to help prospective log home buyers find the right company for them.

The 2007 Annual Buyer's Guide[9] included a Products and Services section that included a table of details about log home companies and the building systems they offer. Updated annually, this information provided potential customers excellent comparisons as to what companies produced particular wood species, log profile styles and sizes, fasteners, design services, construction assistance, and other features and services. Based on well over 100 entries representing companies from both the United States and Canada, one can draw several conclusions about the existing log home built-inventory and new home options.

Compiling the data reveals that log home manufacturers average 75 to 100 homes per year, and handcrafted home builders produce 20 or less on average. Regardless of the location of the company, the market area extends across all of North America. White pine and cedar species dominate production, with Douglas fir, Lodgepole pine, and Engelmann spruce used by roughly half of companies surveyed. Other specialty species are also available, generally tied to industry resources in the region where the producer operates.

Further research of wood resources reveals that the log home industry provides a viable use of wood species that are not typically used for commercial lumber products. The industry can utilize standing dead timber killed by beetle or fire assuming they can gain access to it. The size of the logs is less sensitive because log companies can utilize smaller diameter trees, therefore standing dead that may not be attractive to commercial wood operations are attractive to log builders.

Also, it should be noted that knowledge of the wood species is essential in building and caring for a log system. Aspen or poplar may be available, but are they the right choice for the design?

Regional Variation

Wood species are generally a function of proximity of the mill to the natural resource surrounding it. The local, available source also makes it an economically desirable raw material. Some woods are selected because of their color and figure, while others are chosen for workability (profiling, staining, controlling drying effects) or durability (e.g., natural resistance to decay and insect attack). Some companies use drying and/or treating processes to improve both workability and durability.

To understand the industry, it is advantageous to look at the correlation of log home producers to the indigenous wood species in those regions. The table below divides the United States by the Mississippi River, describing log systems by Handcrafted Log Systems and Milled Log Systems. Based on limited data, this sample shows an interesting contrast.

Characteristic	Handcrafted Log Systems		Milled Log Systems	
	West	East	West	East
Producer Sample	17	11	27	63
Average Home Packages/Yr.	7	7	85	75
Primary Wood Species	Douglas fir, Lodgepole pine, Engelmann spruce	White pine, Red pine	Douglas fir, Lodgepole pine, Ponderosa pine, Engelmann spruce	White pine, Red pine, Southern pine
Specialty Wood Species	Red cedar	Red cedar, White cedar	Red cedar, oak, walnut	Red cedar, White cedar, Cypress
Drying Method	Air dry, standing dead timber	Air dry	Air dry, standing dead timber	Air dry, Kiln dry
Design Moisture Content	<19% MC	varies	<19% MC	<25% MC
Log Stack Heights	>10"	>10"	7" to >10"	6" to >10"
Nominal Log Widths	>10"	>10"	7" to >10"	6" to >10"
Horizontal Joinery	Cope/Notch	Cope/Notch	T&G*, flat on flat, Cope	T&G*, spline, flat on flat, Cope
Corner Style	Saddle notch, dovetail	Saddle notch, dovetail	Saddle notch/ interlock, dovetail, butt & pass, posted	Saddle notch/ interlock, dovetail, butt & pass, notch & pass, posted
Primary Log Style/ Profile	Natural logs, full round, tapered	Natural logs, full round, tapered	Inside: Uniform round / Flat, Round — Outside: Flat, Round	Inside: Flat, Round — Outside: Flat, Round

T&G = tongue and groove; includes single, double and triple T&G joint design.

Figure 6: A View of the Log Home Industry by region and method of construction. Source: Author.

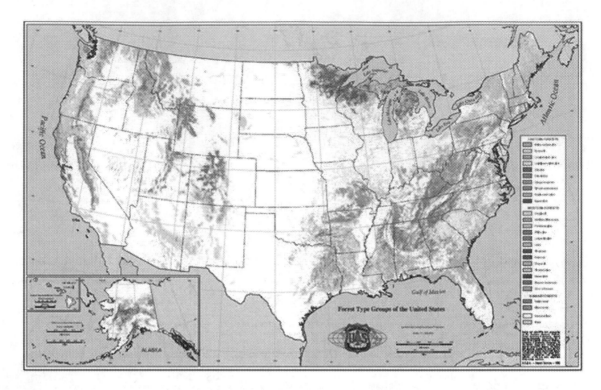

Figure 7: U.S. Forest Service Map of Forest Type Groups. Source: http://www.srs.fs.usda.gov/ pubs/misc/misc_reston.pdf

The map of forest type groups illustrates further the available forests and wood species for log construction. Not surprisingly, the forest cover map has a strong correlation to annual mean total precipitation.

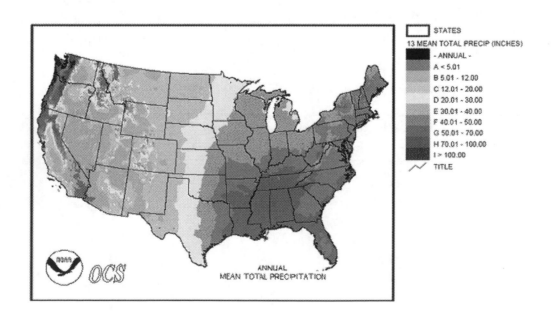

Figure 8: Map of annual mean total precipitation correlates well to the forest cover of the U.S. and the DOE Climate Zone Map. Source: NOAA

Log Yield

Forest harvest management strategies may make small diameter timber available that may not be economically viable for lumber production in a conventional saw-mill process, but it may provide a suitable log for smaller wall-logs. This material is often turned over to chip and pulp processes.

older, larger trees. Reported data on individual wood species provides mature height and diameter of trees, with most commercial species ranging from 1-foot to 6-foot diameters at breast height (DBH). Removal of these trees helps minimize the ability of ground fires to reach the forest canopy (the shorter trees catch fire and spread the flames upward to the canopy). The younger trees are also more attractive to insects.

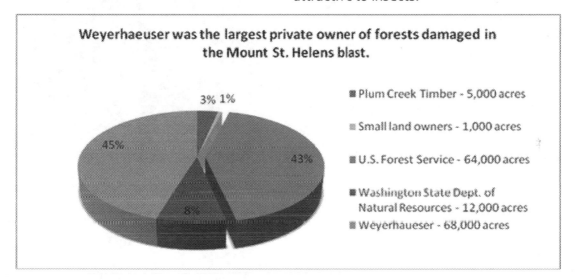

Weyerhaeuser was the largest private owner of forests damaged in the Mount St. Helens blast.

- Plum Creek Timber - 5,000 acres
- Small land owners - 1,000 acres
- U.S. Forest Service - 64,000 acres
- Washington State Dept. of Natural Resources - 12,000 acres
- Weyerhaueser - 68,000 acres

Figure 9: Forest ownership breakdown of the 150,000 acres of forest lands damaged or destroyed by the eruption of Mt. St. Helens. Source: http://www.weyerhaeuser.com/Sustainability/People/ Communities/ForestryEducation/MountStHelens/ForestOwnership

Forest management is a variable due to policies established by the Federal government. Access, harvesting and other aspects of forest management have become controlled by lobby interests rather than agricultural science. With vast tools accessible to its operations, Weyerhaeuser (www.weyerhaeuser.com) has done an admirable job of farming forest lands using sustainable practices to provide a wide variety of wood-based, renewable products. From the natural environmental disaster of the Mt. St. Helens eruption, Weyerhaeuser has been able to reestablish a healthy forest.

It appears that forest health benefits from selective harvest where smaller trees are removed to benefit the healthy growth of

Montana State Representative, Pat Connell, R-Corvallis, was the company forester and resource manager with Rocky Mountain Log Homes, Hamilton, MT. Now a forestry services consultant, he explained that natural resource management works toward an economic harvest based on high grade selection. The current regenerated stands are overstocked, so removing the suppressed (smaller) trees reduces the fire threat under the canopy. This leaves the dominate trees as a seed source. He noted that smaller diameter trees have smaller checks, which means lower maintenance in service (in the log wall).

So, let's look at log size this way: Wall-logs produced from larger diameter trees realize the economic advantage of using boxed heart cants (from sawmills) and peeler cores (produced from veneer manufacturers). Without question, requiring larger sizes in wall-logs to satisfy energy codes produces a major economic disadvantage as larger cants and peeler cores now have to cover the profit that would be provided by side cut lumber/ boards or veneer products—both are generally a higher margin product than the piece used to mill the wall-log. In all cases, these are the raw material for the milled log industry and keep the byproduct "boxed heart" from being sent to the chipper.

Transforming Raw Material into Wall-Logs

Not surprisingly, the mode of log wall production correlates to the size of the individual log profile. Wall-logs and Sawn Round Timber Beams (both defined in ASTM D3957) are produced from raw log with natural taper.

Figure 10: Peeled logs staged for the next step in the process. Source: Author during visit to Hiawatha Log Homes.

- **Sawn Round Timber Beams (SRTB)** is a classification of log timber that allows for natural taper logs to be left full round or that are sawn to produce one flat bearing surface for support of decking or other floor or ceiling. It generally requires a minimum 5" diameter tip. One option is to use 6-40 poles, which means a 6" tip and a 40' length. Typically, that butt diameter will be 11" at an average taper of 1/8" per foot. Statistically, this is about 10% of a typical forest lot—a 12" DBH log. The log home producer will buck that 40' pole down to get smaller diameter porch rafters, use the longer length with big diameter for purlins/rafters/joists, and keeping large butts for posts. Thus the production of log components for a new home offers flexibility without demanding the harvest of a larger diameter tree.

- **Wall-logs** can be produced from a full log like the SRTB or from a sawn timber (cant). They can incorporate the natural taper (common among handcrafted walls) or be milled into a uniform size and shape. Milling a log to a 9" diameter (a popular US milled log diameter due to lower cost), the producer will expedite a log with a 10" tip, which typically means it will have a 15" butt. This log will produce a uniform 9" diameter product and generate a volume of shavings as a byproduct. The purchasing specification for this log is nearly the same as the log that handcrafters have been using which average a 12" diameter. The handcrafted log has a lower carbon footprint as it produces less material as a byproduct and results in a wider average width.

Handcrafters are predominantly using full round or Swedish cope log profiles of 10-inch diameter and larger. They often use the full tree length from a 10-inch diameter tip to the butt (assuming normal taper). The log wall height is maintained to a level dimension by alternating the orientation of the logs so that consecutive log diameters are tip over butt and so on.

there is no industry standard for the amount of wood removed in the profiling process. The different shapes result in average widths (area of the log cross-section/profile divided by the stack height) that range from 70% to 95% of the nominal width.

Figure 12: Douglas fir cants at Buse Timber & Sales Inc., Everett, WA.
Source: Author, 2002 LHC President's Tour.

A graphic of typical log styles is presented below with descriptions to explain how their shape generates a shape factor from the nominal cant (square sawn timber) to the average width of the log profile—95% for a rectangular shape, 88% for a bevel, 83% for a D-log, 77% for a coped round, 71% for full round, and 72% for a milled round. Since the average width is defined as the profile area/stack height (see General Requirements), it could be argued that the size factor also represents the amount of wood fiber remaining after the rectangular cant has been milled into the wall-log.

Figure 11: Douglas fir logs arriving in Rossland, BC Canada for a handcrafted home package.
Source: Bob Warren, Khita Log Builders Ltd.

Manufactured log profiles are often less than 10-inches in width, except for Swedish cope profiles that can range from 7 to 24 inches in diameter. Often produced from sawn timbers (cants), manufacturers create a uniform shape along the full length of the log using planers or other profiling machinery. Without question, the majority of the log wall systems manufactured today are from 4-inch to 10-inch in nominal thickness. Nominal callouts are not appropriate measures for code reference however, because

Full Round	Seated Round	Milled Square	Milled Round	Milled D	Milled Bevel
0.71	0.77	0.95	0.72	0.83	0.88
A full round log may or may not contact the log below it. Chinking and backer rod are used to seal between logs.	The inscribed rectangle is permitted to extend 1/2" beyond the edge of the profile. The depth of the long notch is limited to the Maximum Profile Reduction.	Flat interior face & Flat exterior face. Minimal profile reduction Inscribed rectangle is same as profile.	Round interior face & Round exterior face. The curvature of the face varies significantly between manufacturers. Assumed: The curvature consumes no less than 3/4" on narrow logs and a maximum of 1-3/4".	Flat interior face & Round exterior face. The curvature of the face varies significantly between manufacturers. Assumed: The curvature consumes no less than 3/4" on narrow logs and a maximum of 1-3/4".	Flat interior face & Beveled exterior face. The angle of the face varies significantly between manufacturers. Assumed: The bevel consumes no less than 1/2" on narrow logs and a maximum of 1-1/2".

Figure 13: Various log profiles and descriptions used to generate size factors from nominal cant to average wall-log thickness. These generic profiles can all be milled from cants. Source: Author.

Forest Impacts

The health of the North American forests is an environmental concern facing the log and timber industry. The log home industry utilizes small diameter trees, with many companies helping to remove dead standing timber and reducing the fuel load in the forest.

Forester and State Rep. Pat Connell understands this well. For over 20 years, he practiced what he preached regarding log harvesting, forest management for a healthy community, and use of dead-standing timber. He noted that the log home industry utilized a significant amount of fire-or bug-killed wood that had

virtually no other economic use, except maybe firewood. When the salvage of that fire-killed wood became the target of the classic ecology wars, some mills turned to British Columbia for their supply of house logs. British Columbia's policy was that using the wood was better than seeing it burn up and pollute the sky and watersheds. That extra cost of transporting logs across the border helped drive costs of log homes upward, which priced some people out of the market.

One response is given in *TechLine* issue GR-1[10], March 2004, identifying logs from small-diameter trees (4- to 7-inch diameter) being advantageous due to less susceptibility to warp, available at lower processing cost, and having higher economic value. Using these smaller diameter trees is possible for floor and roof framing in log structures where a minimum 5" diameter is realistic at the tip. However, the use of small diameter logs in the wall is limited because of building energy codes, proportional relationships with the house design, and market demand for larger logs (smaller logs are often associated with camp type buildings).

Economic Impacts

In 2004, log homes were sold in the United States by the more than 400 log home manufacturers and handcrafters and their networks of sales representatives. That number has been reduced by the 2008-2011 economic downturns. How does that affect the forests?

Demand is down as those who want to build a log home are struggling with credit approvals and banking regulations. Appraisals of log homes have always been a challenge, but market comparables filled with foreclosures and dropping resale values limits the ability of appraisers to really know what new construction is worth. This translates into a lower demand which means workers in logging, sawmills, and construction are forced to find other income. With mill closings, the question becomes whether anyone be available to cut and haul trees.[11]

When log homes are produced from small diameter trees or those killed by insect, disease or fire, the revenue benefits forest management by incentivizing ecological restoration, conservation of forest ecosystems and the related benefits of the forests—water purification, water flow regulation, erosion control, stream bank stabilization, carbon sequestration, biodiversity, recreation, and cultural heritage values.[12] An industry that is perfectly situated to help maintain healthy forests has been hit hard by the economy and regulations. What happens next . . .

Western Bark Beatle Impact

In a report on North American forests, the Journal of Light Construction[13] reported the following. The conclusion that these logs are only good for wood pellets is not true—Log home companies can make excellent use of these trees! For log home companies, these trees may enable them to offer wall-logs that are even more environmentally conscious and a contribution to forest conservation. The acceptability of a blue stained log is the only market issue, as the logs are structurally sound if protected from the weather.

> Bark beetles are devastating softwoods in the western United States, with a 95 percent kill rate reported in some lodge-pole pine forests. Entomologists estimate that more than 5 million acres of spruce, pine, and fir in Colorado, Wyoming, Utah, and New Mexico and 35 million acres of forest in western Canada will be decimated by the beetles over the next decade. Forest-management practices may be partly to blame, as mature stands of trees of a single species are more vulnerable than stands with a mix of species and age groups. Already battered by depressed lumber markets, the region's remaining sawmills are now faced with a glut of nearly worthless bug-killed timber, useful only for the manufacture of wood pellets for heating stoves.

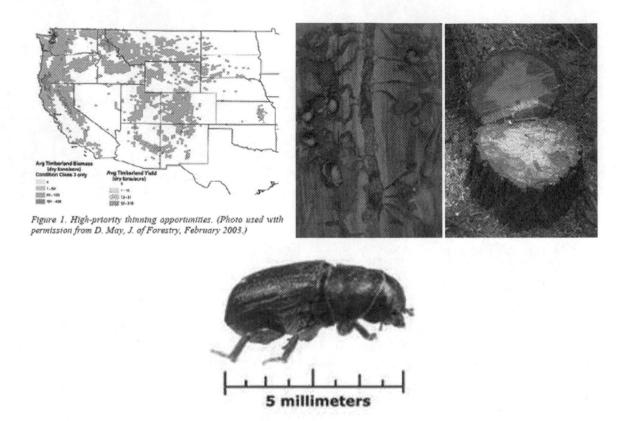

Figure 1. High-priority thinning opportunities. (Photo used with permission from D. May, J. of Forestry, February 2003.)

5 millimeters

Figure 14: Threatened forest lands, pine beetle engravings, and cross-section of a blue-stained log resulting from this small invader. Source: http://www.ext.colostate.edu/pubs/insect/05528.html/.

The only limitation to log home producers on using standing dead timber (wind-downed; killed by fire or insects) is the consumer's acceptance of blue stain. While this is not a structural defect, areas exposed to the exterior should be protected from moisture as a maintenance practice. But as such, the blue stain wood is a low-value tree.

Figure 15: Photos of a log building in Merritt, BC utilizing very large beetle killed Ponderosa (Jan. 2010). Source: John Boys, Owner of Nicola Logworks (www.logworks.ca). John notes, "These majestic trees, so iconic of the inter-mountain desert, are fast disappearing."

ENVIRONMENTAL REPORT CARD

Wood is an amazing material that is used by our society in many ways. There is a long list of solid wood products, but the list of products we use daily range from paper to many extractives and cellulose products that are processed from wood fiber. A tree uses 1.47 pounds of carbon dioxide to grow a pound of wood, and in the process gives off 1.07 pounds of oxygen. If you wonder what you really know about wood, take the Environmental Quiz at http://www.forestinfo.org/

Material	Embodied energy (MJ/kg)
Air dried sawn hardwood	0.5
Kiln dried sawn hardwood	2.0
Kiln dried sawn softwood	3.4
Particleboard	8.0
Plywood	10.4
Glued-laminated timber	11.0
Laminated veneer timber	11.0
Medium Density Fibreboard (MDF)	11.3
Glass	12.7
Mild steel	34.0
Galvanised mild steel	38.0
Zinc	51.0
Acrylic Paint	61.5
PVC	80.0
Plastics (general)	90.0
Copper	100.0
Aluminium	170.0

Process energy requirements (PER) for some common building materials.

Source: Lawson B (1996) Building materials energy and the environment. Towards ecologically sustainable development. The Royal Australian Institute of Architects.

Figure 16: Process energy requirements.
Source: ECOS magazine, Feb-Mar 2006 issue

Wood: The Undisputable Facts

Wood offers a raw material for construction that is a natural resource that is **renewable and sustainable**. Managed properly (which is in the best interests of the paper, lumber, and log home industries), it provides an endless supply of wood fiber as opposed to depleting a finite supply (i.e., fossil fuels). It also **embodies less energy** to generate a usable structural component than steel, concrete, masonry, and composites. It is **not a product of petroleum** such as vinyl, expanded polystyrene, and similar products being promoted for energy conservation and green building. Plastic insulation is a product based on polymers of different petroleum derivatives such as styrene, isocyanurate, and urethane.[14]

The Western Wood Products Association (WWPA) is only one source of information expounding on the benefits of wood:[15]

"For example, a young forest produces 1.1 tons of oxygen and absorbs 1.47 tons of carbon dioxide for every ton of wood fiber, which **stores the carbon**. A typical 2,400 square foot wood-frame house represents 28.5 tons of stored carbon dioxide or the rough equivalent of seven years' of emissions from a small automobile.

As a natural material, wood is **safe to handle and use**, is **biodegradable** and **can be recycled** easily. Wood is converted into thousands of products, from lumber, panels and paper to shoe polish, liquid soaps and cologne.

In building, wood has a **high ratio of strength to weight** and boasts a long history of durability and performance in construction. It features superior **insulating properties against heat, sound and electricity**. Wood **resists oxidation, acids and other** corrosive agents and easily **accepts preservatives, fire retardants and a variety of finishes**."

The process energy requirements (PER) table above is taken from the Feb-Mar 2006 Issue of ECOS magazine[16]. From the website, www.ecosmagazine.com, ECOS is described as being

". . . regarded as one of Australia's most authoritative magazines on sustainability, published since 1974 by Australia's national scientific research agency, CSIRO" (www.csiro.au).

Given the minimal processing involved with shaping a log component for a log structure, this table lends credence to the idea that the manufacture of wall-logs or log joists/rafters/purlins would find itself **within the top four categories for low levels of embodied energy**.

The article further discusses the debate of methane emissions produced by plants and reforestation, but notes that **the climate benefits of carbon sequestration far outweigh all effects of related methane emission**.

Figure 17: Landfill is not the best answer for disposing of wood products. This photo shows wood products from a Sydney, Australia landfill after 19 to 46 years. Source: http://www.fopap.org/FX_2008_WM.pdf.

Opponents to wood products will note that the decomposition of timber and paper products releases carbon emissions. However the authors found that it took roughly 10 years for decomposition of wood-based products in landfills:

". . .research by the CRC showed that timber that had been in landfill for 46 years had only lost between 1.4 to 3.5 per cent of its carbon. Paper, likewise, had lost very little of its carbon over 20-50 year periods in landfill, significantly altering the thinking on carbon storage times." [17]

The Australian CRC for Greenhouse Accounting reported that **decomposition rates are far less than previously thought**.

Table 1–3. Net carbon emissions in producing a tonne of various materials

Material	Net carbon emissions (kg C/t)[a,b]	Near-term net carbon emissions including carbon storage within material (kg C/t)[c,d]
Framing lumber	33	−457
Medium-density fiberboard (virgin fiber)	60	−382
Brick	88	88
Glass	154	154
Recycled steel (100% from scrap)	220	220
Concrete	265	265
Concrete[e]	291	291
Recycled aluminum (100% recycled content)	309	309
Steel (virgin)	694	694
Plastic	2,502	2,502
Aluminum (virgin)	4,532	4,532

[a] Values are based on life-cycle assessment and include gathering and processing of raw materials, primary and secondary processing, and transportation.
[b] Source: EPA (2006).
[c] From Bowyer and others (2008), a carbon content of 49% is assumed for wood.
[d] The carbon stored within wood will eventually be emitted back to the atmosphere at the end of the useful life of the wood product.
[e] Derived based on EPA value for concrete and consideration of additional steps involved in making blocks.

Figure 18: Table 1-3 tells the story of how the carbon footprint of wood compares to other materials. Source: FPL Wood Handbook.

The findings of the Australian study are substantiated further by research provided in FPL 2012 Heath001[18], where the authors' conclusions are as follows:

"Results of this study indicate that improvements in the U.S. industry's carbon and GHG profile can be achieved by focusing on several areas:

- Continue to reduce direct and indirect emissions intensity (GHG per unit production) attributable to manufacturing operations.
- Expand efforts to keep easily degradable forest products out of landfills.
- Ensure that wood harvested and burned for energy in place of fossil fuel is counted properly.

- Make more extensive use of landfill cover systems that capture and use or destroy CH_4.
- Increase the use of forest products, especially in long-lived applications, manufactured from domestically grown wood; in many applications they provide carbon sequestration benefits, and they also avoid missions by substituting for more GHG-intensive products and fuels."

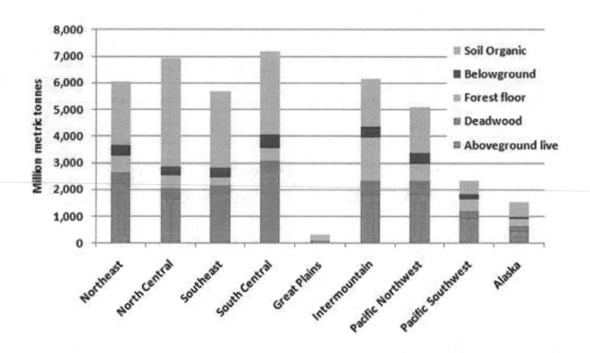

Total carbon in U.S. forests by region and carbon pool.

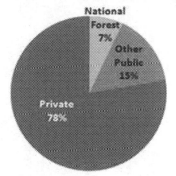

Total carbon in Eastern forests by owner

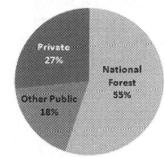

Total carbon in Western forests by owner

Excludes Hawaii and Interior Alaska.

Figure 19: USDA statistics support the nature of our forest resource (carbon storage graphics 20101028). Source: Climate Change Advisor's Office, USDA Forest Service [19]

Life Cycle Assessment

Life cycle assessment (LCA) evaluates the process of producing, constructing, and maintaining a building over a 60-year service life. It quantifies the environmental impacts of the materials and process involved. Green building programs already recognize LCA tools compliant with ISO 14044 or other recognized standards—Section 609 of the ICC700-2008 National Green Building Standard is being enhanced for the 2012 edition, and the ICC International Green Construction Code (IgCC) includes LCA provisions.

Significant recognition of the environmental value of wood is now coming from the U.S. Department of Agriculture (USDA, http://www.fs.fed.us/news/2011/releases/09/green-building-report.pdf).[20] As noted in the USDA press release,

"The Forest Service report also points out that greater use of life cycle analysis in building codes and standards would improve the scientific underpinning of building codes and standards and thereby benefit the environment. A combination of scientific advancement in the areas of life cycle analysis and the development of new technologies for improved and extended wood utilization are

needed to continue to advance wood as a green construction material. Sustainability of forest products can be verified using any credible third-party rating system, such as Sustainable Forestry Initiative, Forest Stewardship Council or American Tree Farm System certification."

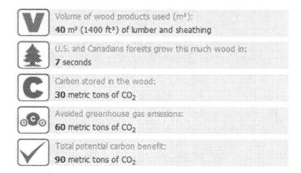

Carbon Summary

Results

V	Volume of wood products used (m^3): **40 m^3 (1400 ft^3) of lumber and sheathing**
🌲	U.S. and Canadians forests grow this much wood in: **7 seconds**
C	Carbon stored in the wood: **30 metric tons of CO_2**
⚙	Avoided greenhouse gas emissions: **60 metric tons of CO_2**
✓	Total potential carbon benefit: **90 metric tons of CO_2**

Equivalent to:

🚗	17 cars off the road for a year
🏠	Energy to operate a home for 8 years

Figure 20: Carbon Summary. Source: WoodWorks® Carbon Calculator

Another source of information is coming from the American Wood Council via their affiliated organization, Woodworks. At the Woodworks website, one can now work with their *Carbon Calculator* (http://www.woodworks.org/resources/span-tables-Online-Calculators.aspx) to estimate carbon impacts on commercial building.

that any specific project should undergo its own specific life cycle assessment by a qualified professional.

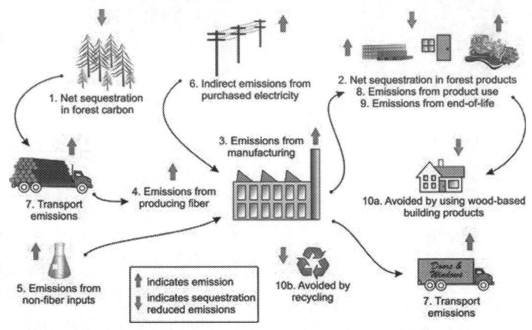

Figure 21: The elements of the U.S. forest products industry for its greenhouse gas profile. All wood grown in the U.S. is included in all elements; imported logs processed in mills are also included in elements 3-10.[21] Source: U.S. Forest Service.

Using the "low-rise" construction type, the next step in the Carbon Calculator is to estimate the extent of structural wood in the design. Some basic assumptions were entered, such as all the lumber/timber is of Spruce-Pine-Fir species group. Very broad material estimates were entered (e.g., a 6" log wall x 1494 sq. feet of wall area provides 747 cu. feet of log wall, 1040 bf of 2x4, 2284 bf of 2x6, and 4567 bf of 2x10) for wood volume. For sheathing, 3/4" Advantek® subfloor and 1979 square feet of 5/8" DF CDX roof sheathing is assumed. For the ranch design, no major beams were required, no siding is required because we are assuming a 6" log wall, and no exterior decks are included. The calculator estimates the amount of sequestered carbon, avoided greenhouse gases, and emission equivalents. It is a compelling analysis, but it properly notes

LCA is already used internationally to evaluate buildings and is becoming more widely adopted in Europe. Based on the home design presented later in UA Alternative Case Study, a 1540 square foot ranch (143 m2) is entered into the NZ Wood HOUSECalc Building Materials Carbon Calculator. Since wood floors are common to log home construction, that is selected (granted, slab-on-grade foundations are prevalent in some regions of the U.S.). The next selection is the exterior wall, where solid wood walls (as produced by one of 4 log home companies in New Zealand) are an option as opposed to steel or wood frame. Exterior cladding is next (brick, wood siding, or non-wood siding), but solid wood walls are recognized as not requiring a cladding.

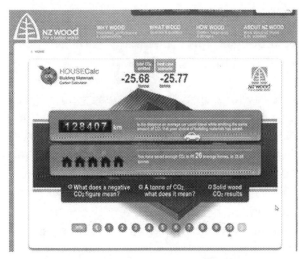

Figure 22: The results of the NZ Wood HOUSECalc Building Materials Carbon Calculator shows significant carbon sequestered using the design and material choices as compared to emissions from driving a car. Source http://www.nzwood.co.nz/house-calculator/.

Next is the window frame which offers a selection of wood (selected) or aluminum. An exterior deck option is available, but no deck area is entered. Trying to stay closer to a U.S. model, the long run steel roof option is selected over metal or concrete tiles. The garage option is not added. Based on the selections and entries made so far, the program allows for all of the other materials installed in the house (e.g., wiring, plumbing, interior doors and other interior finishes).

Materials are a measureable commodity in assessing embodied energy, as is on site construction energy consumption. A simple measure is the length of time required to complete the weather-tight shell. The most efficient building system in this regard would be a modular home, as it is set and closed weather-tight in a single day (a typical ranch or colonial design up to as many as six modules). With a crane on site, structural shells built with large/long logs can be set in two days, with the exterior weather tight within the week. Smaller pre-cut log components do not require the heavy equipment for lifting, but

a larger crew can shorten the time required to enclose the shell, perhaps within a week to 10 days. Random length log packages that are assembled by an experienced crew can be completed in nearly the same time, perhaps a couple days longer.

An LCA effort appears to be a mountain of a task in this economy. But the effort may prove beneficial in ways unknown at this time. Just like log grading, the industry thought it was a waste of time. However, by tying grading criteria to purchasing specifications, material usage by grade in development of house plans, and at other points of integration, we have seen companies dramatically improve the way they produce their log components.

More can be learned and applied to the log components by completing an LCA study and developing an LCA tool. By examining resources and processes, the industry may modify current practices to advance log building as the most environmentally-friendly building system. Funding LCA database work cannot be allowed to be a barrier to demonstrating superior benefits of log homes, but the reality is that funding is scarce at this time.

By incorporating log wall construction in an available, unbiased, and trusted tool like Athena Institute's EcoCalculator, design and code professionals can readily evaluate the log wall systems against other wall technologies. Combined with ICC400 and the IECC, the total building performance can be quantified. Using a life cycle assessment, it would be interesting to compare the total use of energy, both embodied and expected heating demand. Is it possible that the low embodied energy/carbon footprint of log structures would lower the bar? Charting time and energy consumption from zero over the life of a building and its collective elements, how long would it take for involved energy of a log structure to cross the curve of a home built using another wall technology?

Green Building—Applying ICC700 to Log Homes

To a log home practitioner, a green log home means that the logs were freshly cut and installed, with the intent that they season (dry) in place. The use of the term "green building" as it relates to the ICC700 *National Green Building Standard* has required the log home industry to either change its definition or find another way to explain the process of building with unseasoned timber. The interesting note here is that both definitions apply. Log walls contribute points toward green building certification as well.

generated by a log home. Note that this home cannot be certified due to an insufficient point total in Chapters 5, 7, 8, and 10.

A review of a proprietary log wall system[22] was completed to assess points under the NAHB National Green Building Certification Program (NGBCP) in accordance with ICC700-2008 National Green Building Standard. This review revealed that this log home materials package, supported by the company's construction manual and detailed construction plans, was designed to provide 153 points toward a Bronze certification (requiring 222 points). The benefit of the log materials package came

Chapter	Description	Assessed Points	Points required to achieve per Level			
			Bronze	Silver	Gold	Emerald
5	Lot Design, Preparation and Development	0	39	66	93	119
6	Resource Efficiency	**82**	45	**79**	113	146
7	Energy Efficiency	18	30	60	100	120
8	Water Efficiency	2	14	26	41	60
9	Indoor Environmental Quality	**51**	**36**	65	100	140
10	Operation, Maintenance, and Homeowner Education	0	8	10	11	12
	Additional points from any section 37 pts. From Ch. 6 and 15 pts. From Ch. 9 contribute	0	50	100	100	100
	Totals	153	222	406	558	697

Figure 24: Points Required for Certification of an average home with 2 bathrooms to ICC700-2008. An average log home should be able to readily achieve Bronze Certification while Silver level may involve a bit more effort. The costs become increasingly influential when trying to achieve Gold or Emerald Certification. Source: Author.

How do log buildings fare in the ICC700? ICC700 is divided into several areas of concentration, each with a minimum number of points that must be achieved. If an insufficient number of points are applicable to the project in any one of these areas, the project cannot be certified. The table below illustrates points that may be

from efficient use of materials, local or regional source of supply, recycling byproducts, plans and instructions showing how to use the precut/specified lengths of materials, etc. With an attitude for sustainability and then designed and built to the ICC400 standard, log homes can easily provide an above-code structure.

This specific case includes features associated with a precut log materials package. There is a broad range of services available with log material packages, but it is expected that most producers could generate a design specification capable of producing a Bronze certified finished project.

This review demonstrates the ease at which a log structure can be certified to an above-code program. The challenges of meeting changing energy codes will be a factor in the future, but we can see that 2006/2008 codes and standards tolerate log walls. Typical of log structures, it should be easy to keep all heating/cooling distribution inside the thermal envelope, and to seal connecting assemblies (ceilings to walls, walls to floors) to achieve low air infiltration rates (4 ach @ 50 Pascal). Using 90% AFUE furnaces and 0.93 EF water heaters would be a natural choice. Therefore, the remaining issue comes back to the rated R-value of the log wall while roof, foundation/floor, and glazing levels are specified to be 15% above code.

No points are assessed for Chapter 5. It is highly recommended that the homeowner/builder look closely at this section to achieve certification. By bringing in the proper expertise *before* disturbing anything on the lot, it should be very easy to achieve Bronze or Swilver certification to the lot. Site planning (Ch. 5) can be satisfied by locating the home to maximize daylighting, minimizing disruption to the building site throughout the building process, recycling construction debris, harvesting roof rain runoff and employing gray water systems, using trees for shading and indigenous vegetation that can survive on natural climate factors, especially water supply.

Chapter	Description	Assessed Points	EPA Program Benefits[1]	Points required to achieve per Level			
				Bronze	Silver	Gold	Emerald
5	Lot Design, Preparation and Development	0		39	66	93	119
6	Resource Efficiency	**85**	+3-ES	45	**79**	113	146
7	Energy Efficiency	70	+30 or 32 -ES	30	60	100	120
8	Water Efficiency	35	+8-ES, 16-WS	14	26	41	60
9	Indoor Environmental Quality	**53**	+4-ES	**36**	65	100	140
10	Operation, Maintenance, and Homeowner Education	0		8	10	11	12
	Additional points from any section 37 pts. From Ch. 6 and 15 pts. From Ch. 9 contribute	0		50	100	100	100
	Totals	234	+61 or 63	222	406	558	697

[1] ES = **ENERGY STAR**®, WS = **WaterSense**®

Figure 25: Point summary for a proprietary log materials package and a specific design. Source: Author.

By specifying, installing, and verifying ENERGY STAR® and EPA Water Sense® products and systems, this house can gain another 3 points in Chapter 6 (satisfies Silver), 52 points in Chapter 7 (satisfies Silver), 33 points in Chapter 8 (satisfies Silver), and 2 points in Chapter 9 (satisfies Bronze)—243 total points. Therefore, this particular design can achieve Bronze certification if Chapters 5 and 10 are satisfied at verification to at least the Bronze point total. Previously aligned with the NGBCP, the Builders Challenge program under DOE's Energy Efficiency and Renewable Energy Building Technologies Program (EERE BTP) provided additional incentives for builders and their clients to be focused on sustainable design and construction.

To bring more points into the certification,

- Finish the energy conservation measures (Ch. 7) with 50% CFL or 100% dedicated CFL fixtures and occupancy sensors.
- Dual-flush toilets and low-flow 1.75 gal./min. shower heads add points for water efficiency (Ch. 8), not to mention the old-fashioned design element of stacking plumbing.
- While low VOC (volatile organic compounds) paints, adhesives, and sealants help indoor air quality (Ch. 9s), it is more essential in a well-built log home to provide proper, balanced ventilation to remove moisture in bathrooms (on automated switches and timers) and kitchen fumes via a 90cfm range hood that is vented to the outside.
- No points are shown for Chapter 10, but a well-written manual can easily produce 11 points, which is good for Gold!

Resource Efficiency

Recognize the Footprint

Green building programs point to the size of the structure as an element that affects its environmental benefits. It is true on many levels from material demands to occupant use. With energy conservation of log homes, it may be important to study the nature of those many log homes where the consumer is happy with their energy efficient lifestyle.

When Sarah Susanka, FAIA published and promoted her book, *The Not So Big House*, her concepts were (and continue to be) well received by the building industry. One small aspect of her message had to do with the actual size of homes, meaning that big spaces do not mean quality living. Over the history of the log home industry, the vast majority of the built inventory fits into her description, in that most were less than 2,500 sf of floor area. Surveying the plan books of most log home companies, one will see that the majority of the plans are in this category (less than 2,500 sf).

In the UA Alternative calculations (see **UA Alternative Case Study**), the designs range from 1,540 to 1,764 square feet of living area (for the ranch and 2-story designs respectively). This is not abnormal for the existing log home inventory in the United States. The other feature of this that is revealing is the ratio of the log wall to the total thermal envelope in those designs. Obviously, the ranch design has a higher percentage of log walls to the thermal envelope at 27.3%. Change the design to a cape adding frame gable ends, and the percentage drops to 21.5% (29.88 % when log gables are used). Add frame dormers to the cape to get the 2-story design, and the percentage drops to 18.9% (37.33% with log gables and dormers). This demonstrates how the percentage of the log wall to the overall thermal envelope is a big factor in designing the home to comply with the energy codes.

Log home designers should be aware that the smaller footprint will have less environmental impact and garner points in green building programs. More points can be gained by adding living space on an upper floor, and when the upper level walls are built with alternatives to the log wall, the UA calculations benefit. In the UA examples, the 2-story design with log gables and dormer walls will require a 9-inch average log width (vs. 7" for the ranch) to meet the 2012 IECC in Climate Zones 7 & 8, with two or more inches added to the average width applying to Climate Zones 4-6 as well. **Log home design can have a big impact the thermal performance of the home.**

Planning for Construction

Many log home companies provide design services, but the extent of the design work varies. Having plans that define the project enhance the efficiency of the work and the use of resources, thereby earning points. Designing a home that is in a certain size range can also earn points. If the average log home is represented by plans as shown in company catalogs, it could be said that the average log home is less than or equal to 2,000 square feet of living space. This provides 9 points in ICC700.

Detailed construction plans and instructions with framing plans, log wall layup drawings, etc., add 4 points. And companies that take the step of cutting the logs and notching them for placement without further modification by the builder on site gain another 4 points. This reduces on-site material waste and handling. Yet, even when cuts are made on the building site, the wood that is discarded is not thrown into a dumpster. If a use is not found in the building process, this wood will find its way as a fuel source for the builder or homeowner.

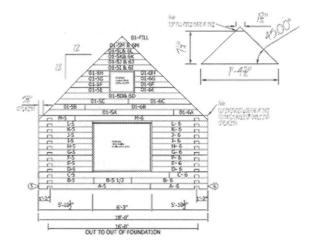

Figure 26: Precut log materials reduce on-site labor and material waste. Source: Robert Orth, Detailed Design Services.

There are many more opportunities for points during the development of construction documents. Assembly details and construction plans provide guidance to the builder by noting

- Installation of foundation perimeter drains, properly sloped finish grade, etc.
- Installation of flashing, drip edge, etc.
- Roof overhangs and covered entries are shown and dimensioned
- Detached garages
- Venting for fuel-burning appliances and/or mechanical compartment with its own air handling.
- No fireplace, woodstove, pellet stove, or masonry heater is installed.

The plans themselves do not provide the points, but the inspection and verification that these items were done are much easier when the plans or construction manuals show what the Accredited Verifier should see.

Advanced Framing Principles

For credit in green building programs and ENERGY STAR, advanced framing techniques can be employed to reduce the impact of thermal bridging in above-grade walls. Due to the continuity of the log wall throughout the exterior wall component, it naturally provides these same benefits.

- All corners insulated to the same extent as the log wall, since the thickness at the corner will typically be no less than the narrowest width of the wall itself.
- All headers above windows and doors are insulated since the log headers are key elements of the log wall.
- Framing is limited at all windows and doors as it is literally only the "buck" or rough opening material.
- All intersections of interior to exterior walls are insulated to the same R-value as the rest of the exterior wall since the log wall covers the intersection or the intersection is built like an interlocking log corner.
- Minimum stud spacing is irrelevant since log walls do not contain cavities requiring insulation.
- Alignment of framing is not an issue since the log wall provides uniform support for the roof and distributes a uniform load across the floor/foundation stem wall. The load path is continuous without concern for spacing of the framing.

Conservation of Resources

Log building adds more to green building through the benefits of solid wood:[23]

- Logs are **renewable, bio-based** materials that make up a large part of the structure. Documentation is required to demonstrate sustainable forestry practices, although it is inherent in the wood industry to do so.
- Log wall systems **that provide sufficient structural and thermal characteristics** used for at least 75% of the gross exterior wall area of the building earn green points. While the quantity of wood fiber is greater than would be supplied for a framed

structure, log walls require fewer different materials and trades to accomplish this.

- **Indigenous Materials:** Logs are often harvested from within 500 miles of the mill resulting in lower transportation energy-use than conventional framing lumber;
- Log walls are solid, and therefore plumbing distribution lines are not installed in exterior wall cavities. In addition, the typical log home with a heated basement and a timber framed roof system has all mechanical and plumbing systems contained within the thermal envelope.
- Less energy and labor are consumed processing the timber for log components between harvest and installation in the wall at the building site resulting in a far **smaller carbon footprint**;
- Fewer (albeit proportionally stronger) fasteners are needed to erect a log-walled building, resulting in lower quantities of metals employed to complete the job (manufactured metals have high embodied energy);
- In the future, when log buildings are demolished there is a **high potential for recycling logs** (log homes would more likely be "deconstructed" for their valuable timbers);
- Log wall thermal performance does not degrade over time
  a. Solid wood walls do not degrade like batt insulation when compressed into a framing cavity;
  b. Movement is controlled and visual, versus the voids created when cellulose settles;
  c. Wood does not off-gas any toxins or degrade with age like foam insulations;
  d. Solid wood walls cannot collect debris, allergens or mold as those conditions are not concealed in a wall cavity;

Minimal Penetrations of the Thermal Envelope

The mass of log walls discourages the use of the exterior wall as a good location for distribution systems or other elements that may appear in a frame wall. Wiring may find itself in the log wall on occasion, but the vast majority of electrical, plumbing and mechanical systems are installed to the interior of the log wall. It can be a challenge to minimize wiring runs in the log wall because of code requirements for receptacles. However, there are options such as running wiring along the bottom plate log, concealing it with trim boards or chair rail or in a power strip above base cabinets.

Sustainable Forestry Practices

With a history that evolved from the forestry and wood products industries, the log home industry has long understood that proper stewardship of its raw material sources was the only way to maintain business. A paper written by the Log Homes Council and published in NAHB's Nations Business News[24], several companies describe this position:

> Like many critics whose understanding of forestry is based on emotion rather than ecology, several first-year students of **Ed Burke**, a professor of wood and forest science at the **University of Montana College of Forestry and Conservation** "think that any cutting of trees is bad." In truth, however, harvesting is the only controlled alternative available to maintaining a healthy forest.
>
> A large number of log home manufacturers only use standing dead timber that has been killed by insects while others harvest

living trees responsibly, either maintaining their own tracts of land or buying from producers who are certified as sustainable.

> "There is a book titled 'Best Logging Practices' that most of us in the industry follow," said **Chris Wood** of **Hearthstone Homes**, a log and timber frame manufacturer in Dandridge, Tenn. "We don't practice clear cutting," Wood continued. "The general public has little idea how well the U.S. Forest Service manages its land. There are restrictions and guidelines in place to protect this valuable renewable resource."
>
> **Kuhns Bros Log Homes** of Lewisburg, Pa. manages more than 2,200 acres of private woodlands with a full-time staff of foresters to ensure the company will have an adequate supply of logs short- and long-term. Also, as a corporate supporter of the Arbor Day Foundation, Kuhns Bros. plants thousands of trees annually in the country's national forests and gives each of its home buyers a foundation membership. "I'm very proud of the way we do business. Sound forestry management will always be a vital part of our operation," said **Tom Kuhns**.

Besides practicing good forest stewardship, the industry has developed ways to recycle or reuse all of the byproducts of the log manufacturing/handcrafting process. This is an opportunity for companies to recover the cost of those byproducts that cannot be incorporated into the log structure. Byproducts include bark removed from the log, shavings from planer operations, and saw dust from cut lines. These are sold for a variety of other uses including mulch, bedding for animals, paper, wood pellets for pellet stoves, etc.

As reported in the Jan/Feb 2011 issue of ASTM Standardization News, two new ASTM International standards will bring continuity to forest management. D7612, *Practice for Categorizing Wood and Wood-Based Products According to Their Fiber Sources* identifies three categories for fiber source—legal sources, responsible sources and certified sources. D7480, *Guide for Evaluating the Attributes of a Forest Management Plan* gives policymakers seven criteria to use in assessing national forest trends and progress toward sustainable forest management. The report notes that green building programs can be modified to use these ASTM standards to require appropriate forest management practices "rather than simply referencing {an} alphabet soup of names."

Alternative Energy Resources

Some companies have invested in alternative energy technologies, such as using solar energy and cogeneration systems to reduce utility costs. Again from the Log Homes Council article:

> Gastineau Log Homes of Bloomfield, Mo. was the first in the industry to develop a solar forced-air kiln to dry its oak logs. The company has been using solar kilns for four years. "In keeping with our desire to be environmentally conscious and our trademark of being a leader and innovator in the log home industry, we designed a drying system that is unique in the log home industry—solar forced-air kilns," said Lynn Gastineau. The

> solar kilns "are environmentally responsible and use virtually no energy except the electricity to run the computers that monitor the system and the air turbines," Gastineau said. "It is kiln drying for the 21st century. With our process, the logs are in the kiln from four to five months at a lower temperature. This is better for the wood-less damage and checking—better for home buyers, less costly and better for the environment."

To cut fuel costs in its mill vehicles, Katahdin Cedar Log Homes has installed a commercial ethanol distiller at its milling facility, which ferments culled potatoes from nearby farms into ethanol. The company produces about 100 gallons of ethanol a day as a supplement at a cost of under $1 per gallon. "We continue to look for new ways to lower our dependence on fossil fuels and keep our costs down," said David Gordon, President. Earlier this year, Katahdin completed construction on a 14 million BTU biomass boiler to recycle wood waste into steam heat for the mill buildings.

Figure 27: Solar Kilns at Gastineau Log Homes, MO. Source: Gastineau Log Homes, Inc., www. oakloghome.com.

Testimony to Durability

In their book, "Log Structures: Preservation and Problem-Solving", authors Goodall and Friedman[25] provide an excellent opening as to the formation and endurance of log buildings:

> "Pioneers and early settlers built with logs because of the simple construction technology involved and the availability of materials. Built from the materials readily at hand—logs, stones, moss, dirt, bark—log structures were very practical for builders a hundred miles from the nearest mill. Log buildings were quick to assemble,

economical, and provided shelter for people as wells as domestic animals. **With simple and periodic care**—patching cracking and broken daubing, replacing missing roof shingles, applying a yearly coat of whitewash—such a structure could be maintained in good condition for at least one lifetime.

In the nineteenth century, many log houses in the East and South were covered with siding to make them appear more permanent and to preserve the logs. Because their structural system is hidden under

board-and-batten, clapboards, or
vertical siding, many such houses
go unnoticed as log structures."

Today's log buildings still rely on good roof systems that remain in place, indigenous woods, and regular maintenance to withstand their environments. Wood experts, maintenance contractors, and preservationists are well acquainted with several factors that impact the durability of log structures.

- Imposed structural loads
- Wood erosion from exposure to the elements—sun, wind and water
- Precipitation and relative humidity
- Evidence of insects.

Imposed Structural Loads

Proper structural design is elemental in that the structure must be designed to meet snow build-up, wind and seismic lateral forces, and loading imposed by the occupants in the expected use of the building. Minimum design loads are available in the model codes, but local conditions may exceed that information. In such cases, the structure is designed to the greater of the two load conditions.

There have been many reports of log homes surviving major natural disasters while other homes have been lost. Some of this success is due to the intrinsic nature of log construction—continuous load path from roof to foundation through the exterior walls, contiguous horizontal members held with fastening systems vs. spaced framing members, etc. Instead of relying on sheathing or let-in bracing to resist horizontal loads, the loads are easily transferred along the logs. In fact, the fastening schedule used is often dictated by the design wind or seismic condition.

Design conditions can be tested in a laboratory, such as racking, bending and resistance to

wind-borne debris, but the log home industry has not invested heavily here because they have witnessed the real thing with minimal damage from tornados, hurricanes, and earthquakes. One company, Anthony Forest Products, did perform a wind-borne debris test on its proprietary glu-laminated log, the PowerLog. The southern pine exterior lamination received the impact of a 2x4 wood stud that was shot from a air-canon to replicate debris blown at a wind force of 100mph or more. After three tests, only one 2x4 missile was embedded enough to stay in the wall while the others bounced off. Contrast this to the report of similar testing on frame walls, ICF and concrete walls.[26] The concrete wall tests had similar results to the log wall, except the end of the missile was never held by the concrete. The missile perforated completely through the framing cavity, even when covered with brick veneer, with minor to no damage to the missile. For ICF (insulated concrete forms) walls, the missile penetrated the exterior finish and foam form, but did not generate significant damage to the concrete. These latter two wall systems, therefore, would require a greater extent of repair than log or concrete walls.

Mass walls provide another advantage!

More information is provided in sections that follow regarding the design and construction of log structures to resist such loads.

A testimony to good design, compliance with codes and standards, and quality construction is taken from a case study provided by Heritage Log Homes, Kodak, TN as reported by Rebecca Ferrar on Tuesday, January 17, 2006 in the News Sentinel:

> "Sheila Mhire thanks God and her sturdy Heritage log house for bringing her home safely through Hurricane Rita. The Sept. 24 storm devastated schools, churches

and other homes in her Grand Chenier, LA community. But the log home built with blueprints and logs from Heritage Log Homes of Sevierville allowed the structure to withstand not only 120 mph winds but also a 15-foot storm surge. Mhire said the home is 11.9 feet above ground."

Figure 28: Before (left) of the Mhire home and after Hurricane Rita hit Grand Chenier, LA. Source: Heritage Log Homes.

Wood's Sacrificial Layer

The durability of wood to erosion from wind, water and sun is analogous to its performance in fire. The outer layers are sacrificed, but the wood underneath remains unaffected and structurally sound. Where log structures have not undergone regular maintenance, one can use a fingernail to scratch away loose fiber that has lost its structure due to ultraviolet light.

While ultraviolet light breaks down the outer fibers of the wood, the cells within are unaffected, almost like char protects inner wood from the damaging effects of fire. But even with wind working to erode those damaged cells from the surface of the wood, the process is very slow. Actually, cleaning the logs to apply a finish will remove more wood fiber at a faster rate.

Figure 29: Many abandoned log homes like this one near Great Basin National Park, Nevada suffer from a roof that failed. Sun-bleached and weathered, the logs remain structurally sound.

The environmental impact on exposed wood has been tested by many for the past several decades. In the high country of the Rocky Mountain region, where low humidity is generally the case, log walls are battered more by ultraviolet radiation and wind erosion than anything else. Where roof structures were not capable of resisting the snow loads, the roof failed but the walls remain.

Rustic style log walls (as shown below) built by sawing a flat top and bottom surface for bearing purposes provide a unique opportunity. Whenever the log above is narrower at the connecting surface of the log below it, there is a potential for long term damage from pooling water. The goal is always to provide at least a 1/8" overhang of one log to the next when working with this style of wall. When that is not possible, a draw knife can be used to remove the "shelf" created on the exterior by the lower log. It is best to bevel about a 45-degree angle on the top exterior edge of the wider log so that the top of the bevel is under the log above.

invitation for growth of fungi that can impact the structure of the wood, and those same elements often attract insect activity. However, wood can be protected from biological attack

Figure 30: Rustic park shelter in Windsor, VT. Source: Author.

Exposed primarily to high snow loads, the Windsor park shelter above has a metal roof that requires little maintenance. The overhangs have provided some protection to the upper logs, and most of the horizontal log interfaces do not have a sufficient ledge to hold moisture. The discoloration at the bottom of the posts and along the foundation indicates that the builder was aware that the building needed to be protected from splash back from roof runoff. Only about 18-20", this distance did a reasonable job of keeping water and snow buildup off the logs.

by eliminating the food source in the wood, removing the water or air, or keeping it in temperatures below about 40-degrees-F. The ECOS Magazine article previously noted shows that wood products buried in a landfill did not decay at the expected rate—was this because of a lack of oxygen limiting fungal activity?

The maps below illustrate how decay and termite hazard coincides with the humidity zones noted on the climate zone map. When the climate is dryer and cooler, it is not

Figure 31: Height above grade reduces effects of roof runoff back splash; even without exterior maintenance, UV degradation is limited to the outer shell of the logs. Source: Author.

Moisture and Humidity

Studies have demonstrated that exposure to air, water, and warm temperatures is an

uncommon to see exposed logs remain in a condition that would allow it to be recycled into another product. However, in warmer and more humid climates the wood must be protected by preservative treatments or on-going exterior maintenance practices.

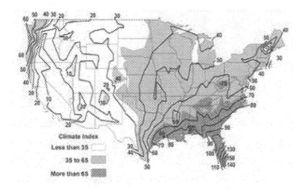

Figure 32: Left—Climate index for decay hazard (higher numbers indicate greater hazard). Right—Northern limits of recorded damage by (A) subterranean termites and (B) drywood termites. Source: FPL Wood Handbook.

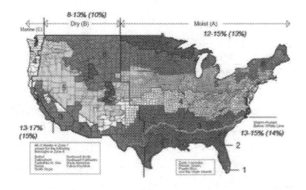

Figure 33: Climate and environmental hazards have direct correlations to relative humidity and temperature. Source: U.S. Department of Energy modified for ICC400.

Inspection and maintenance of the exterior of the log wall is key in warmer, moist climates. The most important maintenance practice is to seal exterior checks (longitudinal cracks resulting when internal stress from wood shrinkage exceeds the bond between wood cells). Sealing the checks restricts the entry of rain water into them. When water gets into the checks, the wood swells, dries, and generates a deeper check. When the check is deep enough that the water is not removed by draining or evaporation, the collected moisture will allow fungi to develop, eventually damaging the wood and requiring replacement of that section of log.

Assuming the log wall is designed, constructed and maintained to minimize degradation due to these conditions, the effect of moisture is reduced by the time the wood is acclimated to its environment (a.k.a., equilibrium moisture content). As a hygroscopic material, it will continue to gain and lose moisture content with its environment and will exhibit small degrees of dimensional change. This is analogous to a solid wood door that is stuck closed on a humid day and swings freely on a dry one. When the moisture content of the wood is greater than the relative humidity, the wood will lose moisture to the air environment and vice versa. One can counter some of this effect by sealing the end grain of wood components with a suitable coating that will not allow vapor to be transported along the longitudinal capillary cell structure.

Insects and Log Homes[27]

The control of insects entering a log home is the same as for any other wood or foam building system. Termites are controlled by treating the ground, adding a termite shield, and raising the foundation stem wall high enough to make mud tubes visible on inspection. Keeping vegetation, firewood, and other insect friendly environs away from the wall is recommended.

The effects of insects in a log structure are limited by the visual inspection methods employed during the log grading process. This is done by quantifying the size and number of holes evident in a piece due to boring insects. Insects that attack the trees in the forest can be severe as previously noted. The logs harvested from a beetle-killed wood lot will likely have blue stain, at a very minimum around the holes where the eggs were laid. The damage that killed the tree was the insect feeding on the cambium layer under the bark.

Some insects, like carpenter bees and carpenter ants will bore into the wood to create a shelter. They do not ingest the wood as termites do. These insects typically attack dead wood in contact with the ground, but if permitted, they will find a log home attractive. There are several wood boring insects that also use standing dead trees and existing wood structures to lay eggs. The LHC Log Grading Program Training & Operations Manual[28] explains this as follows:

> "While some boring beetles, especially the round-headed and flat-headed borers, can cause significant visual and customer relation problems with their relatively large tunnels and often untimely emergence in a finished home, others produce tunnels of such small size that their presence does not affect the structural integrity of the wood.
>
> Most of the boring beetles spend less than two years in a log before emerging as short-lived adults looking for mates and a new standing or downed dead tree to lay eggs in. They will rarely, if ever, re-attack the log they emerged from, so the chances that logs and timbers in service being attacked

or re-attacked by these forest dwellers is quite remote."

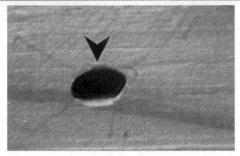

Figure 34: Boring beetle feeding gallery and exit hole. These are limited by the structural grading of log components. Source: Edwin J. Burke, PhD, University of Montana.

Care & Maintenance [29]

In the 1960's and 1970's, some promoted log homes as maintenance free. In a sense, log homes are no more maintenance free than any house with wood siding. Maintenance of a log home varies by climate region and design. For example, homes of all types benefit from gutters, downspouts, and splash blocks in climates with higher average rainfall. Roof overhangs play an integral role with sheltering the wood surface from precipitation. And the exterior finishes available from companies specializing in log home protection are effective at providing UV protection repelling water while still allowing the wood to breath (moisture drawn to the surface by solar gain can pass through—film-forming finishes promote decay beneath the film).

The exposed interior surfaces of a log wall provide a constant opportunity for visual inspection, and indications of problems on the exterior will ultimately show on the interior. Regular inspection of the exterior is also important to insure that water is not penetrating the exterior wood surface.

The sector of the wood coatings industry that has come to support the log home industry has recognized wood's sacrificial layer. They produce coatings that protect the wood surface by sacrificing the applied coating first. The wood will not erode as long as the coating is properly maintained. It is important to maintain the exterior finish as per the recommendations of the manufacturer of the product applied.

Figure 35: Caulking checks on the outside is critical on upward-facing checks. For larger checks, press a backer rod into the check sufficient to caulk up to the wood surface. Source: Right-Perma-Chink; Middle & Left-Sashco.

Checking

Checking is a natural result of drying of wood as cells shrink when water leaves the cell walls. They extend radially from the outside toward the pith for varying distances.

Rapid or extreme drying of the wood surface will create excessive checking. Checking on the exterior of the log wall should be properly treated. Hairline cracks on exterior surfaces that have been recently treated with a water repellant, breathable coating will be protected by the molecular bond of the finish across the check. The finish can be tested by misting water onto the surface; a satisfactory surface will cause the water to bead and roll off while absorption of the mist indicates the need to retreat.

Larger checks will appear in solid wood components and must be sealed to keep moisture from entering the log. Narrow checks (± 1/8") can be caulked, while wider checks should be sealed with a dowel-type backer rod before being sealed with caulk. Some

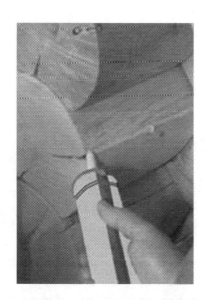

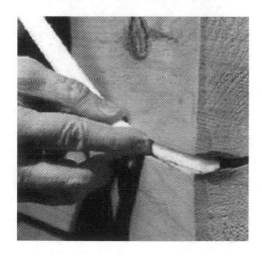

producers use laminated systems to eliminate checking and the associated maintenance.

Drying and erosion from exposure to dry winds can be offset by wind breaks or frequent retreating of the exterior finish in the first few years of occupancy. Given appropriate clearance from the log wall, the heat of a wood burning stove or similar appliance should not be a factor. Locating the appliance near the center of the space has the optimum effect.

Inspection of Log Homes

Durability and performance of log walls are dependent on the inspection, care and maintenance practices applied. Most log home companies describe this effort in their construction manuals, but the supporting members of the industry who produce log treatment and preservation products have provided the best information. In fact, many log producers have partnered with their suppliers of caulking, chinking, interior finish, exterior finish, wood cleaning, and preservative treatment to provide information to homeowners.

One of the best unbiased sources of guidance is the International Association of Certified Home Inspectors, www.nachi.org/loghomes. htm. This organization is diligent in its research on topics and presentation to its members. On their website, they publish the following guidelines for log home inspection:

Inspecting a Log Home

Log Wall Exterior

The inspector shall inspect exterior surfaces of log walls, when such surfaces are visible, looking for:

- the presence of mold, mildew or fungus;
- cracks located at tops of logs and facing up;
- discoloration, graying, bleaching or staining of logs;
- loose or missing caulking;
- separation of joints;
- the condition of chinking, to include cracking, tears, holes or separation of log courses; and
- the condition of log ends.

Other Exterior Concerns

In addition to the items specified in InterNACHI Standards of Practice 2.1 and 2.2, the inspector shall inspect:

- downspout extensions;
- grading and water flow away from log walls; and
- vertical support posts under and on all porches.

Log Wall Interior

The inspector shall inspect interior surfaces of log walls, when such surfaces are visible, looking for:

- separation between logs, including light or air penetration from outdoors;
- separation between exterior log wall and interior partition walls; and
- separation between log walls and interior ceilings.

Other Interior Concerns

In addition to the items specified in InterNACHI Standards of Practice 2.4 and 2.6, the inspector shall inspect:

- slip joints, adjustable sleeves, looped water supply lines, flexible hose sections, and flexible ductwork that are visible as part of the standard heating and plumbing inspections.

<u>Exclusions</u>

The inspector is not required to:

- Inspect or predict the condition of the interiors of logs.
- Predict the life expectancy of logs.
- Climb onto log walls. However, the inspector may inspect log walls by use of a ladder, if this procedure may be done safely and without damaging the walls.
- Inspect components of the porch support system, or of the plumbing or heating systems, that are not readily visible and accessible.

Witnessing the Service Life of Log Homes

Many log homes were built in North America, and many are still in use. Some have been covered over for some reason and rediscovered during renovation work. Why would log homes be covered over?

- Application of a new siding product/ method that would eliminate the need to maintain the seal between the logs.
- Additions to the existing structure using conventional framing methods calling for continuity of the exterior siding.
- Social influences that would identify a small log home as a different class or culture. Applying siding could be one way to dress up the appearance and raise social stature.
- Administration of codes, standards, covenants, and ordinances that require certain architectural specifications for buildings in a particular community.

Google Alerts is a great tool for learning about log buildings that have become the subject of news articles published on the Internet. In addition to the many log buildings in the <u>National Park Service</u>[30], many homes built by pioneers are showing up again in news. Here is an example that demonstrates that **log homes last well beyond the acknowledged service life of buildings,** regardless of the care given to them over the course of their existence.

Captain Timothy Hill House

Best said by quoting the article from the Eastern Shore News:

"CHINCOTEAGUE—The island will have its first listing on the Virginia Landmarks Register.

On June 16, the Board of Historic Resources and the State Review Board at its quarterly joint meeting in Richmond voted that the Captain Timothy Hill House, 5122 Main St., Chincoteague, would be officially listed on the Virginia Landmarks Register and its nomination be forwarded to the National Park Service for consideration for listing on the National Register of Historic Places.

The Hill House, built around 1800, is the oldest known house on Chincoteague. It is a log plank construction with full dovetail joints. This form of architectural construction came to the New World with the Finns and Swedes in the early 1600s by way of the Delaware Bay.

The Hill House before Paul Brzozowski and Louisa Flaningam purchased it in December 2009.

Credit: Louisa Flaningam

Log building was very prevalent in the early days of the country but few have survived. This building is likely one of two still standing in Virginia that was built to have a wooden chimney."

The Capt. Timothy Hill House of Chincoteague, Va., moved for a third time on June 21, 2010.

Credit: Louisa Flaningam

Figure 36: This building demonstrates the ability of log walls to prevail in spite of owner neglect. Open on Thursdays from 1-3 pm., visitors are welcomed to see the numerous sailing ships carved into the log walls. Source: Eastern Shore News

ENERGY POLITICS & REGULATION

In the mid 1970's, the log home industry faced three growing objections from the authority having jurisdiction over the construction of new log structures. First was a demand for graded logs. Second was a call for a fire-resistive rating of the wall assembly. Third was a need for an energy analysis that satisfied the new Federal initiatives for energy conservation.

The Energy Crisis of the 1970's brought the first cry for independence from the interests controlling foreign oil, resulting in the US Weatherization Assistance Program and ultimately the U.S. Dept. of Energy (DOE). One initiative was the development of a new code that set minimum requirements for building energy performance. The primary focus of the new building energy code was the thermal envelope defined as the combination of assemblies and components that separate the interior, conditioned air volume from the ever changing exterior environment.

Why an energy code? Fire and life safety codes have helped improve building design and construction by placing a priority on protecting occupants relative to the hazards normally found for the activity intended for the structure. Plumbing, mechanical and electrical codes similarly exist to protect occupants from potentially hazardous installations. Building codes require structures to be designed to have the capacity to withstand the design loads expected from the environment in which they will be built. Fire codes address the length of time a structure can be expected to remain standing to allow emergency services to arrive and remove occupants from the fire. The distribution codes insure that water, warmth and/or cooling, and power are safely and adequately delivered to the intended locations. Energy codes evolved to limit the extent of resources required to provide a comfortable and healthy indoor habitat. Today, "green" building codes are being developed to insure that the materials and methods required by the other codes are designed to limit the overall use of materials and energy to produce them, providing a responsible environmentally sound structure.

Over many versions of the energy conservation codes, the thermal envelope regularly advanced levels of insulation to meet its goals, although research of the 1970's had identified air infiltration as the bigger culprit for heating fuel consumption. This was largely due to the effort that earlier weatherization programs had established to temper air leakage rates. Even though DOE and other proponents recognize testing to verify performance as the ultimate approach to an energy code, the process begins with calculations that rely on R-Value. Unfortunately, established wood properties do not demonstrate a competitive value for heat transmission through a 1" sample. Wood provides roughly R-1 per inch thickness vs. R-3 to R-7 per inch for rated insulation products (rated = tested in an accredited lab to ASTM standard methods). Log walls require a different set of evaluation criteria that more accurately represents the comfortable, energy-efficient performance expressed by log home owners.

The ARRA legislation (a.k.a., the Recovery Act) provided an incentive to all levels of state and local government nationwide to adopt the 2009 IECC (International Energy Conservation Code). The new and/or revised requirements of this code brought impacts that greatly affect the log home industry.

DOE has established a significant campaign to reduce building energy consumption to meet the Challenge 2030 Net-Zero Energy Initiative identified by architect Ed Mazria in 2002 and promulgated by Architecture 2030, a non-profit organization in Sante Fe, NM. DOE had been developing valuable tools and resources for the building industry for many years, and offers them for free on several sites:

> http://www.energycodes.gov-- The Energy Policy Act of 1992 called on DOE to support the adoption and enforcement of energy codes in the states. This website was created by DOE's Building Energy Codes Program which was funded in 1993.

> http://www.eere.energy.gov-- Information on energy efficiency and renewable energy. This site has an incredible number of links to builder programs and residential building products, appliances, and more.

> http://www.bcap-ocean.org This is the site of the Building Codes Assistance Project, funded by DOE to track and report on state energy code activity. This online code environment and advocacy network is another source for information and educational tools.

> http://www.dsireusa.org-- A valuable website that provides a database of State incentives for renewables and energy efficiency.

The combination of prescriptive code requirements, legislation for rapid adoption and enforcement, and the zealous advocacy of lobbyists threaten to eliminate the log home industry and the American heritage on which it is founded. The speed of change is evident in the two maps below, showing code adoption by state.

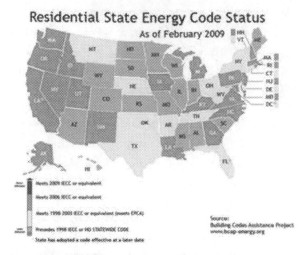

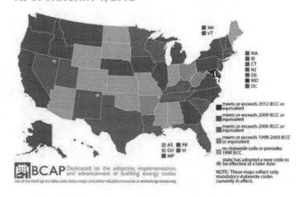

Figure 37: Nationwide reporting of code adoptions. Source: http://bcap-ocean.org/ code-status-residential.

The Evolution of Energy Conservation Codes

With the energy code goals established, DOE started to work more closely with the ICC (International Codes Council) code development process when it was formed from the merger of the regional model code agencies in the U.S. (ICBO, BOCAI, SBCCI and CABO).

ICC's code development process was established on a three-year cycle. The cycle included proposal of code changes, public comment and debate on those proposals, final action by a consensus of building officials,

resulting in a new publication. Through the 2003 edition of ICC's International Energy Conservation Code (IECC, which replaced the CABO Model Energy Code), DOE had been a contributor to the process. That changed a bit in the 2003-4 cycle as DOE arrived with a complete rewrite of the 2003 IECC. First published as the 2004 Supplement, the new IECC was not adopted by many jurisdictions until it was published as the 2006 IECC.

With the 2006 IECC in place, DOE established it as the baseline code for the 2030 Initiative. DOE goals for the development of the 2009 IECC were to integrate changes that would produce new building designs that use 15% less energy than those built to the 2006 IECC. Changes to the IECC for the 2012 edition, now available, targeted another 15% savings in building energy use so that new buildings are 30% better than the 2006 code. And for 2015, the IECC is expected to produce buildings that save 50% more energy than the 2006 IECC baseline.

The log home industry has a history of (and pride in) providing warm, comfortable, and energy efficient homes (as compared to neighboring framed homes). Log home owners consistently list energy efficiency as one of the reasons they purchased and built their log home. The log home industry continues to respond to the changing energy code environment with higher performance windows and doors, insulated foundations, higher levels of roof insulation, and increased mechanical efficiency.

The CABO Codes

The discussion of log homes and energy code compliance has escalated since energy codes were initiated and implemented in the 1970's. The call for heat loss analysis on a wall system that few knew how to evaluate caused enough concern and expense for the log home industry that the Log Homes Council came about. With the advent of the CABO (Council of American Building Officials) Model Energy Code (MEC), the log home industry learned to evaluate log structures to meet/exceed the requirements of the MEC.

Based on the work completed under the DOE Thermal Mass Program (1975-1985), the Model Energy Code (MEC) was modified in 1989 to include an allowance for mass wall construction. The mass wall tables from the original MEC versions remained unchanged through the 2003 IECC. The MEC focused primarily on energy conservation through increasing the insulation of the thermal envelope, although air infiltration had already been identified as the most significant factor in building energy usage.

Originally written by CABO, the One & Two Family Dwelling Code became the International Residential Code (IRC) when ICC was formed. The IRC is the building code for all dwellings under 3 stories, and it contains the energy conservation requirements for these structures in Part IV, Chapter 11. All other building types are covered for elements of life safety by the International Building Code (IBC) and for energy conservation by the International Energy Conservation Code (IECC).

The 2003 IECC

When written, ICC400-2007 Section 305 *Thermal Performance* referred to the 2003 IECC, which contained the table below that benefitted log walls. The entire approach taken for mass wall evaluation in the 2003 IECC was carried forward into ICC400-2007. The process was defined in ICC400, but the user was directed to the IECC for the tables that addressed design conditions. During the development of ICC400, this was the appropriate reference; however, as ICC400 was being finalized through the ANSI public comment process, the IECC code development cycle went through two changes—the 2004 Supplement and the 2006 edition. Therefore, the reference to the IECC in ICC400 Section 305 cannot be found in the 2006 IECC since the referenced table had been removed during the code change cycle and replaced with the "simplified" tables 402.1.1 and 402.1.3 and the provision that log walls are included as "mass walls."

While the 2006 edition of the IECC had become a bit more stringent, log homes were not experiencing great difficulty in complying with it. Log home designs utilized greater roof insulation and better windows than required by the code to offset the imbalance between log walls vs. insulated frame walls (the "trade-off" approach, also known as the UA Alternative).

Heating Degree Days (HDD)	UW REQUIRED FOR WALLS WITH A HEAT CAPACITY LESS THAN 6 Btu/ft2-oF AS DETERMINED BY USING EQUATIONS 5-1 AND FIGURE 502.2(1)										
	0.24	0.22	0.20	0.18	0.16	0.14	0.12	0.10	0.08	0.06	0.04
0-2000	0.33	0.31	0.28	0.25	0.23	0.20	0.17	0.15	0.12	0.09	0.07
2001-4000	0.32	0.30	0.27	0.24	0.22	0.19	0.17	0.14	0.11	0.09	0.06
4001-5500	0.30	0.28	0.26	0.23	0.21	0.18	0.16	0.13	0.11	0.08	0.06
5500-6500	0.28	0.26	0.24	0.21	0.19	0.17	0.14	0.12	0.10	0.08	0.05
6500-8000	0.26	0.24	0.22	0.20	0.18	0.15	0.13	0.11	0.09	0.07	0.05
>8000	0.24	0.22	0.20	0.18	0.16	0.14	0.12	0.10	0.08	0.06	0.04

Figure 38: Equivalent U-Factor for log walls. Source: 2003 IECC Table 502.2.1.1.2(3)

The 2006 IECC

At the 2004 National Workshop on State Building Energy Codes, an update was presented on DOE's Residential IECC Code Change that became the 2004 Supplement to the 2003 IECC.[31] Key points of the rewritten IECC were:

- Climate zones reduced from 19 to 8, with political/geographic boundaries (state, county lines);
- A minimum glazing U-factor established per climate zone, and the window-wall ratio (glazing area as a percentage of opaque wall area) removed. This was explained as saying that if the established U-factor was met, 100% of the wall area could be glazing.
- The density requirements have been omitted from section 402.2.3 for mass walls.
- Mass wall requirements are now listed by R-value (Table 402.1) and u-value (Table 402.1.2). Table 402.1.2 integrates a mass credit for climate zones 1-5, but not for climate zones 6-8, but these u-values are not the inverse of the R-values in Table 402.1.
- The R-value tables show requirements for high-density insulations in framing cavities and include rigid insulation sheathing as an option in colder climates.

With the 2004 Supplement to the IECC, a result of the 2003/2004 Code Development Cycle, the 2003 edition of the IECC was substantially revised and reformatted. The actions resulted in the elimination of four entire chapters (5-7, 9), as well as the appendix of the 2003 IECC. Proponents praised the reduction in the size of the code and the simplification. The 2004 IECC Supplement became the 2006 IECC with some modifications which added many pages back to the code. The IECC had been an option for residential evaluation in addition to the International Residential Code (IRC) largely because they were the same. However, the 2004 Supplement is a drastic departure from what it was (effort to simplify) and is no longer aligned with the IRC.

The effect on the log home industry was interesting. The key change affecting the log home industry was a dramatic simplification of the mass wall criteria and evaluation process, reducing three tables to one. All log walls were grouped together and defined as mass walls along with other mass wall technologies. Mass walls became defined in IECC section 402.2.3 as having 50% or more of the required insulation R-value on the exterior (such as concrete/masonry/earth) or integral in the wall (such as log). However, the tabulated mass wall U-Factors were based on concrete wall applications and the benefit of solid wood walls was lost in the "simplification".

The IECC provides alternatives for compliance. The fastest approach is to simply meet or exceed the thermal properties of each assembly in the thermal envelope—e.g., rated insulation levels for roof, floor and wall cavities. To account for alternative methods and materials of construction, the UA Alternative allows a designer to trade off the thermal ratings of components in order to achieve an overall weighted average that is lower than the product of the prescriptive requirements and envelope areas. This has been the most commonly used approach as it was greatly facilitated by the REScheck® program developed for DOE.

A very important note: **Prescriptive code requirements set the minimum allowable standard** accepted by the code to comply. There is no limit on specifications that are better than those prescribed.

INTERNATIONAL CLIMATE ZONE DEFINITIONS

ZONE NUMBER	THERMAL CRITERIA	
	IP Units	SI Units
1	9000 < CDD50°F	5000 < CDD10°C
2	6300 < CDD50°F ≤ 9000	3500 < CDD10°C ≤ 5000
3A and 3B	4500 < CDD50°F ≤ 6300 AND HDD65°F ≤ 5400	2500 < CDD10°C ≤ 3500 AND HDD18°C ≤ 3000
4A and 4B	CDD50°F ≤ 4500 AND HDD65°F ≤ 5400	CDD10°C ≤ 2500 AND HDD18°C ≤ 3000
3C	HDD65°F ≤ 3600	HDD18°C ≤ 2000
4C	3600 < HDD65°F ≤ 5400	2000 < HDD18°C ≤ 3000
5	5400 < HDD65°F ≤ 7200	3000 < HDD18°C ≤ 4000
6	7200 < HDD65°F ≤ 9000	4000 < HDD18°C ≤ 5000
7	9000 < HDD65°F ≤ 12600	5000 < HDD18°C ≤ 7000
8	12600 < HDD65°F	7000 < HDD18°C

For SI: °C = [(°F)-32]/1.8

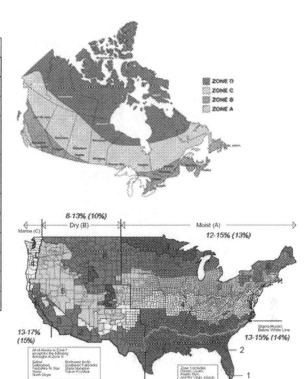

Canadian Climate Zone data is provided on the oee.nrcan.gc.ca website as

- Zone D: > 8000 HDDs
- Zone C: > 5500 to <= 8000 HDDs
- Zone B: > 3500 to <= 5500 HDDs
- Zone A: <= 3500 HDDs

An HDD is the annual sum of the degrees of the average daily temperature for all days below 18°C.

Figure 39: TABLE 301.3(2) from the 2006 IECC has been carried forward to the 2012, along with the Climate Zone Map. Climate Zones Maps of Canada (Source: 0ee.nrcan.gc.ca) and U.S. (Source: U.S. DOE for the 2004 IECC Supplement)

Other significant changes in the 2006 IECC included

- 402.5 Moisture control—Unvented assemblies must have a vapor barrier required on the warm-in-winter side of the thermal insulation.
- Table404.5.2(1)—Minimummechanical system efficiencies are set for electric air-source heat pump, nonelectric furnaces (natural gas) and boilers with prevailing federal minimum efficiency.
- Air exchange rate assuming no energy recovery is defined as a Specific Leakage Area (SLA) of 0.00036, where L is defined in accordance with Section 5.1 of ASHRAE 119 and where SLA=L/ CFA and L and CFA are in the same units.

The log home industry continued to successfully comply with the 2006 IECC by balancing the U-Factor trade-offs in REScheck, which still allowed the option of increased mechanical efficiency.

An important detail in the 2006 IECC was the allowance for upgrading the efficiency of mechanical equipment to offset deficiencies in insulation levels. When insulation levels alone would not offset the variance between code requirement and log wall properties, designers could specify the mechanical efficiency to achieve compliance. This was and continues to be a major point of contention between builders and DOE, however both the 2009 and 2012 editions no longer allow this tradeoff.

The 2009 IECC

For the first time, mechanical efficiency has been taken out of the IECC as a consideration for energy conservation. The impact of this change has been big in the colder climate zones of the United States where nominal 6" milled log walls have performed well for decades. In general, the nominal 6" milled log is no longer an option unless unrealistic levels of roof and foundation insulation are coupled with extreme window performance and changing log gables and dormers to frame.

Other significant changes in the 2009 IECC included

- Removed 402.5, moving vapor barrier requirements to the ICC International Residential Code (IRC).
- Removed the option of using increased mechanical efficiency to offset insulation levels below the prescriptive minimum established for the thermal envelope.
- Added 402.4 Air leakage (Mandatory) by testing (ACH50<7) or visual inspection per Table 402.4.2.

The single biggest change to the 2009 IECC that threatens the log home industry is the elimination of the mechanical efficiency trade-off. The call for testing of air infiltration changed the industry's focus from prescriptive code

compliance to performance path through certified energy audits. At 7 ACH50, most reasonably well built homes comply.

The 2012 IECC

Compliance with the 2012 edition of the IECC is a problem because it incorporates the higher levels of insulation and glazing performance that the log home industry had previously used to offset the deficiency in log wall R-value. A carryover from the 2009 IECC, the exclusion of mechanical efficiency from the UA tradeoff amplifies the problem. The impact of the 2012 IECC on the thermal envelope is highlighted in the tables shown in the section, UA Alternative Case Study.

A significant change in the 2012 IECC is the advancement of the tight house mindset. As Joseph Lstiburek, Ph.D., P.Eng., ASHRAE Fellow, and a principal of Building Science Corporation (www.buildingscience.com) has preached to all audiences, "Build tight, ventilate right." He credits the phrase to a time dating back to the 1970's. Doing so reduces the demand and therefore the required capacities of heating and cooling equipment. It reduces drafts and balances the indoor air pressure with conditioned air.

The 2012 IECC references log walls in a footnote to the air barrier table. Critics noted that log walls cannot achieve the definition of an air barrier, but the definition in the IECC clarifies the point:

"**AIR BARRIER.** Material(s) assembled and joined together to provide a barrier to air leakage through the building envelope. An air barrier may be a single material or a combination of materials."

Log walls demonstrate that they satisfy the **air barrier requirements** of the IECC.

1. Solid wood walls, at 3-inch thickness are thick enough to be considered an air barrier.
2. When log homes are designed and built properly, log joinery maintains an equally air tight seal as the wood itself.

The quality of log home construction is no more questionable than the quality of construction and installation of insulation on any other method of construction.

Based on a blower door test (pressurized to 50 pascals or 0.2 inches of water), a blower door test provides two readings, infiltration rate and air exchange rate. The infiltration rate is the volume of outside air entering the thermal envelope and is measured in cubic feet per minute (CFM). The air exchange rate (a.k.a., air changes per hour or ACH) is the number of times per hour the entire volume of the interior air changes. The 2012 IECC sets ACH ≤ 3 in cold climates, where ACH = CFM*60/volume within the thermal envelope. This equates to a home that meets minimum ventilation requirements of ASHRAE 62-1999, *"Ventilation for Acceptable Indoor Air Quality"* (0.35 ACH by natural or mechanical ventilation).

During testing:

1. Exterior windows and doors, fireplace and stove doors shall be closed, but not sealed, beyond the intended weatherstripping or other infiltration control measures;
2. Dampers including exhaust, intake, makeup air, backdraft and flue dampers shall be closed, but not sealed beyond intended infiltration control measures;
3. Interior doors, if installed at the time of the test, shall be open;

4. Exterior doors for continuous ventilation systems and heat recovery ventilators shall be closed and sealed;
5. Heating and cooling systems, if installed at the time of the test, shall be turned off; and
6. Supply and return registers, if installed at the time of the test, shall be fully open.

If log walls are not resisting heat transfer losses at the same rates as other materials, components and assemblies, the variance must be quantified. Using a UA alternative from REScheck®, the heat loss can be estimated in terms of BTUs and measured in terms of heating fuels.

> **The 2012 IECC changes the mass wall U-Factor for the first time in 6 years, but only for Climate Zones 4 (except marine) and 6. The other major change coming in the 2012 IECC is the requirement to test to insure that air infiltration is limited to 5 ACH50 in Climate Zones 1 &2 or 3 ACH50 in Climate Zones 3-8.**

Changes beyond the Thermal Envelope

For decades, homeowners have provided log home companies with testimonials as to the energy efficiency of their log home. Throughout that time, it was assumed that thermal mass was the key, not just a contributor. In the 1980's, air infiltration was identified as having the single greatest impact on thermal performance, and hence energy conservation. Simultaneously, log homes were fending off the reputation of being leaky construction. If air infiltration was recognized long ago as the prime cause for energy consumption in a heating climate, how could log homes be so comfortable?

ALL IECC Climate Zones (CZ)				Future? DOE Challenge Home	
Component / System	2006 IECC	2009 IECC	2012 IECC		
Duct Tightness	0.80 DSE	8 CFM/100 sf	4 CFM/100 sf	Ducts located within the thermal/air barrier.	
Airtight Level	0.00036 SLA	7 ACH50	5 ACH50 in CZ 1-2 3 ACH50 in CZ 3-8	CZ	ACH50
				1-2	3
				3, 4 except marine	2.5
				5-7	2
				8	1.5
Lighting Efficiency	10% Assumed	50%	75%	80% of lighting fixtures are ENERGY STAR qualified or ENERGY STAR lamps (bulbs) in minimum 80% of sockets	
% Fenestration: Wall to Floor Area (WFA)	18% Assumed	15% Assumed	15% Assumed	Prescriptive: (0.15 / WFA) x ENERGY STAR requirement	
				CZ 1-3	ES SHGC
				CZ 4-8	ES U-Value

Figure 40: Among the many changes over the past three IECC code cycles are these that address performance rather than envelope R-value. Source: Author, consolidated from DOE/ICC documents.

So, with all of the talk of thermal mass, was thermal mass really the factor that made log walls better than framed walls? With the IECC prescribing rated R-Values of insulation that are reaching the point of diminishing returns, the code changes that may have the biggest impact are the tighter requirements above. If air infiltration is truly the big energy hog in homes, perhaps we have the real explanation of how log homes have performed better than framed homes. Perhaps the allowance for the conventional home to pack in the insulation but still allow them to leak like sieves while log walls were airtight is the answer. Perhaps allowing convective airflow within insulated cavities had a bigger impact than acknowledged by the insulation folks. Have we been taken for an expensive ride for the past 30 years so that insulation manufacturers can profit?

Log walls are frequently criticized regarding air leaks because of the number and extent of joints in the wall assembly. This narrow view of log walls is further promulgated by DOE on their EERE website (http://www.energysavers. gov/your_home/designing_remodeling/index. cfm/mytopic=10180), noting

> Log homes are susceptible to developing air leaks. Air-dried logs are still about 15%-20% water when the house is assembled or constructed. As the logs dry over the next few years, the logs shrink. The contraction and expansion of the logs open gaps between the logs, creating air leaks, which cause drafts and high heating requirements.

To minimize air leakage, logs should be seasoned (dried in a protected space) for at least six months before construction begins. These are the best woods to use to avoid this problem, in order of effectiveness:

Cedar → Spruce → Pine → Fir → Larch

Since most manufacturers and experienced builders know of these shrinkage and resulting air leakage problems, many will kiln dry the logs prior to finish shaping and installation. Some also recommend using plastic gaskets and caulking compounds to seal gaps. These seals require regular inspection and resealing when necessary.

While not entirely incorrect, this information illustrates a bias that DOE should discontinue. Yet, it should be noted that over the course of history, infiltration issues have been controlled by using full length logs, larger logs, and chinking with readily available materials to seal the joints. For new log construction, the discussion **Quantifying the Components of Settling** sets parameters for building that manage the joinery in log walls to keep them airtight. This is further demonstrated in <u>Rated Energy Performance</u>.

The best response to critics regarding air infiltration in log homes is to ask, "What percentage of conventional, wood-frame homes built in the same time frame has air infiltration?" As we learn more from blower door testing on the built inventory of homes, we are finding that there are a high percentage of homes with air infiltration rates that are no longer acceptable by today's standards. What is the difference between log and stick homes regarding air infiltration? A well-built log home demonstrated superior control of air infiltration—how do you blow air through solid wood? However, there are log homes that are not built to be airtight just as older wood framed homes were not. As builders focus on the issue, both forms of construction will certainly advance to meet the upgraded performance standards.

Comparisons of thermal performance of solid wood walls (or any thermal mass wall) versus conventional frame construction depicted in the building codes are inappropriate without reporting air infiltration rates.

Controlling air infiltration in log buildings is synonymous with water infiltration, and both are best managed at the exterior exposure to the outside air. Modern log homes are designed and produced to account for movement in the wall system. The log profile is designed to shed water on the exterior surface onto the surface of the log below without capillary action between logs. To further control the joint between logs and the potential for movement at that point, a combination of joinery design and sealants (dry gaskets and/or wet applied caulk) are used. In service, maintenance practices are included in homeowner manuals that instruct the owner to perform periodic inspections of the log wall, covering such topics as how to fill and seal exterior seasoning checks.

Log buildings will have the same trouble spots as any other type of construction, but the structure itself can be tested when it first made airtight, before any finishes have been started. A blower door test of the "weather-tight shell" will allow proper sealing at a time when that application is at its least cost.

Look at the common areas for leaks before critiquing the log wall. Gaps in basement walls can account for as much as a third of the energy costs lost to air infiltration. Convective loops that begin in the basement can run up interior wall cavities, chases, and other locations up to the attic, cooling interior wall finishes that now absorb interior heat and drawing heated air through outlets and other openings in the interior walls. Closing the loop at the basement level using a method that qualifies as an air barrier (not packing fiberglass batt in holes) is the key. Tightly sealed fireplace doors are referenced in the 2012 IECC, but what about chimneys? Chimney flues also need to be sealed against air and vapor as well as providing a firestop to the structural elements.

"Over the past 10 years I have conducted hundreds of blower door and thermal imaging surveys on log homes throughout the country. I typically only get called in to assess and repair "problem log homes". In the vast majority of these homes it is not the logs that are the big problem. It is usually problems with the roof system, poor or inconsistent air / vapor barriers, canned lights, etc. It is very frustrating. These same problems exist in countless

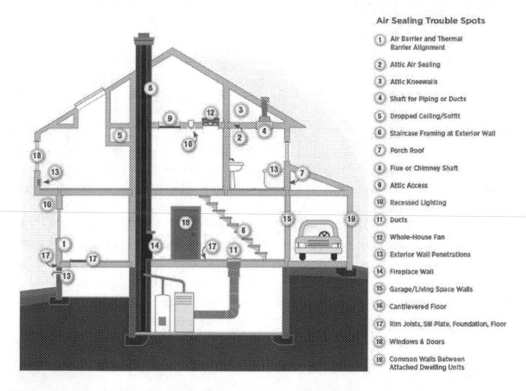

Air Sealing Trouble Spots

1. Air Barrier and Thermal Barrier Alignment
2. Attic Air Sealing
3. Attic Kneewalls
4. Shaft for Piping or Ducts
5. Dropped Ceiling/Soffit
6. Staircase Framing at Exterior Wall
7. Porch Roof
8. Flue or Chimney Shaft
9. Attic Access
10. Recessed Lighting
11. Ducts
12. Whole-House Fan
13. Exterior Wall Penetrations
14. Fireplace Wall
15. Garage/Living Space Walls
16. Cantilevered Floor
17. Rim Joists, Sill Plate, Foundation, Floor
18. Windows & Doors
19. Common Walls Between Attached Dwelling Units

Figure 41: Illustration of Air Sealing Trouble Spots in *ALL* Residential Construction. Source: EERE Air Leakage Guide[32]

Proof of the performance of log structures comes from Tracy Hansen, President of Stormbusters Inc., in Jackson, WY. In a conversation with Mr. Hansen, he provided the following from his experience with log structures:

thousands of frame homes as well but I have never heard a homeowner, contractor, or architect say "I'll never have a "frame home" they are just too problematic."

State Energy Codes

Facing a realization that many families in their states may lose jobs as log home companies go out of business due to energy code adoption, several states have made amendments to their energy codes to provide for log walls. Granted, the greatest help has come from those states that recognize their forestry resource as vital to health of the State. However, these states are providing guidance to others across the Nation as we adopt the new versions of the IECC.

- Footnote "d" of that table: "The wall component shall be a minimum solid log or timber wall thickness of 3.5 inches (90 mm)."

New Hampshire

The 2006 IECC is currently enforced with an amended version of the 2009 proposed to the State Legislature. Upon approval, log homes will be handled as follows:

Building Section	Required R or U Values	YOUR PROPOSED STRUCTURE	
		Write Planned R and U Values	Brands / Models / insulation type and thickness (if known)
Above Grade Wall R Value[ii]	**R-20** Cavity Insulation only *or* **R-13** *plus* **R-5** Cavity *plus* Continuous Insulation R-13 (Thermally Isolated Sunrooms only)		Log walls must comply with ICC400 with an average minimum wall thickness of 5" or greater and must have overall glazing of U-.31 or lower and heating AFUE of 90% (gas) or 84% (oil) and all other component. Check if ☐ Sunroom ☐ Log Walls

[ii]R-13 + R-5 means R-13 cavity insulation plus R-5 insulated sheathing. If structural sheathing covers 25 percent or less of the exterior, R-5 sheathing is not required where the structural sheathing is placed. If structural sheathing covers more than 25 percent of exterior, the structural sheathing must be supplemented with insulated sheathing of at least R-2."

Washington & Oregon

2008 OR SC-Chapter 11: Table N1101.1(1) Prescriptive Envelope Requirements includes log walls specifically, with an increase in flat ceiling insulation from R-38 to R-49 but allowing R-38 to the outside of the log wall in vaulted ceilings.

Vermont

The 2011 VT Residential Building Energy Standard was officially adopted on July 1st. The standard will not become effective until three months after final adoption and "shall apply to construction commenced on and after the date they become effective." So the effective date for RBES will be October 1st.

TABLE 402.1.3
LOG HOME INSULATION AND FENESTRATION REQUIREMENTS BY COMPONENT[a]

FENESTRATION U-FACTOR[b]	SKYLIGHT U-FACTOR	MAXIMUM GLAZING AREA[c]	CEILING U-FACTOR	MASS WALL U-FACTOR[d]	FLOOR U-FACTOR[e]	BASEMENT WALL U-FACTOR[f]	SLAB U-FACTOR & DEPTH	HEATED SLAB U-FACTOR[g]	CRAWL SPACE WALL U-FACTOR
0.30	0.55	20%	0.020	Log	0.026	0.050	0.066, 4 ft	0.066	0.050

For SI: 1 foot = 304.8 mm.

a. U-factors are maximums.
b. The fenestration U-factor column excludes skylights.
c. Glazing area includes window and skylight opening area, plus actual glazed area of glass in doors. Sunrooms are exempt from this requirement.
d. Log walls must comply with ICC400 with an average minimum wall thickness of 5" or greater, and have a heating AFUE of 90% (gas) or 85% (oil). Boilers must have a modulating aquastat or outdoor temperature limit control.
e. Or insulation sufficient to fill the framing cavity, with U-0.05 as the absolute minimum.
f. Foundation U-factor requirements shown in Table 402.1.3 include wall construction and interior air films but exclude soil conductivity and exterior air films. U-factors for determining code compliance in accordance with Section 402.1.4 (total UA alternative) of Section 405 (Simulated Performance Alternative) shall be modified to include soil conductivity and exterior films.
g. Required beneath the entire slab.

Idaho

Changes to the state energy code include section "402.6 Residential Log Home Thermal Envelope." This section stipulates that log homes comply with the same requirements for air leakage, maximum fenestration U-Factor and Solar Heat Gain Coefficient, controls, sealing, and all mandatory provisions. In addition to REScheck analysis or simulated performance alternative paths, the prescriptive path is provided in Table 402.6. The table allows for a 5-inch minimum average log thickness when high efficiency equipment is used; otherwise, the log wall must be 8-inches.

Minnesota

The code calls for a minimum 7-in. diameter log with 0.31 overall glazing U-factor or better (2009). This statement has been interpreted as covering need and reasonableness, meaning that the state cannot put an industry out of business, dictate or restrict the type of construction.

> 16B.59 POLICY AND PURPOSE. The State Building Code governs the construction, reconstruction, alteration, and repair of buildings and other structures to which the code is applicable. The commissioner shall administer and amend a state code of building construction which will provide basic and uniform performance standards, establish reasonable safeguards for health, safety, welfare, comfort, and security of the residents of this state and provide for the use of modern methods, devices, materials, and techniques which will in part tend to lower construction costs. The construction of buildings should be permitted at the least possible cost consistent with recognized standards of health and safety.

APPLYING THE IECC TO LOG HOMES

The log home industry is in peril because of the legislative pressures to meet or exceed the minimum requirements of the ICC International Energy Conservation Code.

Proponents for the higher R-values suggest that increasing log wall thickness is the answer. However, steady-state R-values for wood would require unnecessarily large logs that would significantly increase the cost of a log home. Cost increases are associated with several aspects of log building:

• Increased volume of wood fiber

- Additional handling and tooling to account for the additional weight
- Greater tree waste because natural taper of the tree limits available use to shorter lengths from the butt end
- Reduced environmental benefits of log construction as the need for larger timber requires older trees.

Looking at the continuing code changes (the IECC is scheduled per the ICC standard 3-year code development cycle), one can see that the U-Factor requirements for mass walls did not change remarkably over the various editions. Hence it is the other elements of the thermal envelope that have impacted the ability of log homes to meet the energy code requirements.

Climate Zone	City	HDD	2006 IECC U-Factors				2009 IECC U-Factors				2012 IECC U-Factors			
			Glazing	Floor	Roof	Mass Wall	Glazing	Floor	Roof	Mass Wall	Glazing	Floor	Roof	Mass Wall
1	Miami, FL	139	1.2	0.064	0.035	0.197	1.2	0.064	0.035	0.197	0.50	0.064	0.035	0.197
2	Mobile, AL	1702	0.75	0.064	0.035	0.165	0.65	0.064	0.035	0.165	0.40	0.064	0.035	0.165
3	Greenville, NC	3129	0.65	0.047	0.035	0.141	0.50	0.047	0.035	0.141	0.35	0.047	0.03	0.141
4 except marine	Louisville, KY	4514	0.40	0.047	0.03	0.141	0.35	0.047	0.03	0.141	0.35	0.047	0.03	0.098
4 marine	Portland, OR	4522	0.35	0.033	0.03	0.082	0.35	0.033	0.03	0.082	0.32	0.033	0.026	0.082
5	Omaha, NE	6300	0.35	0.033	0.03	0.082	0.35	0.033	0.03	0.082	0.32	0.033	0.026	0.082
6	Laconia, NH	7956	0.35	0.033	0.026	0.06	0.35	0.033	0.026	0.06	0.32	0.033	0.026	0.057
7 & 8	Anchorage, AK	10871	0.35	0.033	0.026	0.057	0.35	0.028	0.026	0.057	0.32	0.028	0.026	0.057

Figure 42: Comparing prescriptive U-Factor changes to common elements of log homes illustrates where in the thermal envelope changes have been made to reach the 2030 accord.

The additional costs would greatly limit the ability to continue selling affordable log homes with current products, forcing log home companies to make hard decisions and sending repercussions throughout the log supply network, with all ancillary products and services similarly affected.

It is easy to see the continued tightening of glazing U-Factors. Since log home companies have always worked to stay ahead of these minimum requirements, they will rely on their window manufacturers to continually provide more efficient windows and doors that exceed the code minimums. What's coming down the road?

DOE's Challenge Home requirements indicate even tougher glazing requirements:

Measure	Hot Climate Zones (1-2)	Mixed Climate Zones (3-4, except Marine)	Cold Climate Zones (4 Marine—8)
SHGC	0.25	0.27	any
U-Value	0.4	0.3	0.27

Prepare for it now.

Floor insulation is a possibility, but experience has shown that improving the performance of the foundation wall provides a bigger benefit for log building. Insulated concrete forms (ICF), precast insulated panels (e.g., Superior Wall Systems), and other methods are preferred for better thermal envelope performance.

Roof insulation for log homes is similar to any home regardless of wall construction. The arguments of what is the best type of insulation are beyond the scope of this work, but the advances in use and requirement of foam insulations should be noted. For cathedral beam and deck roof systems, log home builders have used rigid insulation with strapping (for airspace and nail-base) over roofing felt and decking for years. They like the ability to use higher R/inch material, seal and overlap seams, etc. Some have moved to structural insulated panels (SIPs) over the timbers to save on-site labor, using the panels to provide insulation and structure at once (allowing use of paneling or gypsum as the finish ceiling). In either case, the required thickness of the foam panels will impact the thickness of the fascia.

Mass walls have not seen the same changes over the last several code cycles due to the mass wall benefits—no air leakage through the wall component and the ability to store heat gained from the interior to offset losses to the outside. These two concepts will be discussed again later. It is important to note here, though, that the columns containing the mass wall U-Factors reflect the benefit of opaque wall areas and not the insulation value. These U-Factors are slightly higher than their frame wall counterparts except in the colder climate zones (6-8).

Code Interpretations & Application of R-Values

Log wall assemblies reflect the lower R-value/inch of wood as established by ASHRAE standards and ASTM test protocols. However, the comparison to the rated, steady state R-value of insulation products installed in or on a wall cavity construction does not reflect the performance demonstrated by log walls—mass walls with integral insulation.

Interpretations of IECC requirements for log wall performance are often incorrect. Frequently enough, the interpretation is that a log wall must meet the rated insulation R-values provided in Table 402.1.1. This is neither accurate nor intended by the code, but the industry is put in a position of debating the issue that the frame wall requirements represent the rated insulation R-value rather than the effective overall value that accounts for the lower R-value of framing members.

Code requirements for minimum wood frame wall R-value are for the insulation only. The wood framing component of the wall can vary from 23% to 25% of the wall area, reducing the overall R-value of the wall. Log walls maintain the overall R-value across the entire wall area. Solely due to the framing factor therefore, mass walls in Zone 6 (R-19 batt) should be reduced to R-15; mass walls in Zones 7 and 8 should be reduced to R-16.

Wall assemblies constructed of solid material (e.g., log, brick, masonry/concrete, or straw bale) do not conceal a cavity, perform altogether differently, and can only be compared on the basis of the overall U-Factor as provided in IECC Table 402.1.3, where the framing factor for frame walls is applied. ICC400 uses this code requirement for overall U-Factor and applies it to Table 502.2.1.1.2(3) as published in the 2003 IECC to establish the log wall benefit.

The 2004 and later editions of the IECC specify cavity insulation R-values that do not account for any of the framing material thermal shorts through the insulation. According the "*Thermal Performance and Wall Ratings*" by J.E. Christian and J. Kosny of Oak Ridge National Laboratory (ORNL, http://www.ornl.gov/sci/roofs+walls/articles/wallratings/index.html), the whole wall R-value can be as low as 70.2% of the in-cavity R-value. ORNL has demonstrated that the whole wall R-value is a better criteria than the clear-wall and much better than the center-of-cavity R-value methods used to compare most types of wall systems. The value includes the effect of the wall interface details used to connect the wall to other walls, windows, doors, ceilings and foundations.

The IECC threatens to severely restrict the market and buyer profile of the log home industry because it uses prescriptive tables that compare the thermal properties of log walls to rated insulation products, not the wall assembly. To move away from R-Value and focus on the overall U-Factor of the wall assembly, the following two tables have been created. These two tables show the overall U-Factor for various widths of log wall made from wood species of various densities. The color coding in the tables match that of the DOE Climate Zone Map. Generating these maps at 12% equilibrium moisture content for the wood will produce the wall U-Factor that will appear in the DOE REScheck® program when a size and species of log is selected.

CLIMATE ZONES DEFINED AS MARINE, MOIST AND WARM-HUMID
U-Factor of Log Wall (Uw) by Average Width (WL) and Specific Gravity

Specific Gravity (Gu)	Average Width											
	5 in.	6 in.	7 in.	8 in.	9 in.	10 in.	11 in.	12 in.	14 in.	15 in.	16 in.	18 in.
0.29	0.115	0.098	0.085	0.075	0.067	0.061	0.056	0.051	0.044	0.041	0.039	0.035
0.30	0.118	0.100	0.087	0.077	0.069	0.063	0.057	0.053	0.045	0.043	0.040	0.036
0.31	0.121	0.103	0.089	0.079	0.071	0.064	0.059	0.054	0.047	0.044	0.041	0.037
0.32	0.124	0.105	0.092	0.081	0.073	0.066	0.060	0.055	0.045	0.045	0.042	0.038
0.33	0.127	0.108	0.094	0.083	0.075	0.068	0.062	0.057	0.049	0.046	0.043	0.039
0.34	0.130	0.111	0.096	0.085	0.076	0.069	0.063	0.058	0.050	0.047	0.044	0.040
0.35	0.133	0.113	0.098	0.087	0.078	0.071	0.065	0.060	0.052	0.048	0.045	0.041
0.36	0.136	0.116	0.101	0.089	0.080	0.073	0.066	0.061	0.053	0.049	0.046	0.042
0.37	0.139	0.118	0.103	0.091	0.082	0.074	0.068	0.063	0.054	0.051	0.045	0.043
0.38	0.142	0.121	0.105	0.093	0.084	0.076	0.069	0.064	0.055	0.052	0.049	0.043
0.39	0.145	0.123	0.107	0.095	0.085	0.077	0.071	0.065	0.057	0.053	0.050	0.044
0.40	0.147	0.126	0.110	0.097	0.087	0.079	0.072	0.067	0.058	0.054	0.051	0.045
0.41	0.150	0.128	0.112	0.099	0.089	0.081	0.074	0.068	0.059	0.055	0.052	0.046
0.42	0.153	0.131	0.114	0.101	0.091	0.082	0.075	0.070	0.060	0.056	0.053	0.047
0.43	0.156	0.133	0.116	0.103	0.093	0.084	0.077	0.071	0.061	0.058	0.054	0.048
0.45	0.162	0.138	0.121	0.107	0.096	0.087	0.080	0.074	0.064	0.060	0.056	0.050
0.46	0.164	0.141	0.123	0.109	0.098	0.089	0.082	0.075	0.065	0.061	0.057	0.051
0.47	0.167	0.143	0.125	0.111	0.100	0.091	0.083	0.077	0.066	0.062	0.059	0.052
0.48	0.170	0.146	0.127	0.113	0.102	0.092	0.085	0.078	0.068	0.063	0.060	0.053
0.49	0.173	0.148	0.129	0.115	0.103	0.094	0.086	0.080	0.069	0.065	0.061	0.054
0.51	0.178	0.153	0.134	0.119	0.107	0.097	0.089	0.082	0.071	0.067	0.063	0.056
0.53	0.184	0.158	0.138	0.123	0.111	0.101	0.092	0.085	0.074	0.069	0.065	0.058
0.54	0.187	0.160	0.140	0.125	0.112	0.102	0.094	0.087	0.075	0.070	0.066	0.059
0.55	0.190	0.163	0.143	0.127	0.114	0.104	0.095	0.088	0.076	0.072	0.067	0.060
0.56	0.192	0.165	0.145	0.129	0.116	0.106	0.097	0.089	0.078	0.073	0.069	0.061
0.57	0.195	0.168	0.147	0.131	0.118	0.107	0.098	0.091	0.079	0.074	0.070	0.062
0.62	0.209	0.180	0.158	0.141	0.127	0.115	0.106	0.098	0.085	0.080	0.075	0.067
0.70	0.230	0.199	0.175	0.156	0.141	0.129	0.118	0.109	0.095	0.089	0.084	0.076

For SI: 1 inch = 25.4 mm.
MCs = 13%

IECC Edition	2006	2009	2012 proposal
Climate Zone 1, 14% EMC	0.197	0.197	0.197
Climate Zone 2, 14% EMC	0.165	0.165	0.165
Climate Zone 3, 13% EMC	0.141	0.141	0.141
Zone 4 Moist, 13% EMC	0.141	0.141	0.098
Zone 5 Moist, 13% EMC	0.082	0.082	0.082
Climate Zone 6, 13% EMC	0.06	0.06	0.057
Climate Zones 7-8, 13% EMC	0.057	0.057	0.057

Figure 43: Color-coded comparisons of log wall average thickness to comply with IECC Mass Wall prescriptive U-Factors generally East of the Mississippi River

CLIMATE ZONES DEFINED AS MARINE, MOIST AND WARM-HUMID
U-Factor of Log Wall (Uw) by Average Width (WL) and Specific Gravity

Specific Gravity (Gw)	Average Width											
	5 in.	6 in.	7 in.	8 in.	9 in.	10 in.	11 in.	12 in.	14 in.	15 in.	16 in.	18 in.
0.29	0.115	0.098	0.085	0.075	0.067	0.061	0.056	0.051	0.044	0.041	0.039	0.035
0.30	0.118	0.100	0.087	0.077	0.069	0.063	0.057	0.053	0.045	0.043	0.040	0.036
0.31	0.121	0.103	0.089	0.079	0.071	0.064	0.059	0.054	0.047	0.044	0.041	0.037
0.32	0.124	0.105	0.092	0.081	0.073	0.066	0.060	0.055	0.048	0.045	0.042	0.038
0.33	0.127	0.108	0.094	0.083	0.075	0.068	0.062	0.057	0.049	0.046	0.043	0.039
0.34	0.130	0.111	0.096	0.085	0.076	0.069	0.063	0.058	0.050	0.047	0.044	0.040
0.35	0.133	0.113	0.098	0.087	0.078	0.071	0.065	0.060	0.052	0.048	0.045	0.041
0.36	0.136	0.116	0.101	0.089	0.080	0.073	0.066	0.061	0.053	0.049	0.046	0.042
0.37	0.139	0.118	0.103	0.091	0.082	0.074	0.068	0.063	0.054	0.051	0.048	0.043
0.38	0.142	0.121	0.105	0.093	0.084	0.076	0.069	0.064	0.055	0.052	0.049	0.043
0.39	0.145	0.123	0.107	0.095	0.085	0.077	0.071	0.065	0.057	0.053	0.050	0.044
0.40	0.147	0.126	0.110	0.097	0.087	0.079	0.072	0.067	0.058	0.054	0.051	0.045
0.41	0.150	0.128	0.112	0.099	0.089	0.081	0.074	0.069	0.059	0.055	0.052	0.046
0.42	0.153	0.131	0.114	0.101	0.091	0.082	0.075	0.070	0.060	0.056	0.053	0.047
0.43	0.156	0.133	0.116	0.103	0.093	0.084	0.077	0.071	0.061	0.058	0.054	0.048
0.45	0.162	0.138	0.121	0.107	0.096	0.087	0.080	0.074	0.064	0.060	0.056	0.050
0.46	0.164	0.141	0.123	0.109	0.098	0.089	0.082	0.075	0.065	0.061	0.057	0.051
0.47	0.167	0.143	0.125	0.111	0.100	0.091	0.083	0.077	0.066	0.062	0.059	0.052
0.48	0.170	0.146	0.127	0.113	0.102	0.092	0.085	0.078	0.068	0.063	0.060	0.053
0.49	0.173	0.148	0.129	0.115	0.103	0.094	0.086	0.080	0.069	0.065	0.061	0.054
0.51	0.178	0.153	0.134	0.119	0.107	0.097	0.089	0.082	0.071	0.067	0.063	0.056
0.53	0.184	0.158	0.138	0.123	0.111	0.101	0.092	0.085	0.074	0.069	0.065	0.058
0.54	0.187	0.160	0.140	0.125	0.112	0.102	0.094	0.087	0.075	0.070	0.066	0.059
0.55	0.190	0.163	0.143	0.127	0.114	0.104	0.095	0.088	0.076	0.072	0.067	0.060
0.56	0.192	0.165	0.145	0.129	0.116	0.106	0.097	0.089	0.078	0.073	0.069	0.061
0.57	0.195	0.168	0.147	0.131	0.118	0.107	0.098	0.091	0.079	0.074	0.070	0.062
0.62	0.209	0.180	0.158	0.141	0.127	0.115	0.106	0.098	0.085	0.080	0.075	0.067
0.70	0.230	0.199	0.175	0.156	0.141	0.129	0.118	0.109	0.095	0.089	0.084	0.076

For SI: 1 inch = 25.4 mm.
MCs = 13%

IECC Edition	2006	2009	2012 proposal
Climate Zone 1, 14% EMC	0.197	0.197	0.197
Climate Zone 2, 14% EMC	0.165	0.165	0.165
Climate Zone 3, 13% EMC	0.141	0.141	0.141
Zone 4 Moist, 13% EMC	0.141	0.141	0.098
Zone 5 Moist, 13% EMC	0.082	0.082	0.082
Climate Zone 6, 13% EMC	0.06	0.06	0.057
Climate Zones 7-8, 13% EMC	0.057	0.057	0.057

Figure 44: Color-coded comparisons of log wall average thickness to comply with IECC Mass Wall prescriptive U-Factors generally West of the Mississippi River

One can readily see the issues of comparing only the mass wall U-Factors in the IECC to a "prescriptive" log wall U-Factor. In New England, where the nominal 6-inch log wall has been built since the 1930's, prospective home buyers will have to purchase twice as much wood! As we will see in the next section, this is not true and leads to misleading conclusions. One such conclusion was reached by a highly regarded and respected ENERGY STAR® provider:

Default R-values provided by the EPA are R-1.4/inch for softwoods and R-0.71 for hardwoods. For log homes to achieve the minimum mass wall requirements of R-15, the **minimum, average log wall thickness must be:**

- **11 inches** for softwood logs,
- **21 inches** for hardwood logs,
- Or, the wall must utilze other means of insulation in addition to the logs to

achieve minimum insulation standards.

Using the IECC requirement for a mass wall to have a U-Factor of 0.06, one can get to the R-15. Divide by the 1.4 and round up and one gets the 11". Using <u>Figure 45</u>: Color-coded comparisons of log wall average thickness to comply with IECC Mass Wall prescriptive U-Factors generally East of the Mississippi River one can see this rationale. But let's look at a better alternative . . .

Log Walls in REScheck®

RE*Scheck*® is the most widely used software to demonstrate compliance with state and local energy codes. Its reports are widely accepted by building officials. The program and support are sponsored by the U.S. Department of Energy and are free to download from <u>www.energycodes.gov</u>. Formerly called MECcheck and used to demonstrate compliance with the Model Energy Code (MEC), REScheck has been continually updated to support the International Residential Code (IRC), and the International Energy Conservation Code (IECC), and a number of state codes. REScheck residential compliance methods offer two ways to demonstrate compliance: the trade-off approach and the prescriptive packages approach.

Since REScheck was developed, most log home companies have used it to demonstrate code compliance, and this has held true through the 2006 IECC versions. In fact, the Log Homes Council worked with REScheck developers to integrate the information developed for ICC400 into the program. After REScheck version 3.7.1, the program calculates thermal parameters based on the variables as defined by ICC400 and the Wood Handbook (USDA 1999). In the Technical Support Document released for REScheck 3.7.1, changes relating to log walls are described.

"Prior versions of REScheck required users to input only the log wall width and the insulation R-value. REScheck then implemented an average calculated density used to compare the wall with the thermal mass requirements of the International Energy Conservation Code (IECC). For a wall to receive the mass wall credit in the IECC, it needed a heat capacity (HC) of 6 Btu/ft^2 F, which generally requires a weight of 20 lb/ft^2. Lighter walls with 5" and 6" diameters did not receive the credit, demonstrating the compliance difficulties of smaller log walls."[33]

To demonstrate compliance of log homes, other components of the thermal envelope need to have better ratings to offset the deficit of solid wood walls versus the requirements set in IECC's Prescriptive Tables (e.g., glazing U-factor, floor/basement, and mechanical efficiency). With the increased requirement for basement insulation in the 2009 IECC and the removal of mechanical tradeoffs, REScheck may no longer be an effective tool to demonstrate UA tradeoffs in cold climates.

Completing a REScheck Analysis

REScheck comes with an excellent area take-off tool, appropriately named AreaCalc. A simple program, it has features that simplify entry of the details of a home design. AreaCalc opens from a drop down menu under "Tools." Similarly, the entered data transmits back into the open REScheck file by selecting the menu item "Tools/Transfer Data to REScheck."

With the data transfer complete, the log wall specifications are chosen so that the program assigns the appropriate U-Factor for the log wall accounting for wood species and average width. While the dialog box refers to nominal width, the intention is to round the average log width (area of log profile divided by stack height).

REScheck was expanded for log walls to include average widths from 5" to 10" in one-inch increments, and then in two-inch increments to 16" wide logs. Because of this incremental approach, the log width is referred to as nominal, but the intent is to use the closest average width (determined by dividing the area of the log profile by its stack height). In addition, REScheck lists 31 different wood species that can be selected. The R-value of the wood is established for each species based on its specific gravity calculated at 12% average moisture content. As such, REScheck assumes that the entire wall, less openings, will perform at that R-value. Mass effect is calculated when the wall is greater than 7" in thickness; it is

not an increase in listed R-value, but changes the Maximum UA permitted by the applicable code.

On REScheck's Envelope tab, each element transferred over from AreaCalc must be adjusted to specify insulation level, placement of windows and doors into appropriate walls, etc.

When all of the entries have been adjusted so that the Design UA values sum to less than or equal to the Maximum UA permitted by the code, the house is compliant. The green bar across the top of the Compliance Certificate indicates code compliance (red otherwise) while the highlighted area shows how the design compares to the code. There is no requirement for a design to be more than 0.0% better than code.

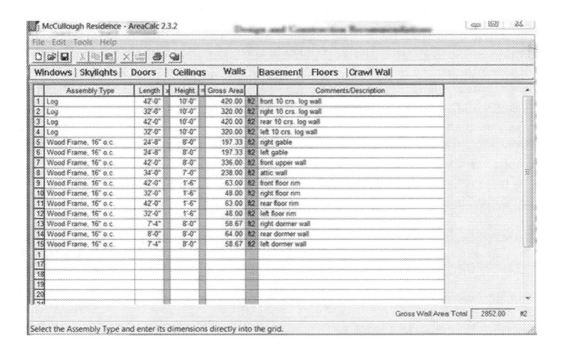

Figure 45: AreaCalc makes take-offs easy, even when separating walls for solar orientation.

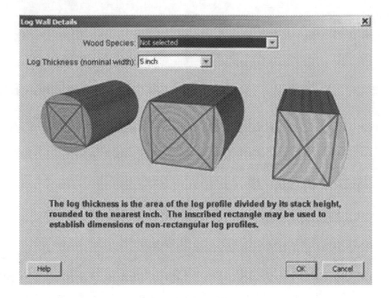

Figure 46: REScheck Log Specification Window

It is important to understand that the window above refers to log thickness as "nominal width". This appears to be a misnomer, but it actually refers to the fact that the developers found such little difference in the U-factor for fractions of an inch thickness that they simplified the matter by using 1-inch increments. Unlike lumber standards where actual dimensions are consistent with respective nominal sizes, wall-logs vary greatly in shape and size. ICC400 establishes the average thickness as the area of the log profile (section) divided by its stack height and is rounded to the nearest inch in REScheck. In other words, a nominal 6x8 S4S timber is 5-1/2" wide x 7-1/2" tall. This dimension

and resulting average width would be similar for a 6x8 rectangular wall-log, or it would be somewhat less for one that has a round profile on the outside. A fully round log with a notch or cope for seating one on another may require a 7" diameter to have an equivalent average width.

As a practical matter, it would be safe to assume that the REScheck nominal log thickness be interpreted as a rounded version of the average width. A 5" log thickness would be any average width from 4-17/32" to 5-1/2", and so on for the other widths.

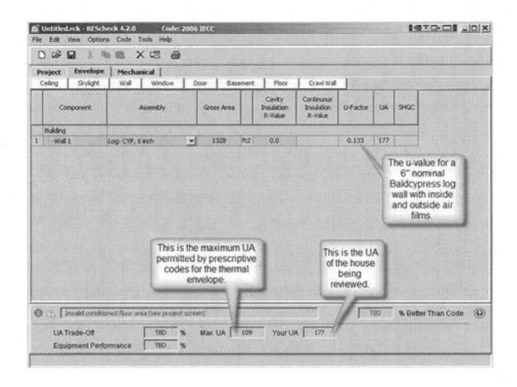

Figure 47: REScheck Envelope Screen

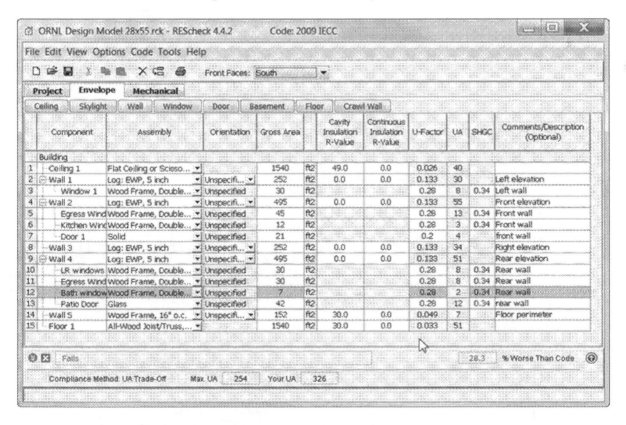

Figure 48: Sample of a completed envelope in REScheck. Insulation levels, log input and/or window performance needs to be modified to achieve compliance.

Reporting options include the Compliance Certificate and Inspection Checklist which are submitted to the authority having jurisdiction, and the Energy Efficiency Certificate which is to be permanently posted on the electrical panel of the home.

To establish an understanding of the future of compliance with the IECC, two test cases are presented. One is a simple log cabin design, the other is a model used for simulating energy code results. The test cases focus on Climate Zone 6, where the most significant change is in the foundation wall requirement (see tables below). Therefore, the thermal envelope requirements for zone 6 construction according to both the 2006 and 2009 IECC are equal as follows: Fenestration U-factor of 0.35, ceiling

R-value of R49 (R38 in cathedral ceilings), R19 frame walls, and R30 floors. This leaves only the building configuration, solar orientation, percentage of glazing and the mechanical efficiency as elements to study. In each case, the building configuration will be oriented to generate the least solar benefit.

Two scenarios were tested in REScheck 4.2.2. For comparative purposes, the building site will be located in Susquehanna, PA (7049 HDD), which is in climate zone 6. The reason for this selection is that it can be compared on the basis of the 2006 IECC as well as earlier versions without state amendments. Both Wisconsin and New Hampshire have adopted amendments which make comparisons using this version of REScheck difficult.

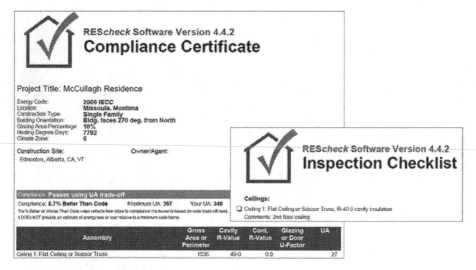

Figure 49: REScheck provides an option to print these certificates.

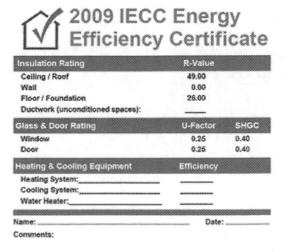

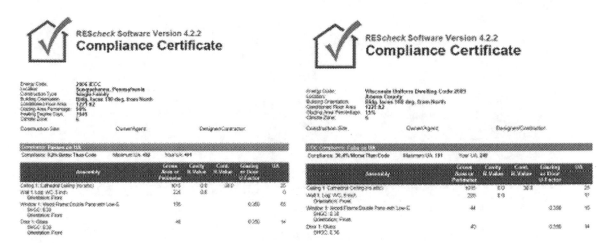

Figure 50: REScheck reports are color-coded to show compliance. Green equals code compliant; red does not comply.

The comparative result of the REScheck® calculation is the UA, or summation (weighted average) of each assembly U-Factor multiplied by the square foot area of the assembly. The IECC defines the U-Factor as follows:

> "U-FACTOR (THERMAL TRANSMITTANCE). The coefficient of heat transmission (air to air) through a building component or assembly, equal to the time rate of heat flow per unit area and unit temperature difference between the warm side and cold side air films (Btu/h · ft2 · °F) [W/ (m2 · K)]."

UA Alternative Case Study

To generate an understanding of the impact of the IECC, the same base design was selected as used in the ORNL reports (http://www. ornl.gov/sci/roofs+walls/articles/wallratings/ index.html). A reference building was used to establish the location and area weighing of all the interface details. This base house design is used for building energy code modeling, such as ASHRAE 90.2, in analyzing different recommended insulation levels.

- Specifications: 28-ft wide x 55-ft long (1540 sf of floor area, 166-ft. perimeter, 8-ft. walls), 154 sf of glazing (10%), flat ceiling, 4 corners, 9 partition wall intersections

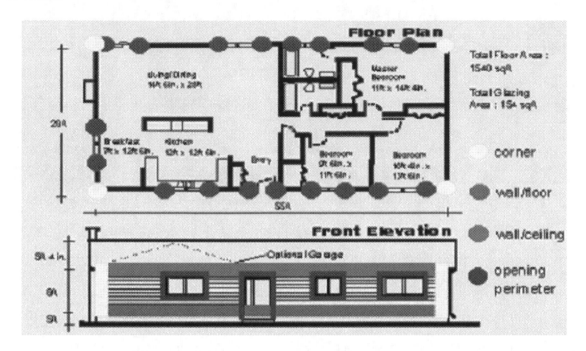

Figure 51: Base House Design Used for ORNL Analysis

To understand the situation better, let's look at the log home of 2006—a nominal 6" log wall, fenestration U-Factor of 0.32, above average roof insulation, batt insulation sized for 2x6 walls (R21), and an R20 foundation wall around a heated basement. Using the prescriptive path to define a log thermal envelope to meet the IECC requirements is not possible in colder climate zones. Therefore, in Climate Zone 4 and higher, a UA tradeoff method is required. It will be slightly different for the various climate zones. The following analysis examines this relationship of the log home thermal envelope and the various editions of the IECC.

Proposed Design

		Ranch Design	Cape Design	2-Story Design	
Log wall = Mass wall	Footprint	28'x55'	28'x42'	28'x42'	
Lw = Avg. width (profile area/stack height)		1-story	21' loft	Dormers at loft	
Gu = Specific gravity	Living Area	1540	1554	1764	sq.ft.
MCs = EMC = 12%	Volume	13,860	22,092	24,444	cu.ft.
	Ceiling	Flat	12:12 cathedral	12:12 & 5:12	
	Flat Ceiling Area	1540	0	0	sq.ft.
12 :12 pitch	Cathedral Area	0	1663	1471	sq.ft.
9 ft. wall height	Exterior Wall Area	1494	1260	1260	sq.ft.
14 ft. to ridge	Gable Wall Area	0	392	392	sq.ft.
8 ft. wall height	Dormer Wall Area	0	0	536	sq.ft.
0.917 ft. wall height	Perimeter of floor frame	152	128	128	sq.ft.
9 ft. wall height	Foundation Wall Area	1494	1260	1260	sq.ft.
	Floor/Slab Area	1540	1176	1176	sq.ft.
	FG clad insulated hinged entry door	21	21	21	sq.ft.
	Glazing (wdw/door) Area	196	226	283	sq.ft.
	Window: Wall ratio	13%	14%	13%	

Figure 52: Area calculations for the ORNL model home taken from a ranch design to a cape, to a 2-story design.

Starting with the ORNL model, we expand testing UA Alternative analysis (similar to REScheck) to a cape design (changing to a 12:12 cathedral ceiling with a half loft) and a 2-story design (by adding shed dormers at the loft). The goal was to keep the living area to approximately the same square footage while expanding the volume enclosed by the thermal envelope.

The table (right) examines the ranch design in Climate Zone 4 (Louisville, KY). Using the color code from the DOE Climate Zones Map, it shows the Proposed Design component descriptions, and areas. The **shaded** cells denote the changes from the requirements of the previous code. The shaded values for Exterior Log Wall UA and Total UA represent UA values that are lower than the proposed design. The %-values in the Total UA row compare the IECC UA to the Proposed Design UA.

The 2006 and 2009 IECC were satisfied by the design with 5-inch logs (dense softwood, Gu=0.48-Southern pine, 12% MCs) and industry standards for insulation and glazing. However, the 2012 requires a more stringent mass wall requirement. To comply with the 2012 IECC, the cape design will need a 6-inch wall thickness using a medium density softwood (Gu =0.39-Lodgepole pine). This will be true of all three proposed designs.

Changing the same table to Omaha, NE provides a look at Climate Zone 5. Without making changes, the Proposed Design fails as the respective code UAs are lower. To meet Climate Zone 5 requirements,

- The glazing U-Factor is dropped to 0.30 because the code requirement dropped from 0.35 to 0.32 in 2012.

- The other components of the proposed design were left the same, but the design UA remained too high.
- Testing a lower wood density of the 6-inch log wall to that of Eastern white pine (0.35) shows compliance to the 2006 and 2009 IECC, but it will not satisfy the 2012. Increasing to a 7" log did not comply, so the of wood species

was changed to cedar (Gu = 0.31). Another option is to increase average log width to 8" so that medium density softwood (Lodgepole pine, Gu 0.39) can be used.

Already in Climate Zone 5, we see that the other elements of the thermal envelope are having a detrimental impact on the viability of

Component / System	Ranch Design			2006 IECC		2009 IECC		2012 IECC	
	Area	U-Factor	UA	Req'd. U	UA	Req'd U	UA	Req'd. U	UA
IECC Climate Zone 4 (except marine)									
Fenestration	196	0.32	63	0.40	78	0.35	68	0.35	68
Hinged Solid Door	21	0.28	6	0.40	8	0.35	7	0.35	7
Skylight			0	0.60	0	0.60	0	0.55	0
Solar Heat Gain Coefficient		0.40		NA		NA		0.40	
Ceiling Flat	1540	0.026	40	0.030	46	0.030	46	0.026	40
Cathedral	0	0.026	0	0.030	0	0.030	0	0.026	0
	R-49 flat/R-40 cathedral			R-38		R-38		R-49	
Wood-frame wall Dormer walls	0	0.057	0	0.082	0	0.082	0	0.057	0
	R-21			R-13		R-13		R-20 or 13+5	
Wood-frame wall Gable ends	0	0.057	0	0.082	0	0.082	0	0.057	0
	R-21			R-13		R-13		R-20 or 13+5	
Exterior log Wall 5 in. (Lw)	1277	0.171	218	0.141	180	0.141	180	0.098	125
	Gu= 0.48			R-5		R-5		R-8/13	
Wood-frame wall Floor perimeter	152	0.049	7	0.082	12	0.082	12	0.057	9
	R-30			R-13		R-13		R-20 or 13+5	
Basement / Crawl Wall	1494	0.044	66	0.059	88	0.059	88	0.059	88
12' KF	R-20			R-10/13		R-10/13		R-10/13	
Slab				R-10, 2-ft. deep		R-10, 2-ft. deep		R-10, 2-ft. deep	
Total UA			400	2.8%	412	0.5%	402	-18.3%	338

Component / System	Ranch Design			2006 IECC		2009 IECC		2012 IECC	
	Area	U-Factor	UA	Req'd. U	UA	Req'd U	UA	Req'd U	UA
IECC Climate Zones 4C & 5 / NRCA Climate Zone A									
Fenestration	196	0.30	59	0.35	69	0.35	69	0.32	63
Hinged Solid Door	21	0.28	6	0.35	7	0.35	7	0.32	7
Skylight			0	0.6	0	0.6	0	0.55	0
Ceiling Flat	1540	0.026	40	0.030	46	0.030	46	0.026	40
Cathedral	0	0.026	0	0.030	0	0.030	0	0.026	0
	R-49 flat/R-40 cathedral			R-38		R-38		R-49	
Wood-frame wall	152	0.049	7	0.060	9	0.057	9	0.057	9
	R-30			R-19 or 13+5		R-20 or 13+5		R-20 or 13+5	
Mass wall 6 in. (Lw)	1277	0.113	144	0.082	105	0.082	105	0.082	105
	Gu= 0.35			R-13		R-13/17		R-13/17	
Basement / Crawl Wall	1494	0.044	66	0.059	88	0.059	88	0.050	75
12' KF	R-20			R-10/13		R-10/13		R-15/19	
Slab				R-10, 2-ft. deep		R-10, 2-ft. deep		R-10, 2-ft. deep	
Total UA			322	0.6%	324	0.6%	324	-7.7%	299

the log wall. One might suggest an R-60 roof, since the ranch design is a flat ceiling, but that only produces a 3UA reduction, hardly enough when the Proposed Design is at a UA of 322 and the 2012 IECC is at 299UA. The roof itself, at R-49, has a UA of 40, which is less than that of the log wall, windows, and foundation. Therefore, the most economical approaches would appear to be gained in those areas. This is not true, however, since all three are more expensive per rated R-value than the cost of roof insulation installed in a flat ceiling. So, we change the ICF walls to a panelized concrete wall (e.g., Superior Wall Xi system) with 2-1/2" of XPS insulation on the outside, and 24" on center stud bays that allow an additional 6" of insulation, saving 23UA!

Moving into Climate Zone 6 using the location of Laconia, NH, we carry forward the change in foundation. New Hampshire enjoys a long and rich heritage of log homes, with many 6x8 D-style log homes built over the past 50 years. Largely built out of Eastern white pine, we start there to see how these energy-efficient homes (so claimed by their occupants) compare to the code. However, we see quickly that additional help is required:

1. First we move to an R-60 flat ceiling and an R-49 cathedral, saving the 3UA.
2. Another less expensive move is to use a door that has a U-Factor of 0.20, saving 2UA.
3. Dropping the window U-Factor to 0.28 saves another 4UA.
4. The cost to UA savings ratio for adding exterior sheathing to the frame walls is too much to consider on the cape and 2-story designs, so the log wall must change to 7" average thickness to meet the 2006 and 2009 IECC.

The final UA needed to comply with the 2012 IECC can come from a couple places. Due to the increase in frame wall area of the cape and 2-story designs, the change from the ranch design to one of the others can make this happen. Sticking solely to the ranch design will require a lower density log species or a window with a U-Factor of 0.27 or less.

Component/ System	Ranch Design			2006 IECC		2009 IECC		2012 IECC	
	Area	U-Factor	UA	Req'd U	UA	Req'd U	UA	Req'd U	UA
IECC Climate Zones 6 / NRCA Climate Zone B									
Fenestration	196	0.28	55	0.35	68	0.35	68	0.32	63
Hinged Solid Door	21	0.20	4	0.35	7	0.35	7	0.32	7
Ceiling Flat	1540	0.024	37	0.026	40	0.026	40	0.026	40
Cathedral	0	0.022	0	0.026	0	0.026	0	0.026	0
	R-60 flat/R-49 cathedral			R-49		R-49		R-49	
Wood-frame wall Dormer walls	0	0.057	0	0.082	0	0.057	0	0.048	0
	R-21			R-13		R-20 or 13+5		R-20+5 or 13+10	
Wood-frame wall Gable ends	0	0.057	0	0.082	0	0.057	0	0.048	0
	R-21			R-13		R-20 or 13+5		R-20+5 or 13+10	
Wood-frame wall Floor perimeter	152	0.049	7	0.06	9	0.057	9	0.048	7
	R-30			R-19 or 13+5		R-20 or 13+5		R-20+5 or 13+10	
Mass wall 7 in. (Lw)	1277	0.098	125	0.060	77	0.060	77	0.060	77
	GU= 0.35			R-15		R-15/19		R-15/19	
Basement / Crawl Wall	1494	0.029	43	0.050	75	0.050	75	0.050	75
	Xi Superior Wall System			R-10/13		R-15/19		R-15/19	
Slab				R-10, 4-ft. deep		R-10, 4-ft. deep		R-10, 4-ft. deep	
Total UA			271	6.6%	280	2.2%	277	-0.7%	269

Finally, we move to Climate Zones 7 & 8. As previously noted, Anchorage, Alaska provides a good model. Thankfully, we find that the situation hasn't changed from Zone 6 above. The numbers are a little tighter, and we have to make up 6UA to pass the 2012 IECC.

Component / System	Ranch Design			2006 IECC		2009 IECC		2012 IECC	
	Area	U-Factor	UA	Req'd. U	UA	Req'd U	UA	Req'd.U	UA
IECC Climate Zones 7 & 8 / NRCA Climate Zone 0&D									
Fenestration	196	0.28	55	0.35	69	0.35	69	0.32	63
Hinged Solid Door	21	0.20	4	0.35	7	0.35	7	0.32	7
Ceiling Flat	1540	0.024	37	0.026	40	0.026	40	0.026	40
Cathedral	0	0.022	0	0.026	0	0.026	0	0.026	0
	R-60 flat/R-49 cathedral			R-49		R-49		R-49	
Wood-frame wall	0	0.057	0	0.0062	0	0.057	0	0.048	0
Dormer walls	R-21			R-13		R-20 or 13+5		R-20+5 or 13+10	
Wood-frame wall	0	0.057	0	0.0062	0	0.057	0	0.048	0
Gable ends	R-21			R-13		R-20 or 13+5		R-20+5 or 13+10	
Wood-frame wall	152	0.049	7	0.057	8	0.057	8	0.048	7
Floor perimeter	R-30			R-21		R-21		R-20-5 or 13+10	
Mass wall	1277	0.098	125	0.057	73	0.057	73	0.057	73
7 in. (Lw)	Gu= 0.35			R-19		R-19/21		R-19/21	
Basement / Crawl	1494	0.029	43	0.059	88	0.050	75	0.050	75
Wall	XiSuperior Wall System			R-10/13		R-15/19		R-15/19	
Total UA			271	5.2%	286	0.7%	273	-2.3%	265

Engelmann spruce (Gu = 0.33) is an available species in the Northwest, as is cedar (Gu = 0.31) and Lodgepole pine (Gu = 0.39). Unfortunately, Lodgepole pine will require an increase to an 8-inch average wall thickness and still doesn't get us down to a UA of 265 (changing to an 8" white pine does). With a desire to stay with the smaller log, the species is changed to the spruce, producing only a savings of 5UA vs. the 6 required. Changing the window U-Factor from 0.28 to 0.25 will produce the 6UA, so it would appear that the best solution is the lower cost of the window efficiency upgrade or the larger white pine log.

The Effect of Air Infiltration on Energy Use

Developing the case study further, we can see that the overall energy demand of the sample house is greatly affected by air infiltration. This example shows the relative importance of the change to the 2012 IECC and substantiates air infiltration as being a bigger factor than the insulated thermal envelope in the quest to the 2030 Initiative.

In the case study used, this log home has a UA of 290 which complies with the 2006 IECC as opposed to the 2009 IECC UA requirement for 273, and 2012 UA of 265. Using the worksheet that follows (not intended for equipment sizing, only for estimating annual fuel costs), the 2006 code compliant house will cost $3,170 per year in propane to heat the house (only heating, $2.95/gal, 80% efficient boiler). This is only $143 more in heating fuel costs than the 2009 IECC compliant house and only $210 more than the 2012 version.

Taking this a step further, the worksheet looks at the other factor of the energy codes, air infiltration. The case as shown sets the air infiltration equal to ASHRAE's ventilation level of 0.35 air changes per hour (ACH) for a healthy indoor environment in Climate Zone 6. This works out to be slightly more than the 7 ACH50 requirement of the 2009 IECC. This value must be confirmed by a blower door test, a step that is highly recommended. Reducing air leakage to 5 ACH50 or about 0.25 ACH natural, the calculated savings per year is $209. So, merely by tightening up the house by 2 ACH50, the building performs at a savings equal to the 2012 IECC prescriptive UA. To reinforce the reason that the IECC in 2012 drops to 3 ACH50, note that the calculated annual savings would be $419.

These calculations are good for demonstrating the example, but are not sufficient to design a house and heating system. They do not include the energy used for water heating, cooking, appliances, or the air changes due to exhaust ventilation. However, the relationships are real and the exercise shows that uncontrolled air infiltration of homes prior to the 2009 IECC consumed more fuel than was saved by increasing the R-value of the thermal envelope. Is that true for log homes? No. Log homes were already being built to better insulation standards and were airtight in addition. This explains the dramatic differences between log homes built in the 70's, 80's and 90's as opposed to their conventionally framed counterparts. Add the comfort afforded by the mass of the log wall, and it is understandable why homeowners love their log homes.

Can log homes be leaky? Absolutely, just like any framed house. But which one will be easier, hence less expensive, to repair to become airtight? Since nothing has to be removed to seal a log wall, how can this be a difficult question?

In Summary

Working through the previous exercise was essential to fully understanding the impacts of the IECC code change cycles on the log home industry. As shown, the selection of materials is one critical decision point, but the design of the structure and component choices also make a difference. It certainly demonstrates that the prescriptive U-Factor for mass walls should not be directly applied to the U-Factor of log walls to demonstrate compliance.

A much more economical model for the thermal envelope of log homes is achieved by using the UA Alternative path.

Each of the tables above was produced in a spreadsheet to show direct comparisons. Then the tables were verified using REScheck 4.4.2 (noting that the ducts are contained in the heated living space). It is important to recognize this so that individuals who are so inclined can duplicate this exercise in REScheck themselves by entering the Proposed Design criteria and the insulation choices.

An important point to address here is compliance with "above-code" programs and a look at future changes. The primary above-code programs include ENERGY STAR, the National Green Building Program (in accordance with ICC700), and LEEDS-H. Since the codes are moving faster than these programs, it is important to look ahead.

- **ENERGY STAR** is currently on Version 3.0—It appears that the primary components are aligned with the 2012 IECC with the following exceptions:
  o Doors have U-Values of 0.21 for opaque/solid, 0.27 up to a 1/2-lite portion, and 0.32 for more than 1/2-lite.
  o Window U-Values are reduced to 0.30 in Climate Zones 4C through 8 and 0.32 in CZ4. This glazing change alone affects the overall UA by 10 points in CZ4, 9 points in CZ5, and 7 points in CZ 6-8.
  o Many other elements are addressed by ENERGY STAR V3, but they are beyond the scope of this study.
- **ICC700** is being updated for 2012.
  o Section 701.1.3 of ICC700-2008 allows ENERGY STAR compliance to satisfy the requirements to the Bronze level without any further work in Chapter 7.
  o The ICC700-2012 proposal for 701.1.3 provides for Bronze qualification for ENERGY STAR Version 3.0 Qualified Home or equivalent.

The exercise above demonstrates that log structures can be built in compliance with the thermal envelope requirements of the 2012 IECC, which is identical to Chapter 11 of the 2012 IRC.

- **Glazing**: As seen in the ENERGY STAR V3 summary, further changes to glazing requirements may cause problems. At what point will window companies have no option for better glazing performance than the IECC requirement? If there is no possibility of improvement in the glazing area, the log wall requirement becomes an 8" E. white pine log wall in CZ6, and 9" medium density softwood (Gu = 0.38) CZ7&8. Climate Zone 5 is not included here, since the discussion revealed that a different foundation system could save 23 points.

In his presentation to the DOE Energy Codes workshop in 2010, Dr. Joe Lstiburek noted that using glazing with good thermal performance is a key decision. He explains that when glazing area of up to U-0.30 makes up less than 15% of the floor area, solar orientation is not an issue.

Again, it is important to restate that regardless of the code or the above-code program, it is NOT necessary to build a log wall that has an overall R-value of 17.5 (for a U-Factor of 0.057). It has been clearly demonstrated by UA tradeoff analysis that home with an R-10.2 log wall can comply with these codes and programs.

Cost Implications of Log Width

Beyond the energy savings of a requirement for wider log walls is the impact it will have on the prospective home buyer. Comparing the incremental cost of additional wall thickness against the present value of energy costs that would be saved must be included in the analysis. Multiple log home company sources estimated that meeting the prescriptive requirements of Table 402.1.1 as written in the 2009 IECC would cost $5,000 per log wall materials package in Climate Zone 5 and Marine 4, with increasing expense to achieve Zone 6-8 requirements.

The **ability to maintain current products** is critical to the industry. The change from a nominal 6-inch wide log wall to a nominal 8-inch typically adds an average of $5,000 per log wall package (an approximately 2,000 sf home with 152 lineal feet of log wall).

Looking at the log width from the standpoint of incremental cost, the following worksheet helps show the relationship. Beginning with a nominal 6x8 log, only the width of the log is changed in the analysis. The raw material cost varies with size somewhat as well, as cant pricing needs to cover the expected profitability that would come from side cut products. The incremental cost increase does relate mostly to the width of the log since fastening and joinery/seal would not require a change. With wider logs, additional fasteners may be a good idea to limit movement during seasoning in place, but this was not factored into the worksheet. Using the examples established in prior worksheets, the first task is to compare the cost per square foot of wall area and then relate that to R-value. Based on this first analysis, it would appear that the increased cost of wider logs is not significant because the "R/$-sf" rate is lower. This would be a misleading indicator though, because the cost factor is significant. The second portion of the worksheet demonstrates that the actual cost of the wider logs results in an expense that is greater than the incremental width. While the change to an 8-inch width adds about $5,000, the change to a 12-inch width is substantially more than twice the cost of the 6-inch width. This cost factor is not reasonably offset by energy savings and is not warranted.

Calculate Incremental Log Cost　　　　　　　　　　　**Sample Case** | **Your Product**

Cost per square foot of wall:

$H_L =$ | 7.5 |　$12/H_L =$ lineal feet log per sf wall = | 1.6 |

Enter the unseasoned specfic gravity　　　　　　　　$Gu =$ | 0.35 |

Calculate the performance factor (Fp):

W, nominal	H, nom.	BF/LF	$/LF*	$/sf	R-Value	R / $-sf
6		4.00	$ 9.00	$ 14.40	8.85	$ 0.61
8	8	5.33	$ 11.50	$ 18.40	11.49	$ 0.62
10		6.67	$ 16.50	$ 26.40	14.08	$ 0.53
12		8.00	$ 19.50	$ 31.20	16.95	$ 0.54

*$/LF includes all cost factors, including but not limited to fasteners, sealants, treatments, packaging, freight, etc.

Calculate the Investment cost factor (FI):

	W, nominal	$/sf	SF log	Log cost	Cost Factor
28x55 Ranch	6	$ 14.40		$ 18,389	1.00
	8	$ 18.40	1277	$ 23,497	1.28
	10	$ 26.40		$ 33,713	1.83
	12	$ 31.20		$ 39,842	2.17

Figure 54: Incremental cost of log wall thickness portrayed in a fairly simple manner.

The National Association of Home Builders published the Affordability Pyramid to illustrate the impact of such cost increases on the buying public. If building a new log home costs an additional $5,000, how many potential buyers will have to look elsewhere (e.g., resale, apartment)? With only 2% of the overall market, additional costs to build new log homes have a significant impact on buyer decisions.

Based on conventional assumptions and underwriting standards, it takes an income of about $27,000 to purchase a $100,000 home. In 2009, about 84.9 million households in the U.S. are estimated to have incomes above that threshold and can, therefore, afford homes priced at least that high. The remaining 29 million can't afford to buy a home unless it's priced under $100,000. These 29 million households form the bottom step of the pyramid.

Of the 84.9 million who can afford a home priced at $100,000, 61.6 million can also afford a home priced at $175,000. The difference is 23.3 million households who can afford to pay a top price of somewhere between $100,000 and $175,000 (the second step on the pyramid).

Figure 55: U.S. Affordability Pyramid (NAHB)

This study shows that for 354 U.S. housing markets with over 91 million households, a $1,000 price increase for a median priced new home would price more than 133,000 households out of the market (from 0.019% to 0.547% depending on metro area).

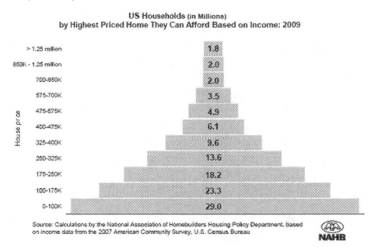

Such an increase in expense will effectively shut down a market, an industry, and a complete network of suppliers, services, and builders who specialize in log wall technologies.

Canadian Study

Using life cycle costing for 34 Canadian zones and both round-scribed and rectangular-milled logs, it was found that a 4" (100mm) wall was the optimum milled log thickness when comparing incremental cost of additional wall thickness against the present value of energy costs that would be saved.[34] Although costs for fuel and electricity have risen since this 1996 report, this report still provides significant relational data for log wall evaluation. For example, this report established a size factor for rectangular milled logs and round scribed logs of 0.97 and 0.77, respectively. These factors are supported earlier.

The study reported that the incremental cost for building with wider logs was significantly greater than the incremental savings in fuel cost. Reporting heating costs for this cold climate, incremental heating costs (electric heat) accounted for the majority of the life cycle cost per conditioned floor area. Where the wall thickness was a 4-inch milled rectangular log (100mm) had a factor of four times the incremental heating cost a 12" diameter round scribed log (305mm). Using a 6-inch (150mm) width, the incremental cost factor drops to about 1.5 times. Marginal incremental heating costs were shown when the log sizes were 10-inch (250mm) rectangular and 18-inch round. At a 12-inch rectangular log and 19.7-inch (500mm) round log, the incremental life cycle cost is entirely that of the log wall.

In the Ontario climate zone B with electric heating of a 2-story home on a full basement, the incremental cost of increasing the log width one size (150mm rect., 355mm round) cuts the incremental heating cost in half. One more step in width (200mm and 410mm respectively) doubles the incremental construction cost and again halves the heating cost. There is no question that the greater log widths will have a dramatic impact on incremental life cycle costs to heat the home, but the study reinforces the idea that the incremental life cycle costs to construct the wider walls will limit the ability of the market to support it.

REAL WORLD PERFORMANCE OF LOG HOMES

The cry for assistance and relief come because our history of log homes and log building do not match the predicted energy consumption portrayed by energy code advocates who are focusing on conventional construction methods.

A Qualified Testimonial

In September, 2010, at my urging, I received a letter from Michael P. Burnetter, P.E., Senior Engineer, Energy Services, Codes Division of the State of New York Department of State. Mr. Burnetter offered his view of log homes and energy conservation from a professional and personal perspective:

> For close to 2 decades my family and I lived in a Northern Products white pine log home (with solid 6 inch depth logs from outside to the warm inside) which required a surprisingly low amount of fuel to heat and tended to stay cool enough to avoid a need for cooling here in New York. Given this direct experience with servicing the utility bills and yet keeping the home warm during our cold northern winters, I can honestly say there is much truth in the industry information which indicates the thermal mass provides much benefit over lighter weight materials. Concurrence is thus found with the document called the "The Energy Performance of Log Homes—http://www.loghomes.org/uploads/EnergyPerformanceWP_2010.pdf" which lists conclusions from a DOE Sponsored Thermal Mass Studies stating that:

> "Log walls, despite lower-appearing steady-state R-values, have been shown to provide equal or superior annual heating and cooling performance when compared to lightweight wood frame walls of higher steady-state R-values and that the homogeneous assembly of the log wall has fewer thermal short-circuits than lightweight wood- or steel frame walls. This property leads to closer agreement between steady-state calculated thermal transmittance levels and their actual thermal performance. Both calibrated testing and sophisticated computer modeling have confirmed this observation."

This testimonial from Mr. Burnetter supports the many, many happy log home owners who do not have his technical knowledge base. The following is just one example of a consumer's perspective, where he is told that his oak log walls are no longer a viable building method in the northern tier of states in the U.S. . . .

> "As for the performance of denser log homes in northern climates . . . I have a log home owner north of Minneapolis who is building a spec home in northern WI in Zone 7. We have finally decided we are going to have to frame out the inside of the log wall in some rooms to get it to pass REScheck. We have been working with the customer on this calculation and alternatives . . . [He sees no need for this.] Said his house is warmer and easier to heat than his neighbors and it is all BS. (His words!) This is not scientific but real world!"

This action is becoming far too prevalent and is the incorrect answer—see Adding Insulation to the Log Wall. The pressure to incorrectly apply insulation to log walls is due to overzealous administration of R-Value.

Log Home Performance Studies

Studies of log home thermal performance consistently demonstrate a benefit of solid wood walls versus other wall technologies. The tests largely address the thermal mass characteristics, but perhaps they are identifying symptoms of the dynamic performance of a mass wall combined with the limitations of code compliance based on heating degree days (HDD). The IECC codes define climate zones partly by heating degree days as an average over the year. Perhaps the following statement from Wikipedia describes why actual field studies perform better than calculated estimates . . .

> "Heat requirements are not linear with temperature,[2] and heavily insulated buildings have a lower "balance point". The amount of heating and cooling required depends on several factors besides outdoor temperature: How well insulated a particular building is, the amount of solar radiation reaching the interior of a house, the number of electrical appliances running (e.g. computers raise their surrounding temperature) the amount of wind outside, and individuals' opinions about what constitutes a comfortable indoor temperature. Another important factor is the amount of relative humidity indoors; this is important in determining how comfortable an individual will be. Other variables such as wind speed, precipitation,

cloud cover, heat index, and snow cover can also alter a building's thermal response."

(2) Valor, E.; Meneu, V., Caselles, V. (2001). "Daily Air Temperature and Electricity Load in Spain". Journal of Applied Meteorology 40 (8): 1413-1421. Bibcode 2001JApMe . . . 40.1413V

The log home industry reached out to many who could study the benefits of log walls.[35] The research performed achieved similar results as this document, that the full impact of solid wood walls is not fully understood. 15 years of side-by-side studies have not provided significantly usable data due to issues of equating differences in orientation, structure, and occupant habits.

NBS Thermal Mass Effort

Upon forming in 1977, the Log Homes Council (LHC) immediately focused on thermal testing under a National Bureau of Standards (NBS, now the National Institute of Standards and Technology—NIST) program that concluded in 1983. In conjunction with the National Concrete and Masonry Association (NCMA), The Brick Industry Association (BIA) and others, the test reports contributed to the thermal mass credit that appeared first in the 1989 Model Energy Code (MEC). The summary of research on the topic is best summarized in the LHC document, *The Energy Performance of Log Homes.*[ix] In this LHC white paper, author Bion Howard provides information pertinent to the NBS testing and the response by ASHRAE (American Society of Heating, Refrigerating and Air-Conditioning Engineers).

As early as 1967, thermal mass effects were identified. J. F. Van Straaten, in the classic book *Thermal Performance of Buildings* identified a distinct property of building physics that discussed a function of heat storage capacity and resistance to heat flow of a structure's various assemblies like its walls, roof, and foundation. In late 1974, the NBS developed a building energy-simulation computer model called "NBSLD—Computer Program for Heating and Cooling Loads in Buildings." It was capable of dynamic simulations based on weather, rather than just more traditional steady state calculations. Using the NBSLD model, engineers at the Illinois-based Portland Cement Association (PCA) compared an equivalently sized and shaped frame building with a masonry building. They calculated that the lightweight walls (with 30% greater R-value) had peak cooling loads 38% to 65% higher than for the masonry building. The overall building seasonal heating loads were 12.3% less for the masonry building and the seasonal cooling loads were 17.4% less.

By late 1982, the DOE Thermal Mass Program was underway, and NBS presented initial results of an instrumented field test comparing frame, masonry and log-walled residential-scale test buildings located in Maryland. The NBS test buildings were designed to be similar in every respect except their wall constructions. Researcher Doug Burch reported mass-wall buildings including concrete masonry and log home construction appeared to save heating energy compared to a well insulated light frame wall building. **The log wall test building performed better than both the insulated wood frame house and the interior insulated block wall house, both of which had higher steady state R-values.**[36]

The NBS data also showed that while the tested log wall R-values tended to be lower than predicted steady state R-values compared to the other buildings, the measured heating and cooling performance of the log walled test home was much better than predicted in computer models. This was a clear indication that **the steady state calculations used by the engineering community was consistently over-predicting log wall heat losses.**[37]

Work on measuring heat capacity effects by NBS continued through 1984, when detailed ASHRAE papers were published on both observed heating and cooling thermal mass "behavior." The log wall ("Cell #5") in the two reports showed energy savings compared to the insulated frame building (with much higher wall R-value)—According to the NBS data, energy savings were 45% for heating (cumulative heating load) and 37% for cooling, which was slightly better than recorded for the exterior-insulated block building.[38]

Based on computer extrapolations of the field test data and the absolute difference in kWh heating demand, NBS compared the exterior insulated masonry building with the insulated frame building tying the heating results to other climates. The range for the log wall home (not directly reported by NBS) can be expected to be somewhat less, since in winter the highest performing exterior insulated block building saved about 22% heating compared to the log wall building.[39] Results indicated

- 3.3% heating savings based in cold climates (e.g., Madison, WI); for log walls, 2.5% is estimated.
- 62% heating savings based in mild climates (e.g., Los Angeles, CA); for log walls, 48% is estimated.

The conclusions drawn by Howard from his research are

1. Steady state R-values are significantly lower than demonstrated heating and cooling performance,
2. The homogeneous assembly of log walls has fewer thermal short-circuits that framed (cavity) wall construction.
3. The "integral" thermal mass and insulation properties of log walls are

nearly as effective as exterior insulation on concrete and masonry walls per unit of insulation and heat capacity. This is largely due to the fact that the latter mass walls have higher heat capacity with higher heat flow conductivity.

4. Adding insulation to the interior of mass walls negates the benefits of the heat capacity of the wall.

In addition to the NBS Testing, the argument of testing log walls for heat flow using the ASTM Hot Box method is supported by the quote below from DOE (http://www.energysavers. gov/your_home/designing_remodeling/index. cfm/mytopic=10170):

"Compared to a conventional wood stud wall [3½ inches (8.89 cm) insulation, sheathing, wallboard, a total of about R-14] the log wall is apparently a far inferior insulation system. Based only on this, log walls do not satisfy most building code energy standards. However, to what extent a log building interacts with its surroundings depends greatly on the climate. Because of the log's heat storage capability, its large mass may cause the walls to behave considerably better in some climates than in others.

Logs act like "thermal batteries" and can, under the right circumstances, store heat during the day and gradually release it at night. This generally increases the apparent R-value of a log by 0.1 per inch of thickness in mild, sunny climates that have a substantial temperature swing from day to night. Such climates generally exist in the Earth's temperate zones between the 15th and 40th parallels."

1984 New Mexico Studies

From 1982 to 1984, the New Mexico Energy Research and Development Institute (NM-ERDI) operated another instrumented test home site in Tesuque Pueblo, New Mexico, under the DOE Thermal Mass program. In addition to wood frame, log walled and concrete block construction, three traditional Southwestern adobe wall houses were constructed with increasingly thick walls, up to 15 inches thick. Roofs were insulated to R-30, the foundations to R-15.4, and the same size, U-factor, and shading coefficient windows were installed after first calibrating the test houses with no fenestration (windows and doors) installed.

The log wall research house used 7-inch walls (R-9 calculated) while the insulated wood frame test house used 4.5-inch thick (2x4 with typical ½" interior wallboard and exterior sheathing) R-11 insulated walls, corrected for framing versus cavity-insulated areas. The measured air change rates of both frame and log houses were about 0.1 air changes per hour. (Note: Typical homes have air change rates of 0.35 to 0.5 per hour, so the test buildings were very tight.). Despite identical steady state load coefficients, the log wall house used the least heating energy of all the test houses. The log walled test house showed 27% lower heating demand during spring 1983 than the higher R-value frame house.[40]

1990 Energy Related Performance Testing of Minnesota Log Homes

The MN study made a valuable contribution to log wall performance by noting, "The identification of tight foundation and wall systems concurrent with considerable air leakage through cathedral ceilings and at the tops of walls could be conducive to conditions of combustion appliance back drafting. Combustion air inlets were not found at most of the sites." ---- It would be reasonable to acknowledge the need for combustion air inlets and balanced ventilation systems in such air-tight construction.

The following is taken from the Summary of the report, "Energy Related Performance Testing of Minnesota Log Homes".[41]

"A survey of the air leakage characteristics of 24 Minnesota log homes was performed during the 1989-1990 heating season. The results of this research were originally published in June 1990; minor edits were made to post the document on the department Web site in May 2005.

The sample consisted of buildings from two to eight years old of three types: kit homes (8 examples), hard-scribed non-chinked homes (14 examples), and hand-scribed chinked homes (3 examples). The sample was identified by contacting long-time builders. Each home was blower door tested to quantify air tightness and surveyed by infrared thermography to identify major heat loss areas. Estimates of annual heat loss through envelope components were calculated. The homes were all occupied, but due to the confounding variable of wood heating, no data on historical energy use could be collected.

The results for these homes showed little air leakage between logs or at the rim joists. More air leakage was found at log corners and window and door frames. Most of the air leakage was through cathedral ceilings and at the tops of log walls (at the intersection with the roof). For this limited sample size, no definitive difference in air tightness was evident of the three types of log homes. However, three of the four homes that were identified as "owner built" had the greatest air leakage of the sample."

The infrared thermographic surveys indicated that under certain conditions, small sections of insulated 2x6 walls (such as dormers) had greater heat conductivity than the adjacent log walls, even though their theoretical conductivity is less. Similarly for cathedral ceilings, the presence of air leakage suggests that their thermal performance is considerably less than their design R-value would indicate. Calculations of annual heat loss indicated that infiltration is generally the largest heat loss of these buildings.

The identification of tight foundation and wall systems concurrent with considerable air leakage through cathedral ceilings and at the tops of walls could be conducive to conditions of combustion appliance back drafting. Combustion air inlets were not found at most of the sites."

Oak Ridge National Laboratories

Oak Ridge National Laboratory (ORNL, http://www.ornl.gov/sci/roofs+walls/) research has demonstrated several findings about the use of R-values to establish energy conservation.

- Hot-box test results for wood and steel-framed wall assemblies with studs installed at 16-in. o.c. are significantly lower than the rated insulation R-value. The use of advanced framing techniques and simplified building configurations (less framing due to fewer corners, point loads, blocking) improve the wall assembly by reducing the amount of framing material as a percentage of wall area.
- Using thermal mass in buildings can significantly reduce annual energy demand—Estimated energy consumption savings generated by application of massive walls in residential buildings can reach 5 -20%. Mass walls eliminate thermal bridging, allow continual visual inspection as construction does not conceal voids, gaps, or improperly installed insulation.
- In moderate climates, integrated insulation and mass (log) walls demonstrated notably better energy performance than wood frame walls of the same R-value.

Thermal mass benefit in cold climates is theoretically reduced where the external climate remains substantially below the interior design temperature for extended periods of time. These studies do not account for solar gain—log wall surfaces have been shown to read over 100-degF during winter exposure in cold climates.

New Zealand's Solid Wood Building Initiative

In 2007, New Zealand's Pine Manufacturers Association conducted a thermal mass study.[42] The study concluded that the use of solid wood walls, instead of wood frame walls, reduces home heating and cooling demand in Auckland and Christchurch. Bellamy concluded that

"The energy savings due to solid wood's thermal mass will not only depend on location and wall R-value, it will also depend on the amount of 'free' solar heat within the home. This is largely determined by the size and orientation of windows. The model house in this study had a relatively large area of north-facing windows, so large amounts of solar heat. It seems likely that the potential energy savings reported here are near the upper end of the energy savings that can be realised in New Zealand homes."

The study notes that solid wood walls contribute to a reduction in indoor humidity in hot and humid climates, reducing energy used for cooling, as the occupant experiences the desired comfort level at a higher temperature. This also may contribute to reduced ventilation demand without sacrificing perceived air freshness

Rated Energy Performance

Using RESNET or BPI certified Home Energy Raters, builders and homeowners can choose to use the Simulated Performance Path of the IECC (Section 405). Many log home builders/producers have chosen to take advantage of EPA's ENERGY STAR program which involves testing for air infiltration. Even as the requirements for various programs are adjusted to maintain their standards against the IECC, the log wall can benefit from taking the performance path to energy conservation.

One program developed by Sascho is the "Insector Detector" program that uses thermographic analysis and blower door testing to evaluate log buildings. This excellent program was designed to help log home owners seal their homes to keep insects outside, but the obvious benefits for energy conservation were realized early. While these reports are not intended to comply with Home Energy Rating Systems (HERS), they do identify areas of the log home that need to be sealed. The important detail here is that a sampling of their reports shows that log homes comply with the 2009 IECC requirement for less than 7 ACH50. Two reports on handcrafted log homes (10-14" diameters) reviewed for this discussion ranged from 5 to 6 ACH50. One report reached nearly 9 ACH50 on a rectangular hewn log with dovetail corners. The report notes that the seal between the log wall and the ceiling was responsible for the high air leakage rate. This demonstrates the value of this work. Had the test been done when the structural shell was completed, the builder could have rectified the situation very easily.

Figure 56: Thermographic studies in combination with blower door tests will identify areas for sealing, like this area above the log wall and between rafters. Source: Tracy Hanson, Stormbusters, Inc.

A review of various reports provides a list of common areas for attention during construction. After making the log structure weather-tight, caulking is the primary option for sealing culprits. However, gaskets applied during construction provide the best long-term solution. Like other forms of wall constructions, seals need to be at—the attic access door, along the ridge of cathedral ceilings, from the top of the wall to the ceiling, at the bottom of the wall to the floor, around recessed lighting, around beam pockets, pattern of tongue and groove (T&G) ceilings over walls, etc.

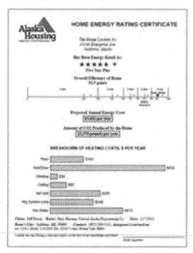

Figure 57: The basis for ratings varies with different programs. This log home with 12-14" logs achieved Five Star Plus with an overall efficiency of 92.5 points against the BEES Standard. This home tested to an air leakage level of 1.6 ACH50, which exceeds the required 3 ACH50 of the 2012 IECC and includes a ventilation warning (air leakage is not sufficient for acceptable indoor air quality). Source: Haven Timber Homes, www. haventimberhomes.com.

ENERGY STAR Certifications

ENERGY STAR certifications have been a reality for log homes through the 2009 IECC and ENERGY STAR Version 2.5. It is unsure where Version 3.0 will take things, as the EPA has raised unusual standards to the program. If the basis remains to be the HERS rating, we can see that 5 Stars Plus Verified Condition with a 56 HERS index should still be a certified home under V3.

With the assistance of NH BPI-Certified Sustainable Energy Engineer, Tom Werst, a comparison was made between wall systems on a single home design using REMRate software. The mandatory requirements for all ENERGY STAR Version 2.5 Qualified Homes were assumed to be met (duct leakage tests and insulation verified, mechanical ventilation, and 2009 IECC insulation levels), including an air leakage rate of 5 ACH50. With a 2x6 wall filled with Icynene spray foam insulation, the HERS index came in at 60. Changing to a 6" log wall, the HERS index changed to 69; a HERS index of 67 with a 7" log wall; and a 65 HERS index with an 8-inch log wall. While this is a quick, somewhat unscientific review, it does approximate the marginal influence of the wall component, and indicates that less efficient wall thermal performance can be offset in other areas of the thermal envelope.

Figure 58: This home achieved 5 Stars Plus had a blower door test result of 350 cfm50, which is about 1 ACH50. Another home in NH has a HERS index of 59 and 2.05 ACH50 air leakage. Source: Coventry Log Homes, www.coventryloghomes. com.

Performance Path: Field Surveys vs. HERS Ratings

The log home industry has discussed the concept of using customer data and field surveys to demonstrate the energy efficiency that homeowners have realized. The expense of time and financial investment has stymied the effort. It appears to be a natural response to consumer testimonials supporting the cause. However, in his report to the Log Homes Council, Bion Howard, President of Building Environmental Science & Technology, notes:[43]

> Like automobile gas mileage ratings, the actual delivered efficiency of any home regardless of construction plan will often differ from calculations, "energy ratings" or other predictions and evaluation methods and computer program modeling. Occupancy, actual weather conditions, and maintenance of heating and cooling systems often affect overall performance.

There are many variables associated with occupant lifestyle that would have to be isolated to provide any kind of statistical accuracy worthy of establishing comparable benchmarks from field surveys.

While field surveys may be unfeasible, there is a true comparable for building performance—HERS ratings and ENERGY STAR® Certification. The IECC has provided for performance path compliance since it was developed. This path relieves the building official of some responsibility, as the ENERGY STAR inspections provide the same inspection services accompanied by blower door testing and/or thermographic studies

> **The ENERGY STAR Challenge: Design a Better World**
> *EPA supports the American Institute of Architects (AIA) national call-to-action to reduce fossil fuel energy associated with CO2 emissions when designing, constructing and operating buildings.*
> *View the 2009 Designed to Earn ENERGY STAR Challenge projects from architecture firms that are designing a better world!*
>
> **Building Design Guidance**
> *These guidelines are a strategic management approach, not a technical reference, to incorporate energy performance in the building design process. It is a set of suggested actions for design professionals and building owners to establish and achieve energy goals. These guidelines encourage best practices for energy design as part of the overall design process, and can help translate design intent to top energy performing buildings..*
>
> - Start Right – *Set energy goal and assemble design team*
> - Pre-Design – *Investigate energy design concepts*
> - Schematic Design – *Simulate and compare energy strategies*
> - Design Development – *Confirm that your design energy meets the target*
> - Construction & Bid Documents – *Include energy goal in specs*
> - Follow Through – *Commission building, rate operational performance, and apply for*

Figure 59: ENERGY STAR challenge

To demonstrate the confidence of the log home industry as to its energy conservation performance, an alliance with ENERGY STAR and a commitment to designing ENERGY STAR compliant log homes is highly recommended. Given the precedent of commercial buildings in the ENERGY STAR program, log buildings could develop a similar program with the assistance of the US EPA and the American Institute of Architects. [44] Only the use of energy rating programs such as RESNET® or ENERGY STAR® can provide comparative benchmarks for performance in the various climate zones.

Evolution of Alternative Log Wall Products

Can you imagine a solid concrete log wall? There are companies promoting the benefit of concrete over wood because there is no decay. And they can form wood grain appearance and even extended knots into the concrete.

How about corrugated steel pipe that is painted brown and tied together with steel bar? Good for fire resistance?

With log walls under attack as insufficient for purposes of the thermal envelope, innovators in the industry are looking elsewhere for answers. One such innovator is using an interesting spin in their marketing—"Is your log home built for 1972 or 2012? Many things have changed since 1972, including the ways homes are built, how banks evaluate them (and finance them) and how building codes regulate them." There is some truth to that statement, but the inference that log walls will not meet 2012 codes is a matter of perspective.

WYSIWYG

Log walls are truly **"WYSIWYG"**—it does not conceal the conditions known to occur with cavities and layers of materials, and it responds to movement. While similar movement in framed, rigid constructions result in drywall

90

cracks or other changes where pressure is released, ICC400 Section 303 specifically covers the adjustments necessary to accommodate movement. Occupants view the interior of the log wall regularly, providing constant inspection opportunities.

Figure 60: This photo shows an interior water stain at a cedar knot which has allowed water to weep through it. This situation is remedied by sealing the knot on the exterior surface.
Source: Author.

Issues generated from the exposure to the outside are often revealed on the surface of the log wall. Periodic visual inspection will readily expose everything from insect activity to water infiltration, both of which are readily repaired without deconstruction. While there are horizontal seams between the logs, these are designed and constructed in accordance with ICC400, and if needed, they can be addressed on the exterior to further protect the joinery. Normal maintenance of sealing exteriors insures a continuous water plane.

To comply with the energy codes as written, log home builders and designers resort to drastic measures such as adding insulation to the inside of the log wall. It is added to the inside so that the structure and log corners are maintained. This meets the code requirement, but it conceals a dynamic wall structure with two undesirable results—it eliminates the benefit of thermal mass to the conditioned space, and it conceals the wall. The latter may seem like a ridiculous claim, but layered elements of frame wall construction are where all of the problems begin—is there proper ventilation to remove moisture? Is there an adequate vapor barrier to keep moisture from forming? Did the builder seal or flash over the interior insulation to make be certain that water from above (e.g., roof leaks, wall joints, etc.) cannot get behind the insulation?

To maintain the best thermal performance, the log wall would be exposed to the interior and the insulation would be applied to the exterior. But, this creates a structural issue at the corner, an important element in log wall design. It also conceals the wall and requires special flashing above to make certain that the wall is protected from potential degradation of trapped moisture.

Truly, the best insulation for a log wall is the wood itself, allowing the radiant benefit to the inside and the solar gain on the outside to temper energy needs throughout the year. It is possible that a compromise would be to add insulation to only the North walls that will not have solar exposure for heating. In primarily cooling design conditions, the wall's thermal mass is a benefit and the conductive performance is satisfactory.

Adding Insulation to a Log Wall

In the October/November 1991 issue of Mother Earth News[45], Harry Yost describes how log home occupants learned to use leaky structures to add an external layer of insulation to a log wall:

> "The propensity for moisture-laden air to move outside has been utilized in the past to make a log house better insulated. In the far north, where winter temperatures

may stay below freezing for months, it was a common practice to seal the house from the inside. This was done by putting several containers of water on the stove and bringing them to a boil. The vapor traveled to the outside through the cracks. It immediately froze on contact with the outside air, effectively scaling the house until the outside air temperature again was above 32 degrees Fahrenheit. This cut down on drafts and made for a snug house, at least until the weather warmed up."

Yost accurately explains that pioneers were looking for shelter, not energy efficiency. They would add wood to the fire to warm up. But he also notes that adding insulation to the outside of the wall and improving the insulation in the roof are keys to meeting energy conservations standards [then of the Model Energy Code].

Probably the most popular and realistic option to solid wood walls has been the application of log siding, false log corners, and interior paneling on structural walls built with conventional framing, structural insulated panels (SIPs), or the like. This has been a response to the settling issue of solid wood walls, and lately has been a response to energy codes. The care and maintenance is no different than for any application of siding—back priming, proper fastening, and solid substrate.

The new generation of log products to improve R-Value is the foam core log. There's an interesting discussion on the blog at http://www.hearth.com/econtent/index.php/forums/viewthread/54792/#612518 as to options. In structural lumber and engineered wood products, Weyerhaueser (http://www.woodbywy.com/insulatedseries/) has launched a line of insulated components—"*integrated,*

preassembled headers, rim board and corners framing components deliver higher insulating values, reduce thermal bridging, and optimize materials and labor."

Keeping to the theme, the following are alternative wall systems that emulate log walls but do not employ solid wood walls.

> http://www.timberblock.com/index.php—Timber Block laminates log siding to 4-1/2" closed cell polyurethane core foam blocks to create a continuous R-30 wall panel. Their entire presentation is geared to better R-value and no settling—meaning no air infiltration. Bolting provides compression to keep the panel together, but the load bearing capacity of the log siding skins is marginal. Concerns not addressed on the website:

o Structural—point loads, lateral loads, uniform loads from floor/roof.

o Warranty—third-party inspection of closed panel construction, third-party testing to verify performance.

o Delaminating—Coefficient expansion and contraction of differing materials [foam and wood] and the stress generated by the radius bend on siding.

o Fire rating—15-minute thermal barrier does not exist at narrow joinery of log siding.

o Maintenance—log siding will still require the same level of maintenance as any other wood exposed to the weather.

http://www.summitlog.com/foamcore.htm—A new approach to technology dating back to National Log of Columbia Falls, MT. Established in the early 1900's, National Log (and sister company, Air-Lok, Albuquerque, NM) milled uniform diameter wall-logs and drilled a 2" diameter hole the full length of the log. This was done to relieve the stresses created as the wood dried, but offered an opportunity to fill it with foam. Summit enlarged the concept to a 3" to 4" hole filled with polyurethane.

http://www.greatlakeslaminators.com/r-values-of-logs/—Great Lakes Laminators is using a rectangular,

cant approach to the foam core log. They laminate planed products to foam cores or can create a cant that can be run through a planer/molder. Joinery is still a question.

http://www.singloghomes.com/prod_log.php—Sing Log Homes promotes a system used by some narrow log producers who rely on double-wall construction. In this case, Sing uses heavy planking with double tongue and groove joinery.

http://www.wisconsinloghomes.com/log-homes/insulated-building-system/—This trademarked system is similar to many others on the market that apply various thicknesses of half-log/log siding/paneling to an insulated frame wall.

Figure 61: Alternative log wall examples—clockwise from top left: Timber Block, Summit Log, Great Lakes Laminators, Sing Log, and Wisconsin Log Homes

Being a solid wood advocate, it is a struggle to recognize a log wall made from an alternate material. There was a report of a Florida builder who used corrugated steel pipe and painted it brown. Then there is the EverLog System—"worry free concrete logs." A product review was completed by the very experienced and respected Beaudette Consulting Engineers, Inc., Missoula, MT who has engineered thousands of log homes. The review verified many of the claims on the website (http://everlogs.com/). To some, this concrete sandwich panel approach is the answer.

Figure 62: EverLogs™—A log look from a concrete sandwich panel.

Other wall systems have been patented that integrate methods for installing foam insulation within the log profile. Following are a few examples.

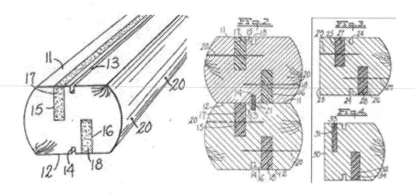

Figure 63: Vito M Vizziello of Connecticut patented this variation in 1975 (3,992,838)

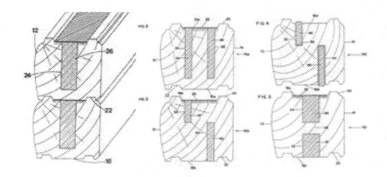

Figure 64: Johann H. Farmont of California patented this slotted approach in 1980 (4,344,263)

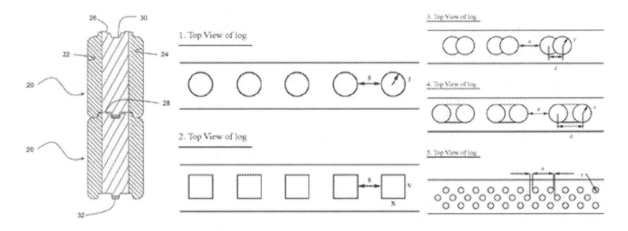

Figure 65: Ronald A. Wrightman of Canada brought a different twist in 2009 (US 2010/0043323 A1)

ICC400-2007, AN INDUSTRY MILESTONE[46]

In 2000, the International Log Builders' Association (ILBA) was working to complete its *Log Building Standards for Residential, Handcrafted, Interlocking, Scribe-fit Construction.* Founded in 1974, ILBA is a worldwide organization dedicated to furthering the craft of handcrafted log building, to the advancement of log builders, and to the promotion of the highest standards of their trade. ILBA writes and distributes educational materials, provides educational services related to the craft of log building, and establishes scholarship trust funds.

With the desire for broader acceptance of their standard, the ILBA approached the National Evaluation Service, Inc. (NES). This was about the time that the regional model codes were merging into the International Codes Council (ICC). In the meantime, the Log Homes Council (LHC) had developed a guideline for the U.S. Dept. of Housing and Urban Development for review and approval of log buildings for Federal financing programs. After a joint meeting between representatives from ILBA, NES, and the LHC, a decision was made to develop an ICC standard for log construction. Through ICC, the

call was released for a committee to develop a consensus standard on log construction.

ICC established the Consensus Committee on Log Structures (IS-LOG) in 2002. The goal was to create uniformity in evaluation applicable to all log building systems, provide a quick reference for technical data, and promote broader acceptance with growth of ICC adoption at various levels of government. The IS-LOG Committee and development contributors represent the perspectives of industry, designers, builders, building officials and others. A byproduct of the effort was a unique synergy between very different philosophies regarding log construction.

The Significance of ICC400

Log structures employ alternative methods of construction that are fully covered by ICC400. The standard gives code officials an important tool for inspection and understanding log construction, including thermal performance. Carefully written in enforceable language to cover all forms of log construction, the standard explains how to respond to design conditions, but it does not establish those conditions.

ICC400 is the only ANSI-approved consensus standard regarding solid wood walls formed by stacking logs horizontally or vertically. It is a single reference for log design, construction, and inspection that reflects the nature of these unique structures rather than requiring them to comply with standards written for lumber and frame construction practices. Yet, ICC400 only establishes methods of evaluation and construction that will respond appropriately to design (environmental, usage, occupancy) conditions. It requires the use of the ICC I-codes to define those conditions. ICC400 provides

- Enforcement of a grading requirement
- Uniformity in evaluation applicable to all log building systems—greater customer satisfaction and reputation among code entities
- Quick reference for technical data
- Broader acceptance with growth of ICC adoption at various levels of government
- Potential adoption worldwide.

As of the 2007 edition of ICC400, the log home industry had a recognized consensus standard for the first time. The importance of working with ICC is that an ICC Standard Development Committee is required to consist of a balance of industry, design, and governmental members. Professionals from each interest group insure that the Standard meets industry standards and can be readily used in design scenarios. An ICC standard

- provides a venue for continued improvement on a 5-year cycle, a process that invites participation from all interests,
- is vetted through the ANSI (American National Standards Institute) process

to insure that the process produces a truly consensus document,
- invites all interested parties to participate,
- removes all bias to any proprietary product, system or other feature, and
- is written in enforceable language.

References to ICC400 within the I-Codes

ICC400 is referenced in the 2009 ICC International Building Code (IBC), the 2009 International Residential Code (IRC), and by footnote in the 2012 IECC.

IBC Ch. 23 Wood, 2301.2 General design requirements:

> "4. Log Structures. The design and construction of log structures shall be in accordance with the provisions of the International Code Council's IS-LOG Standard ICC-400."

IRC Ch. 3 Building Planning, R301 Design Criteria: R301.1.1 Alternative provisions:

> "3. International Code Council (ICC) ICC-400 IS-LOG Standard for the Design and Construction of Log Structures."

IECC Ch. 4 Residential Energy Efficiency, Table 402.4.1.1 Air Barrier and Insulation Installation, footnote a:

> "In addition, inspection of log walls shall be in accordance with the provisions of ICC400."

A Level Playing Field

The Standard does not favor any style of log wall, but requires that the same evaluation be applied to all. It does not concern itself with a particular method of joinery, rather it requires that joinery to meet or exceed the minimum levels of performance established in the Standard.

That was easy to say, but the method of log production complicates evaluation—some logs are produced with a uniform profile (e.g., cross-section) along its entire length while others are produced with the intention of utilizing the full tree and the natural esthetics like taper. This one distinction affects how grading, strength, settling, and other performance properties are evaluated.

Founding Principles for Engineering Log Buildings

While log buildings are historically significant worldwide, the methods of construction have been passed on by traditional means. There are many opinions as to which traditional method is best, how well modern production methods perform, etc. In the past, references were limited to sources such as publications from the LHC, ILBA, trade magazines, proprietary literature, AF&PA/AWC standards, and the FPL Wood Handbook.

Research on wood has been on-going for decades in the United States, with considerable work done by the Forest Products Laboratory (FPL) in Madison, WI. Under the U.S. Dept. of Agriculture, FPL has uncovered and qualified many of the marvelous properties of wood as published in the Wood Handbook.[47] Additional information about the performance of wood is available from the American Wood Council (www.awc.org) and the American Forest & Paper Association (www.afandpa.org). Beyond these references, the regional model building codes published by their respective model code agencies recognized heavy timber construction as a type of construction with particular design and performance implications.

Figure 66: The Wood Handbook and NDS for Wood Construction had been the only early guidelines for design professionals evaluating log structures.

These sources provided the only early guidance for modern design of log structures. Life safety aspects of the building codes were addressed by interpreting and applying available information for lumber, timber, and poles. In many cases, design professionals took an uncertain approach to the structural design because the standards written for rectangular shapes did not apply to the product they were analyzing. Early efforts to generate a reasonable analysis of a log building system became a relatively expensive, with some companies investing in the process of developing an evaluation report.

ICC400 was built on established code formats, derived from industry standards, proprietary programs and wood science. It views all logs objectively and requires all log walls to meet minimum performance regardless of the techniques used to build them.

IMPORTANCE

☑ Federal directives to impose higher R-values on building assemblies via building energy conservations codes threaten to **legislate** solid wood walls out of existence.

ARRA stimulus funding (a.k.a., the Recovery Act) to States is tied to adopting the 2009 IECC and demonstrating 90% compliance with it within 8 years. Supported by political action groups including DOE, architects and others, the 2009 IECC was developed with changes that generate a 15% upgrade to the energy efficiency requirements of the 2006 IECC. The 2012 IECC upgrades are predicted to achieve 30% greater energy conservation than the 2006 code.

There is strenuous opposition to allowing any amendments to the IECC when it is adopted by each State. State code review boards are acting at a rapid pace in order to garner the Federal funds. However, the implications are severe for the log home industry, which does not have the resources to invest in demonstrating that log walls perform better than the steady-state R-values prescribed in the building codes.

☑ Terminating the ability to operate within a range that the market can absorb (width of wall, cost impact, and ability of the consumer to pay for it) will

end the livelihood of those employed by log home producers, builders, suppliers, and service providers. It will further deteriorate the forestry industry.

☑ **Choice?** The real issue is providing an energy efficient / cost effective solution to the constituents that want and dream of the log home lifestyle!"

Log homes with 6-inch nominal wall logs are currently being restricted from building in their traditional markets because of building energy codes. As noted by a client contact operating a sawmill and log home company for 126 years,

> *"We were forced into that change (8") during the last code change. The real issue is providing an energy efficient / cost effective solution to the constituents that like the log home lifestyle!"*

☑ **Natural resources?** Most log wall components are economically produced from small diameter trees and/or the cant/core remaining after producing board, lumber or veneer products. The harvest yield will be negatively affected by calls for increases in size.

☑ **Existing homes?** A real concern comes from improperly insulating log walls, as is discussed in the earlier section, *WYSIWYG*.

The built inventory of log homes in these climate zones are predominantly between 4- and 10-inches average widths.

CLIMATE ZONES 5 & COLDER

A practical application of the points above is provided by examining their impact in a state in climate zone 6, like the State of New Hampshire. In New Hampshire, statistics indicate that log home construction makes up over 7% of new homes in the state, a requirement for a log wall with an average thickness of 5" (nominal 6-inch rectangle or 7-inch diameter) will maintain the jobs and revenue generated by log construction. To understand the impact of increasing average log width, the next nominal increment in width would be 8-inch. That 8" nominal (7" average) log wall thickness would add about $5,000 in material cost (an approximately 2,000 sf home with 152 lineal feet of log wall). In an already difficult economy, this cost increase can be expected to remove a considerable number of potential new home customers from the market. This loss will trickle down through the extensive supply and services network of the log home industry, threatening the income of many families in New Hampshire and beyond.

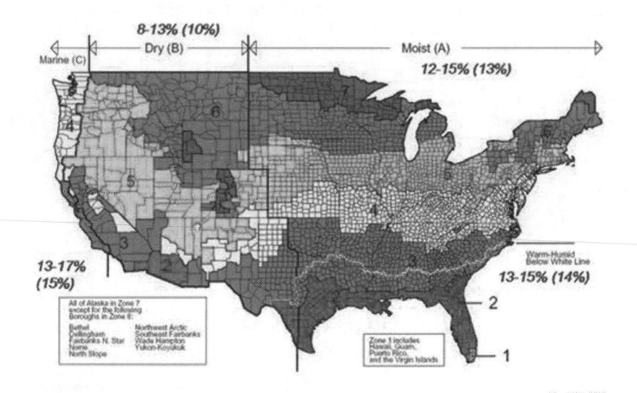

The northern climate zones (5-8) account for about 55% of the log homes built in 2003 and 55% of the dollar volume of log home material packages.[48]

Common log wall components (e.g., a nominal 6" D-log or 8" Swedish cope), will not satisfy prescriptive requirements. Using larger logs means that only the most adamant and financially-viable log home enthusiasts can afford their dream home.

PRIORITIES

Today we spend a lot of emotional energy on the cost of doing things. When it comes to building spaces for living, we can point to the International Space Station as the ultimate in building performance. It took the delivery and connection of three modules to complete an environment that would support the initial three-person crew. An Internet search indicated that estimates to accomplish this are in the $100billion range. Even if you take away delivery and Space Shuttle costs, this ultimate environment is well beyond the means of the average Earth family.

Indications are that future energy codes will emulate the work of ICC's International Green Construction Code (IGCC). Here, all wall technologies are being established as material neutral components of the thermal envelope. This is also being seen in the Canadian Model National Energy Code. What does this mean? Is overall building heat loss not the goal? Can trade-offs not be included?

What then are the priorities and how do we establish a reasonable cost for them? The angst that spawned this work would say that we need an air tight environment with sufficient barriers to maintain conditioned air at minimum fuel/power expenditures regardless of external conditions. Because of a narrow focus on thermal performance, a wall system that has served occupants well for a millennium will be become obsolete?

Re-examining our priorities returns us to the basic human needs—food, water, air, shelter, and comfort. We need to protect the surface of our Earth so that the first three are maintained in adequate quantities. We have shelter well under control—the use of building/life/fire safety codes have repeatedly demonstrated a better way to build. Comfort is relative, but the issue is the energy required to achieve it.

If log structures provide a warm, healthy and perceived energy efficient environment, why should we have to stop building them?

What will be the long term impact of elevating the knowledge base and technology in home building? What is the role of the occupant? Will we automate all mechanical functions via computer to maintain performance? Surely we do not need space age technology to provide energy efficient comfort on Earth.

HYPOTHESIS

Log walls perform as effective components of the thermal envelope.

The theory, therefore, is that completing the following will allow the log home industry to survive:

Recognize ICC400 as the "Log Home Code." The benefit to this is that log wall specific changes can be made in one place. It is assumed that these changes, via the ANSI-consensus process, will also meet the requirements of code developments. This may be a big assumption, since not all interests will keep their eye on the log standard, so it becomes important that the IS-Log Committee maintain a vigilance for the ICC 5-year cycle to update the standard.

Incorporate **blower door testing** to the typical process of construction. Every log building should undergo pressurized air infiltration testing at the time the weather-tight structural shell is completed. Identify problem areas and remedy them before finishes are applied to assure the best results at the code-required blower door test. Complete the performance path approach to compliance with the IECC.

Undertake a **life cycle assessment** (LCA) study to populate the NREL database with information about the production, shipping, construction, and durability of solid wood walls. Added into life cycle assessment tools, such as the Athena Institute's EcoCalculator, log homes will show their environmental benefits.

Address ASHRAE. Recognition of solid wood walls as separate and distinct from other forms of mass wall needs to be identified, updated, and used to **change the IECC requirements for insulation of solid wood walls.** This may include recognition of lower density requirements to establish the log wall as integrated mass and insulation.

Educate building professionals about the benefits of solid wood walls.

The environmental benefit of log building would be enhanced in the U.S. forests by finding support to facilitate better forest management practices that **promote the harvest and use of standing dead timber.**

EVALUATING LOG STRUCTURES USING ICC400

What parameters are applied to log structures to know that they will perform as needed over the life of the structure? If 300 year old log structures are still standing, isn't it obvious?

For those in the log home industry, the answer is clear but individually varied. There are several ways to design and construct a log home, from ancient traditional craftsmanship handed down over the generations to modern engineered and milled structures. There is much to learn from all types of log building rather than pointing to one or another as best. Often, the aesthetic that pleases the home buyer is what matters most (tempered by budget). The only non-proprietary, objective evaluation of log building, regardless of how it looks, smells, feels, or sounds is in accordance with ICC400.

The following is intended to provide commentary to support the use of ICC400. The standard is available in print or electronic download from www.iccsafe.org. Referenced in the International Residential Code (IRC), a copy should be on the shelf next to the IRC in the office of every building department, design office, and contractor!

First published in 2007, ICC-400 IS-LOG *Standard for the Design and Construction of Log Structures* is an ANSI-approved document that represents industry standards and guidelines.

The ICC Standard Committee developed ICC400 with diligence to prepare a document that can be applied to all forms of log wall construction without threatening business success in any way. The ICC also offers on-going review and change to all codes and standards for the purpose of providing the optimum minimum requirements to satisfy life safety and energy conservation. The completion of the 2012 edition of ICC400 reflects the value of the ICC standards process.

THE SCOPE OF ICC400

The administrative provisions explain that ICC400 pertains only to new log structures. It does not establish design loads. It does not address any other requirements covered by other ICC codes such as foundations, roofing, plumbing or mechanicals. Therefore, to complete a log building, other ICC codes will be used to evaluate those elements of the home. While the industry and IS-LOG Committee recognize the need for maintenance of log buildings, the topic of occupant instruction for maintenance was beyond the scope of the standard.

Just as with other materials and methods of construction, log building also requires attention to

- Project planning & preparation—a proven benefit recognized in green building programs
- Design loads and deflection criteria—not all building sites are the same
- Plumb, square and level construction—essential
- Receiving, handling, and protecting materials.

DEFINITIONS

Definitions became a key section for negotiating the meaning of log construction. With an investment of many hours of debate, the IS-LOG committee agreed on a definition of a log for this standard as follows:

> "Log. Wood member that has been stress graded and grade marked or grade certified using rules of an accredited inspection agency in accordance with ASTM D3957, D3737, or D245 and is incorporated into a structure."

There are subtle distinctions to this that may seem to limit the application of the standard. First, all logs must undergo a quality evaluation under an accredited stress grading program. Why is this important? Many companies are selling "log" homes, but they are using only a portion of the log as a veneer or curtainwall, with limited to no load-bearing function. Therefore, while ICC400 may be used to evaluate logs for floor and roof structures, it may not apply to the walls when covered with log siding or half-log construction. If the half-logs perform a structural function, ICC400 applies.

The definitions are focused on terms that are specific to log construction as a building system. They were established to correlate to terms used in other published codes and standards for building. And they serve the invaluable tool of correlating ICC400 terminology to the many terms and definitions used by handcrafters and milled log home builders. ICC400 allows a log structure to be properly evaluated without having to interpret proprietary terms used by a specific log producer/builder.

There are two other definitions that are important distinctions for log building: 1.) The sill log is the first course of the log wall that bears directly on the sill plate of the foundation stem wall; 2.) the bottom log plate is the first course of the log wall bearing directly on the subfloor (e.g., platform framing).

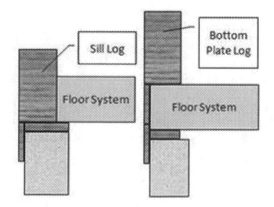

Figure 67: The sill log bears directly on the foundation while the bottom plate log bears on the framed subfloor. Source: Author.

GENERAL REQUIREMENTS

General Requirements evolved into a substantial review of the elements of log building that most engineers do not have at their fingertips. It calls for all logs to be stress graded and requires the grading agency to provide certification of moisture content where a log building system relies on controlling moisture content for performance purposes. This chapter includes specific design stress values associated with two log grading agencies—this information was not previously published. Notching and boring limitations usually adopted from the American Forest & Paper Association's *National Design Specification for Wood Construction* (AF&PA NDS) were modified to represent the normal joinery conditions found in log structures.

In section 303, ICC400 begins to stipulate requirements by offering options for compliance—

- **Prescriptive** path—This is the minimum requirement although structures can be evaluated to a minimum and built to higher, above code specifications. This evaluation path is typically the quickest, least cost option. The downside of this option is that it may be more conservative and not reflect the performance observed in buildings.
- **Calculated/engineered** path—Analysis by calculation to estimate performance or behavior of specific materials or assemblies is a reasonable alternative to the prescriptive path. It is more specific to the log component being used. It requires that the evaluating calculations be presented to the Authority Having Jurisdiction (AHJ—e.g., the building official).
- **Tested/performance** path—By far the most involved both in time and

expense, this option exists to respond to log properties and/or performance that are not adequately represented by other evaluation methods. The empirical data provided demonstrates performance of a given material or assembly under specific conditions. This approach is provided to establish the fire-resistance rating of a log wall (section 303), the necessary provisions for settling (section 304) to insure that the wall remains airtight, and evaluation of the thermal envelope (section 305).

Stress Grading [49]

In the late 1970's, the Log Homes Council retained Steven Winter Associates, Inc. to respond to the call for graded logs used in log buildings to be grademarked. The lumber industry had implemented a visual stress grading process to establish a quality standard that established design stress values. These design values are applied to the section properties of the piece to produce the capacity of the piece. Matching capacity to applied loading verifies use, assembly and structure.

Although lumber and timber grades were established, the American Lumber Standards Committee and certified lumber grading agencies were not willing to take on log grading. Therefore, the need to develop a log grading program began with the creation of a new ASTM standard, D3957 *Standard Practices for Establishing Stress Grades for Structural Members Used in Log Buildings*. Published in 1980, D3957 provided the methods necessary for the creation of design stress values and associated grading procedures that permitted the Log Homes Council to attain accreditation by the National Evaluation Service as a 3rd-party inspection agency, as documented in 1981 as NES QA-154.

As noted in the definition of a log, three ASTM Standards are noted that may apply to the grading of logs—D3957, D3737 for glued laminated timbers, or D245 for lumber and timber. D3737 is required to generate design stress values for logs that are manufactured from "billets" (a.k.a., cants). Billets are the rough timbers created by laminating lumber or smaller pieces of wood into a single structural wood member. D245 is relevant because some logs are essentially rectangular.

Of the 50 pages of ICC400, 27 pages are consumed by design stress value tables for various wood species used for wall-logs and sawn round timber beams. Prior to ICC400, the design values of the two primary, proprietary log grading agencies—the Log Homes Council Grading Program and Timber Products Inspection, Inc.—had not been readily available to engineers.

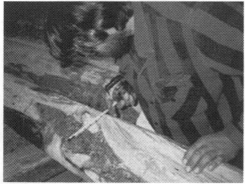

Figure 68: Log profiles are non-rectangular, but an inscribed rectangle is used to establish design stress values and grading criteria. Grading techniques are applied during production and third-party inspection insures consistency. Source: Real Log Homes, www. realloghomes.com.

ICC400 calls for all logs to be stress graded in accordance with an accredited log grading program. **This is the first of two mandatory requirements in the standard**. No provision for an alternative compliance path is made.

Evidence of grading may be in the form of a grademark on the logs or a completed Certificate of Inspection that accompanies the log materials package to the building site. The grademark may be a stamp on a planed surface, a brand hammered into the end or on a face of the log, or even a color code applied to the markings on the logs that indicate where they are to be placed in the wall.

ASTM D-3957 provides two classifications for grading of logs:

- **Wall-logs**
  o Those that span over an opening resist bending both vertically and laterally are graded by criteria that is similar to Beams & Stringers grading—LHC Beam and Header Grades or TP Premium / Select / Rustic.
  o Fully supported wall-logs resist compression vertically, bending laterally and are graded by criteria that is similar to Posts & Timbers grading—LHC Wall Grade or TP Wall Log 40; Wall Log 30.
- **Sawn round timber beams**
  o These products are graded by criteria that consider the natural taper of the log.
  o Logs sawn to produce one flat surface are graded as *Sawn Round Timber Beams,* or *Round Timber Beams* when not sawn.
  o The size (diameter) of the log is determined differently depending on evaluation and application.

When natural logs are used for wall-log applications, the logs are evaluated based on the average diameter, but the wall-log grading criteria are established conservatively by an inscribed square at the tip (smallest) diameter.

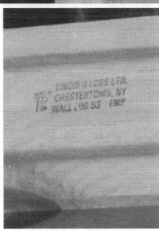

Figure 69: LHC grademark or TP grade stamp indicates that the log has been graded. A Certificate of Inspection verifies the entire load has been graded. Source: Author.

For a bending member, the tip diameter may control due to the reactions at that end. Rafters are typically set with the tip at the ridge. When set over structural bearing, the shear load at the tip may govern the capacity of the piece, but bending can be analyzed as the diameter 1/3 of the overall log length down from the tip. This is a practical approach that acknowledges the taper of the log with the larger butt end

bearing on support at the other end of the rafter.

Sawn Round Timber Beams		
#1	#2	Dia.
Slope of Grain:		
1:14	1:10	(in.)
Maximum Allowable Knot Size		

Max. screw permitted = 0.3"radius

#1	#2	Dia.
1:14 SOG	1:10 SOG	(in.)
1/3	1/2	4
log	log	4 1/2
diameter	diameter	5
1 3/4"	2 3/4"	5 1/2
2 "	3 "	6
2 1/4"	3 1/2"	7
2 5/8"	4 "	8
3 "	4 1/2"	9
3 1/4"	5 "	10
3 5/8"	5 1/2"	11
4 "	6 "	12
4 1/4"	6 1/2"	13

Allowable Knot Accumulation	Up to 3x max. knot in any 12" length
Clusters	Treat as knot
Unsound Knots	1/2 max. knot if surrounded by sound wood and <1.5" deep
	Other Limiting Characteristics
Holes Accumulation	1/2" max. up to 1.5"/sf
Wane & Scars	Not Limited
Decay	firm red heart
Shakes	Up to 1/3 circumference (=dia.)
Splits	Max. length = butt diameter
Checks	Unlimited unless through (see splits)
Pitch & Bark Pockets	
Sapwood Stain	Not Limited
Insect Engraving	
Compression or Cross Breaks	Not permitted in any damaging form.
Warp	Up to 2.5" crook in any 5 feet
Out of Round	Max. of tip diameter x 1.2
Taper	1/8" per foot from tip to 3' from

Figure 70: Sound round timber beams utilize similar grading principles, but the limiting characteristics are different than for wall-logs. Source: Author.

Moisture Content [50]

Change in moisture content directly relates to other wood properties. The greatest impact from MC_D to MC_S is the potential for dimensional change.

The standard recognizes "green" logs in defining the default moisture content of the logs. In Section 302, the prescriptive requirement is set at green which defined as the moisture content of the wood at its fiber saturation point. Section 302 means that all logs are considered green unless otherwise certified to moisture content. Therefore, only those producers who claim that there logs are dried to a moisture content less than the fiber saturation point for that wood species need to verify compliance with this requirement.

Moisture content is differentiated in the standard between the design moisture content (MC_D) and the service moisture content (MC_S). This is specifically done to evaluate how the structure must be designed and constructed to account for the changes in the wood from when it is shaped into its intended form to its finished installation and acclimation to the building site.

Depending on the method of producing the wall logs, the log profile, and the design moisture content, the amount of change in the height of the log wall can be substantial. This change, or settling, may be due to shrinkage (dimensional change), compaction (intentional compression of wood at bearing points), and/or slumping (opening of a notch due to drying). Section 304 covers the provisions for settling due to these changes and contains all of the requirements.

Moisture Migration in Wood

According to Edwin J. Burke, PhD, University of Montana Wood Science Laboratory,

> "Once wood reaches the equilibrium moisture content, there is very little change in the wood due to the flow of water through the log, and its

permeability would be considered quite low."

The equilibrium moisture content (EMC) is a steady-state condition that varies only with relative humidity and temperature. This is further supported in the Wood Handbook (Ch. 3, Sorption Hysteresis) which notes that the *"ratio of adsorption EMC to desorption EMC is constant at about 0.85."* Because water moves 12 to 15 times faster along the grain as it does across it, the best performance is achieved by protecting the end grain exposed at knots and log ends (corners, butt joints, and at wall openings).

The *Textbook of Wood Technology* [51] would indicate that permeability in a horizontal direction through a log wall is much smaller than that in the longitudinal direction. This is because of the large numbers of cell walls through which the moisture would have to migrate. This limited lateral movement (a.k.a., in the radial direction) is also affected by the different *"moisture gradients (i.e., a curve which portrays the rate of change in moisture content in the direction of the water movement)"*, with the outer regions of the log reaching equilibrium moisture content at a faster rate than the center of the piece. This reference of moisture gradients in seasoned wood combined with cell structure supports Dr. Burke's assessment. It should be noted here that not all logs contain the heartwood of the tree; the logs may be milled with the heart or pith occurring off-center or even on the visible face of the log.

Once the log wall has reached equilibrium with its surrounding climate, it will continue to lose and gain moisture depending on the relative humidity and temperature on both sides of the wall, changing gradually over time (another component of the equation). The effect of this movement will not be noticeable after the wood has acclimated, commonly two or three heating/cooling cycles.

There is further support to the idea that the **wood itself provides a sufficient vapor barrier** for the log wall. The International Residential Code (IRC Section R702.7 Vapor retarders) requires Class I or II vapor retarders on the interior side of frame walls in Climate Zones 5-8 and Marine 4. However, the important detail is Exception 3:

> R702.7 Exception 3. Construction where moisture or its freezing will not damage the materials.

The definition of Vapor Retarder Class in the IRC provides three classifications based on testing in accordance with ASTM E96. If a material or assembly limits the amount of moisture that can pass through it, it is defined with a perm rating. A sheet of 1/4-inch thick plywood (Douglas fir, exterior glue) has a perm rating of 0.7, which would place it in Class II with a perm rating of 0.1 to 1.0.

Therefore, the application of the rule for a vapor retarder does not apply to a solid wood wall. It can also be argued that moisture will not be driven through the wood, but the exposed wood will continuously interact with the environment.

Design Moisture Content (MC$_D$)

Design moisture content is the moisture content at time of milling or other shaping for proper fit in the wall, when it leaves the yard, and is used to establish weight for shipping, design loads, etc.

Prescriptive Option: Evaluate as green (at fiber saturation point, MC$_{FSP}$). ICC400 includes a table representing MC$_{FSP}$ for various wood species. Generally taken as 30% for wood, MC$_{FSP}$ does vary.

Table 5–13. Intersection moisture content values for selected species[a]

Species	M_p (%)
Ash, white	24
Birch, yellow	27
Chestnut, American	24
Douglas-fir	24
Hemlock, western	28
Larch, western	28
Pine, loblolly	21
Pine, longleaf	21
Pine, red	24
Redwood	21
Spruce, red	27
Spruce, Sitka	27
Tamarack	24

[a]Intersection moisture content is point at which mechanical properties begin to change when wood is dried from the green condition.

Figure 71: Fiber saturation point of various wood species. Source: FPL Wood Handbook 2010.

Certified Option: Certify specific moisture content under an accredited 3rd-party grading agency. The only way to evaluate log wall performance at a lower design moisture content than the prescriptive percentage is to certify it by adding it to the grademark or Certificate of Inspection that is provided with documentation for the building permit or Certificate of Occupancy.

It is the entirely within the auspices of the grading agency to establish the process of certifying moisture content. The Log Homes Council Log Grading Program based their process on ASTM standards, input from the member companies on how material moves through their operations, and input from manufacturers of instruments used to measure moisture content. This program, properly implemented, not only provides a certification to a given moisture content, but it can improve management of timbers as they flow through the entire operation.

Service Moisture Content (MC$_s$)

Service moisture content is the moisture content when log seasons in place; aka equilibrium moisture content; used for thermal properties (U-Factor, thermal mass).

Prescribed Option

Per Table 304.2(4) and Climate Zone Map

- o The ASHRAE standard for the moisture content of wood exposed to exterior is 12%.
- o Based on the DOE Climate Zone map and ASTM D4933 methods of calculating the equilibrium moisture content, the average MCs in the various regions were established:
  - Dry = average of 10%, ranging from 8% to 13%
  - Moist = average of 13%, ranging from 12% to 15%
  - Warm-Humid = average of 14%, ranging from 13% to 15%
  - Marine = average of 15%, ranging from 13% to 17%.

Calculated Option

The specific service moisture content can be calculated using the methods in ASTM D4933 given historical annual climate data provided for a specific location. Each building site can be evaluated, but the broader stroke of the climate zones will save time.

Installing wall logs that have already been seasoned prior to producing the log profile will tend to show more checking, but demonstrate far less dimensional change and reach EMC quickly. The drier the climate at the building site, the drier the wall logs should be to accomplish this goal. However, while use of green (unseasoned, or considered to be at the natural fiber saturation point at time of milling) wall-logs takes longer to reach EMC, the weight of the structure tends to control movement as the logs season in place, which also tends to limit the size (width) of checks.

It should be noted that exposure to the weather will also impact seasoning and related defects. A log structure that is built with one or more walls unprotected from frequent steady wind will dry and check at an accelerated rate compared to the other walls. This may also be true for walls that have significant solar exposure throughout the year.

Conversely, log structures located in heavily wooded areas can benefit from keeping vegetation away from the structure to promote the drying affects of air flow. Techniques that are affective for limiting fire hazard in rural environments (see *Fire-Resistance Ratings* for discussion of "defensible space" and storage of firewood).

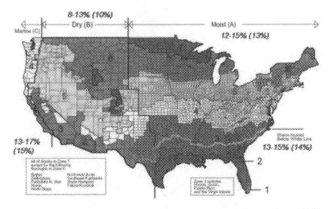

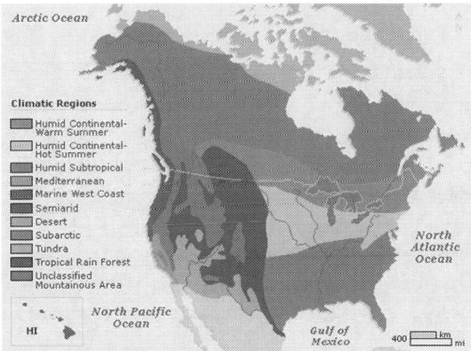

Figure 72: ICC400's Climate Zone Map (Fig. 304.2.2.3) is the same as the IECC Fig. 301.1 Climate Zones. These zones apply beyond U.S. borders. See also *Figure 9:* **Map of annual mean total precipitation correlates well to the forest cover of the U.S. and the DOE Climate Zone Map.**

Design Values

A standard practice for wood construction is to take design values for sawn lumber and glued laminated timbers from the AF&PA *National Design Specification for Wood Construction* (NDS). Beyond the rules-writing grading agencies, ICC400 is the first technical publication that includes design stress values specific to logs used in log structures as per ASTM D-3957. These values are based on the methods defined in ASTM D3957 (logs), D3737 (glued laminated timber), or D245 (lumber).

ICC400 does not limit evaluation to only those species combinations and grading agencies published in the tables. Any design values established by an IAS-accredited grading agency (e.g., Log Homes Council, Timber Products Inspection, VTT of Finland) are acceptable.

Adjustment factors are to be applied to the design stress values per the NDS or Table 302.2(6) as appropriate.

Visual stress grading interprets what is visible on the surface of a piece to determine what grade it is. The grade is associated to a set of design values.

The design values for wood are as follows:

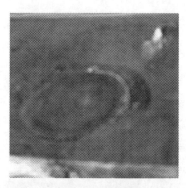

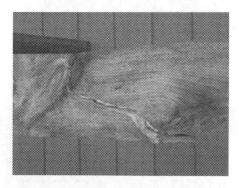

Figure 73: A beam broke when the load was greater than Fb associated with the grade. When a forklift dropped a load of lumber on this rack, the beam broke from the force of the forks hitting it. The break shows the slope of grain and the deviation around the knots. Source: Author.

Fiber stress in bending (Fb): Relates to the strength along the grain allowing for greater spanning capacity. Fb is strongest when the slope of grain is as close to straight (parallel to the edges of the piece) as possible. Its value declines to the worst grade level when the slope of grain is nearly 45° to the edge. It is also affected by the growth of limbs on the tree, where the cells of the tree deviate around the knot (or similar interruption, like a scar). The size, orientation, and accumulation of knots impact both the strength and grade of a log. A Wall-Log will have two values for Fb:

    o   Fb-Vertical will be used to establish the capacity of the log to span over wall openings while supporting roof, floor or other gravity loads.

    o   Fb-Horizontal will be used to establish the capacity of the log to span between supports (in this case, supports are intersecting walls, pilasters or other elements that support the load at the ends of the logs).

Fiber stress in tension parallel to grain (Ft): Relates to the strength along the grain to hold connected elements together such as a wall tie, collar tie, or bottom chord of a truss. Ft, like Fb, correlates strength to the slope of grain and allowable knot size.

Fiber stress in shear parallel to grain (Fv): Due to the natural occurrence of checks, splits and shake in wood, the standard value for Fv always assumes a reduction factor of 50%. This means that Fv already accounts for a check that goes through the log.

Fiber stress in compression perpendicular to grain (Fc⊥, or Fc, perp.): Relates to the strength across the grain. This is critical where a point load (e.g., post, joist, beam, etc.) bears on a log, in log-on-log joint design, and where a log bears on a supporting element.

Fiber stress in compression **parallel to grain (Fc‖, or Fc, para.):** Relates to the strength along the grain to resist loads placed on one end and transmitted to a supporting element on the other end. Examples where Fc, para. Is important would be mining timbers or a post supporting a beam is an example.

Modulus of Elasticity **(E):** Relates to the stiffness of the wood, most commonly recognized as the bounce in a floor.

Prescribed Option

Section properties for wall-logs are determined using the largest rectangle that can be inscribed within the profile. Per ASTM D3957,

"A wall-log is to be graded as the largest piece of rectangular lumber that can be embedded in the wall-log without protrusion from any wall-log surface except that each corner may protrude up to 1/2- in. in either or both directions."

Grade Category	DESIGN STRESS VALUES		Beam	Header	Wall	Utility
Category	Stress Grading: Per Log Homes Council Grading Rules.		Beams & Stringers		Posts & Timbers	
SOG	Slope of Grain		1 in 14	1 in 10	1 in 6	1 in 4
Knot Size	MAXIMUM ALLOWABLE KNOT SIZE	6.63" Narrow Face	1-3/4"	2-1/2"	4 "	4-3/4"
	Ref. 2.2	6.88" Wide Face	1-3/4"	2-1/2"	4 "	5 "
		Kerfed Face	1-3/4"	2-1/2"	4 "	5 "
	Visual Stress Grading Criteria and Values	Ref. 2.11				
Fb	bending, Face <8"	Note: Size Factor (Cs) has been	psi	1100	925	600	400
Fb	bending, Face 8"&>	applied to Fb, bending stress value	psi	1050	875	575	400
Ft	tension	psi	725	600	375	250
Fv	shear	psi	120	120	120	120
Fc, perp.	Compression perp. to grain (taken as Mean Stress at 0.04 in. Deformation)	440	440	440	440
Fc, para.	compression parallel to grain	psi	850	725	550	500
E	modulus of elasticity	psi	1,200,000	1,200,000	900,000	900,000
	For SI	1 lbf/in² (psi) =		6.894 kPa		

Figure 74: TimberLogic's *Log Wall Performance Estimator*[52] includes grading criteria and associated design stress values on the summary page. Source: Author.

Section Properties

Section properties are determined using the largest rectangle that can be inscribed within the profile or per specific engineering. Applying the properties to the design stress values produces the capacity of the log component to resist applied loads. Matching capacity to load is a key ingredient to value engineering practices.

When logs are notched or milled to create the desired joinery between logs, the removed area will impact the inscribed rectangle. For example, a full round log will have an inscribed square (each side = 2*cos45*radius+1"). When the joinery removes area from the top and or bottom of the log, the inscribed figure becomes a rectangle.

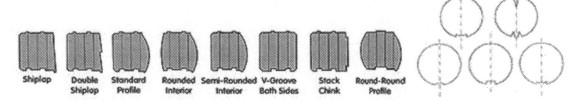

Shiplap • Double Shiplap • Standard Profile • Rounded Interior • Semi-Rounded Interior • V-Groove Both Sides • Stack Chink • Round-Round Profile

Figure 75: Machine-profiled options can be of solid or laminated wood; scribe-fit construction options. Source: Right- Anthony Forest Products; Left-International Log Builders Association)

Rectangular Timbers Graded as Wall-Logs for Use as Joists, Rafters, & Beams				
Face Width Inscribed Rectangle (in.)	Grade:			
	Beam 1:8 SOG	Header 1:8 SOG	Beam 1:8 SOG	Header 1:8 SOG
	Maximum Allowable Knot Size			
	Narrow Face		Wide Face	
3	3/4"	1 1/4"	3/4"	1 1/4"
3 1/4	1 "	1 1/2"	1 "	1 1/2"
4 1/8	1 1/4"	1 3/4"	1 1/4"	1 3/4"
4 1/2	1 1/4"	2 "	1 1/4"	3 "
5	1 1/2"	2 "	1 1/2"	3 "
5 1/2	1 1/2"	2 1/4"	1 1/2"	2 1/4"
6 5/8	1 3/4"	2 1/2"	1 3/4"	2 1/2"
7 3/8	1 3/4"	2 3/4"	2 "	3 "
7 7/8	1 3/4"	2 3/4"	2 1/4"	3 1/4"
8 3/8	2 "	2 3/4"	2 1/4"	3 1/2"
8 3/4	2 "	3 "	2 1/2"	3 1/2"
9 1/2	2 "	3 "	2 1/2"	4 "
10 3/8	2 "	3 1/4"	2 3/4"	4 1/4"
10 7/8	2 1/4"	3 1/4"	3 "	4 1/2"
11 3/8	2 1/4"	3 1/4"	3 1/4"	4 3/4"
12 3/4	2 1/4"	3 1/2"	3 1/4"	5 "

Round Wall Log Profiles			Maximum Allowable Knot Size			
Coped Log Diameter	Maximum Profile Reduction [in.]	Face Width Inscribed Rectangle	Grade:			
			Beam 1:14 SOG	Header 1:10 SOG	Wall 1:8 SOG	Utility 1:4 SOG
6	1 1/8	4 3/4	1 1/4"	1 3/4"	2 1/2"	3 "
7	1 5/16	4 7/8	1 1/4"	2 "	3 "	3 1/2"
8	1 7/16	5 5/8	1 1/2"	2 1/4"	3 1/4"	4 "
9	1 9/16	6 3/8	1 3/4"	2 1/2"	3 3/4"	4 3/4"
10	1 3/4	7	1 3/4"	2 1/2"	4 1/4"	5 "
11	1 7/8	7 3/4	1 3/4"	2 3/4"	4 3/4"	5 3/4"
12	2	8 1/2	2 "	2 3/4"	5 "	6 1/4"
13	2 3/16	9 1/8	2 "	3 "	5 1/2"	6 3/4"
14	2 5/16	9 7/8	2 "	3 "	6 "	7 1/4"
15	2 7/16	10 5/8	2 "	3 1/4"	6 1/4"	7 3/4"
18	2 7/8	12 3/4	2 1/4"	3 1/2"	7 3/4"	9 1/4"

Figure 76: Reference tables created for grading round and square log profiles. Due to the nature of measuring knots on round logs, the allowable knot size is rounded to 1/4" (1/8" is the minimum realistic tolerance for visual inspection in production). The slope of grain requirements are shown per the Log Homes Council Log Grading Program. Source: Author.

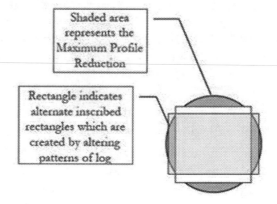

Shaded area represents the Maximum Profile Reduction

Rectangle indicates alternate inscribed rectangles which are created by altering patterns of log

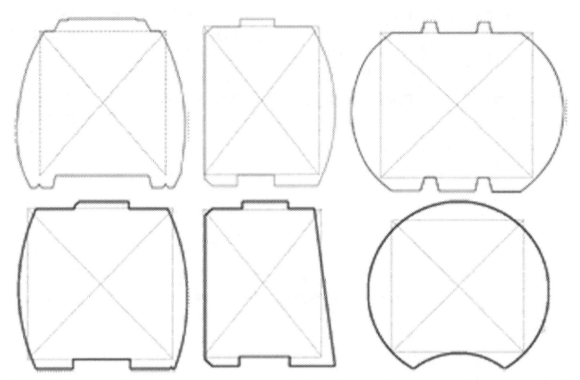

Figure 77: Inscribed rectangles are used to establish grading criteria and may be the prescriptive option to determine section properties. Source: Author.

For the section properties of Unsawn/Full Round and Sawn Round Timber Beams, the following table provides the equations. Use the average log diameter to establish the radius.

Property	Sawn Round Timber Beams	Unsawn (Full Round) Timber Beams
Area of Section (in^2)	2.8461*radius^2	3.1416*radius^2
Section Modulus (in^3)	0.6159*radius^3	0.7854*radius^3
Moment of Inertia (in^4)	0.5612*radius^4	0.7854*radius^4

Figure 78: Formulas for section properties of Sawn Round Timber Beams. Source: Compiled by Author.

Calculated Option

Calculation Option: Engineered composite analysis can be completed that incorporates the entire profile (beyond the inscribed rectangle), and therefore may produce greater section properties.

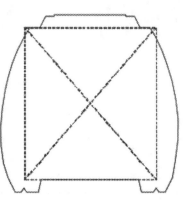

Variable	SECTION PROPERTIES		Ref. 2.3	Vertical	Horizontal
H_L	Stack height	in		7- 3/16	
W_n	Least width dimension	in			5- 7/8
	Calculated fire-resistance rating:		Ref. 4.1		1-hr.
W_L	Average width (A/H_L)	in			7-19/64
B_LP	Profile bearing width	in			5- 7/8
	Bearing capacity			31020 plf	
A	Area of cross-section	in^2		52.428	
IR	Inscribed Rectangle	in		6-5/8	6-7/8
C_F	Size Factor applicable to Fb, bending stress value			1.000	1.000
S	Section modulus	in^3		64.069	56.547
I	Moment of inertia	in^4		230.299	179.4

Figure 79: TimberLogic's *Log Wall Performance Estimator* defines the section properties on the summary page. Source: Author.

Properties Related to Capacity: **Sample Case** | **Your Product**

To get the capacity of the piece, multiply the design value by the section property
Sawn Round   10" dia. SRTB

Design Value Look up in Table	#1 SRTB 302.2(3)	Sect. Prop.		302.2(2)	Capacity lbs.	Design Value	Sect. Prop.	Capacity (lbs.)
Fb, bending (psi)	1100	S, in^3	section modulus	76.99	84,689			
Ft, tension (psi)	600	S, in^3	modulus	76.99	46,194			
Fv, shear (psi)	130	A, in^2	area	71.15	9,250			
Fc⊥, compression perp. (psi)	390	B_LP, in.	bearing area	3	1,170			
Fc, compression parallel (psi)	725	A, in^2	area	71.15	51,584			
E, elasticity (psi)	1100000	I, in^4	moment of inertia	350.72	3.9E+08			

Wall-Log Look up in Table	Header Grade 302.2(5)	Sect. Prop.		7.7"x7.5"	Capacity lbs.			
Fb, bending vertical (psi)	875	S, in^3		72.192	63,168			
Fb, bending horizontal (psi)	875	S, in^3		74.12174	64,857			
Ft, tension (psi)	575	S, in^3		72.192	41,510			
Fv, shear (psi)	125	A, in^2	7.7x7.5	57.754	7,219			
Fc⊥, compression perp. (psi)	350	B_LP, in.		3	1,050			
Fc, compression parallel (psi)	725	A, in^2		57.754	41,871			
E, elasticity (psi)	1100000	I, in^4		270.72	3.0E+08			

Figure 80: Log Capacity Worksheet (Design Stress Values x Section Properties). Source: Author.

Note that wall-logs are assessed in bending in both directions—the vertical condition supports gravity loads while the horizontal condition resists lateral loads imposed by wind and seismic activity. For spanning conditions like rafters and joists, the vertical condition is all that is considered, although restraint against twisting is required at bearing points. Post capacities are illustrated below, showing how post height, grade and section properties can affect the allowable load placed on the post.

"As applied to wood, the ratio of the ovendry weight of a sample to the weight of a volume of water equal to the volume of the sample at some specific moisture content, as green, air-dry, or ovendry."

The specific gravity of the wood controls many other values used to evaluate how wood will perform—from movement to thermal performance to connection design.

- Load capacity calculations are based on Section 3.7 of the 2001 NDS.
- Load capacities assume all posts are vertical and only loaded vertically with 0" eccentricity and both ends of column pinned
- Post height is limited by available stock length or 1/d, the slenderness ratio (for solid columns shall not exceed 50).
- Assume Ke=1.0 for pin-pin connections

Nominal Callout	Grade / Species	Post Height					
		5 ft.	10 ft.	12 ft.	16 ft.	20 ft.	24 ft.
6x6	Wall Grade & Btr. Eastern Softwoods (ESW)	13746 lbs	11672 lbs	9440 lbs.	6020 lbs.	4032 lbs.	NA
6x6	Header Grade & Btr. Eastern Softwoods (ESW)	18173 lbs	15470 lbs	12559 lbs.	8014 lbs.	5371 lbs.	NA
6x8	Wall Grade & Btr. Eastern Softwoods (ESW)	17807 lbs	15120 lbs	12229 lbs.	7799 lbs.	5223 lbs.	NA
6x8	Header Grade & Btr. Eastern Softwoods (ESW)	23542 lbs	20041 lbs	16244 lbs.	10381 lbs.	6958 lbs.	NA
8x8	Wall Grade & Btr. Eastern Softwoods (ESW)	27003 lbs	25279 lbs	22917 lbs.	17181 lbs.	12315 lbs.	8992 lbs
8x8	Header Grade & Btr. Eastern Softwoods (ESW)	35637 lbs	33399 lbs	30027 lbs.	22817 lbs.	16385 lbs.	11975 lbs
8 RTB	#1 RTB Grade & Btr. Eastern Softwoods (ESW)	28492 lbs	27345 lbs	25755 lbs.	21262 lbs.	16286 lbs.	12279 lbs
10 RTB	#1 RTB Grade & Btr. Eastern Softwoods (ESW)	45537 lbs	44514 lbs	43133 lbs.	39034 lbs.	33218 lbs.	26918 lbs
12 RTB	#1 RTB Grade & Btr. Eastern Softwoods (ESW)	66317 lbs	65361 lbs	64102 lbs.	60449 lbs.	54960 lbs.	47835 lbs

Figure 81: TimberLogic's *Span Table Report* illustrates the significance of grade and cross-sectional area on the capacity different rectangular posts. Holding to one grade of round timber beam isolates the change section properties. Source: Author.

Specific Gravity

Specific gravity is important in wood engineering for several reasons. It is often used as a way to group different species that have similar properties. As specific gravity increases,—unit weight increases, connection values increase, and U-Factor increases (hence R-Value decreases). ASTM D9 defines specific gravity as

Compliance Options

Prescriptive Option: The specific gravity is established based on unseasoned wood per ASTM D2555 or Tables 302.2 (3) and (5). For oven-dry logs, see the NDS Table 11.3.2A Assigned Specific Gravities.

Testing Option: ASTM D2395 can be employed to measure specific gravity of a sample of log, but existing wood science is relatively accurate.

Calculation Option: As shown below.

	PERFORMANCE ESTIMATES	Climate Zone:		Initial	Dry	Moist	Warm-Humid	Marine
MCs	Service Moisture Content = EMC	Ref. 2.41	%	30	10	13	14	15
G	Specific Gravity @ MCs			0.38	0.407	0.403	0.402	0.4
Weight	Log weight	Ref. 2.42	plf	11.21	10.17	10.34	10.41	10.45
	Wall mass		psf	18.72	16.98	17.27	17.38	17.45

Figure 82: TimberLogic's *Log Wall Performance Estimator* defines the specific gravity and related properties on the summary page. Source: Author.

Calculate specific gravity

			Sample Case	Your Product
Look up the wood species in Tables 302.2(3) or 201.2(5)			Eastern w. pine	
Enter the unseasoned specfic gravity	Gu		0.35	
Find the fiber saturation point in Table 304.2	MC_{FSP}		30 %	

Enter the target moisture content

and calculate G=Gu / [1(0.265aGu)] , a=(MC$_{FSP}$ – MC$_S$)/MC$_{FSP}$

			Sample Case	
milled green	MC$_D$	30 %	0.35	
	MC$_S$, ASHRAE	12 %	0.37063	
	MC$_S$, Dry	10 %	0.37307	Remember that MC is a %, so the value is actually x/100, or 0.xx
	MC$_S$, Moist	13 %	0.36942	
	MC$_S$, Warm-Humid	14 %	0.36821	
	MC$_S$, Marine	15 %	0.36702	

Figure 83: Specific Gravity Worksheet. Source: Author.

Log Density

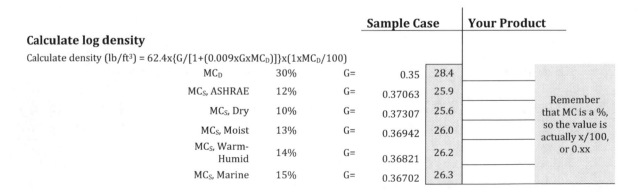

Calculate log density

Calculate density (lb/ft^3) = 62.4x{G/[1+(0.009xGxMC$_D$)]}x(1xMC$_D$/100)

				Sample Case		Your Product
	MC$_D$	30%	G=	0.35	28.4	
	MC$_S$, ASHRAE	12%	G=	0.37063	25.9	
	MC$_S$, Dry	10%	G=	0.37307	25.6	Remember that MC is a %, so the value is actually x/100, or 0.xx
	MC$_S$, Moist	13%	G=	0.36942	26.0	
	MC$_S$, Warm-Humid	14%	G=	0.36821	26.2	
	MC$_S$, Marine	15%	G=	0.36702	26.3	

Figure 84: Log Density Worksheet. Source: Author.

Log Weight

	Sample Case	Your Product
Establish the Log stack height (H_L)		
8x8 nominal H_L	7.5	
Establish the average log width (W_L)		
Area contained within the log profile, A (in.^{2}) =	57.754	
$A / H_L = W_L$ (in.)	7.7	

Calculate log weight

	%	Density	x $W_L/12$ = psf	x A/144 = plf	x $W_L/12$ = psf	x A/144 = plf
MC_D	30%	28.4	18.22	11.39		
MC_S, ASHRAE	12%	25.9	16.62	10.39		
MC_S, Dry	10%	25.6	16.43	10.27		
MC_S, Moist	13%	26.0	16.68	10.43		
MC_S, Warm-Humid	14%	26.2	16.81	10.51		
MC_S, Marine	15%	26.3	16.88	10.55		

Figure 85: Log Weight Worksheet. Source: Author.

Notching & Boring

ICC400 illustrates typical limitations for notching and boring conditions when the structural log spans between bearing points. This is consistent with notching and boring limits for other lumber and timber standards (per the NDS—American Wood Council's National Design Specification for Wood Construction).

Log walls involve notching in many other regards. The need for a broader analysis of notching limits was required to address intersecting log wall sections such as at corners or where an interior wall is tied to the exterior wall by interlock joinery. For this reason, notching is permitted to remove up to 2/3 of log cross-section. The substantiation comes from the fact that the wood removed for the notch is then filled by another log.

Figure 86: A notched log corner—the notch in this case is permitted to remove up to 2/3 of the cross-section of the log. Source: F. Lee Hyslop, Cedar Creek Homes.

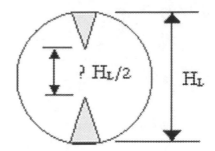

Figure 87: Kerfing limit. Source: Author.

Net section is a principle element where notching, boring and kerfing take place. It refers to the remaining wood available to resist loading at the point where the area of the notch, bore or kerf occurs.

In addition to notching and boring, a log section can be reduced by kerfing. Kerfing removes wood strategically with the intent of relieving stress due to shrinkage as the log dries. It is a successful technique but has limitations. When the kerf is a simple saw cut, the width of the kerf is subtracted from the allowable knot size on the kerfed face when the kerf if deep enough to penetrate the inscribed rectangle. Sometimes, round logs have a groove notched into the top to relieve drying stresses and another in the bottom for bearing and joinery purposes. This is also referred to as kerfing, and the extent of kerfing is limited to one-half the stack height of the log (H_L).

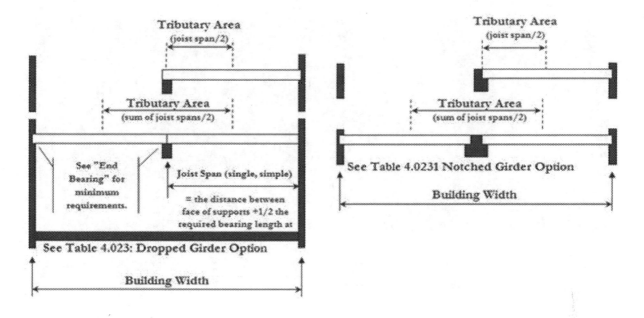

Figure 88: Net section of notched girders (to receive joists) will have the same capacity as net sections with joists bearing on top of the girder. Source: Author

Treating, Handling & Storage

Wood treatments and handling and storage considerations are covered very briefly. This information is provided for completeness of the evaluation of the log wall system and identifies pertinent codes and standards for more information.

Wood treatments include wood preservation and fire retardant treatments. The ability of wood to accept preservatives, fire retardants, and finishes often varies with the species. The Wood Handbook provides information relating to these properties by wood species. The single most common treatment of log components in a log yard is a biocide that will inhibit sapstains. The next most common treatment in the industry today is the application of borate salts (e.g., Timbor®) that will diffuse through the wood to inhibit anything that consumes the wood. Borates are non-toxic to humans and EPA-certified. They are applied via pressure treatment, submersion in dip tanks, spray-applied, and in rod form. These are inserted into holes bored into corners or other

locations for future benefit—if water ever reaches the borate rod, rather than providing water to an inviting food source, the salts diffuse in the water and collect in the wood cells, making the wood unappetizing.

Handling and storage of log components is important. Logs range from smaller profiles of low density woods to very large high density woods. Each log home producer has had to handle the logs they are selling, and they can advise any builder how to safely handle the log components. This is important to make sure notched log sections and other joinery details are not damaged by mishandling. Storage instructions will commonly require that the log components remain covered until needed for installation, with covered bundles keep up off the ground so that they will not sit in rain puddles or snow.

Figure 89: Log building benefits from proper storage and staging of log components. Source: Right- Real Log Homes; Left-Southland Log Homes, www.southlandloghomes.com.

The handling and storage instructions are commonly provided with the log components in two effective ways:

1. A construction manual that outlines proper techniques.
2. A company representative or construction superintendent arrives on site to guide the process.

Mechanical Connections & Fasteners [53]

The topic of fasteners and wood is a big one requiring a summary discussion. The variability of wood requires conservative safety factors to insure that the design capacities will hold true in 95% of the cases. The variability in craftsmanship during the installation of the fasteners is also a factor. The combination results in a fairly conservative approach to the design of wood connections and the selection of fasteners to do that job.

ICC400 relies on the AF&PA National Design Specification for Wood (NDS®) to address the topic. The capacity of the wood connections is found in the NDS Chapter 11 for Dowel-Type Fasteners or may be found on evaluation reports for proprietary products that have better properties than those reflected in the NDS. A preferred source for those evaluation reports is the ICC Evaluation Service, Inc. (www.icc-es.org), although several other independent organizations provide product evaluation services.

The selection of a fastener will vary greatly on the design of the log wall and log profile. Spikes and drift pins were early fasteners of choice because they were readily available. Lag screws become more popular choices as log builders focused on tighter connections between logs. The fasteners were/are produced in large volume with limited quality control in place to insure fastener properties. Based on years of tests, these commodity type fasteners are given conservative design values due to the large variability in their physical properties.

Proprietary self-boring screws have nearly replaced the spike (ring shank or spiral) due to ease of installation and better connection value. These screws entered the log home industry in the mid 1990's when the OlyLog® (http://www.fastenmaster.com/) was introduced. Today, the OlyLog has considerable competition and manufacturers have invested in ICC Evaluation Service Reports to document and vet their claims of capacity and performance. Proprietary fasteners are produced under specific quality control methods that minimize variability in their physical properties, insuring higher strengths per fastener, and thus per connection. In addition to their increased design values, the self-drilling features of the proprietary fasteners make them a viable alternative to lag screws. Lag screws are still a popular fastener, but lead holes are still recommended.

In lumber connections, the full capacity of the fastener can be used as long as the wood doesn't exhibit degradation due to splitting around the fastener. Connection capacity can degrade quickly when this is the case, so wood connection design includes a recommended lead hole, or pre-bored hole for the fastener. This allows the fastener to bear on the wood after installation, but driving the fastener is not displacing the wood fiber.

Drilling a lead hole and managing end and edge distances are more important for lumber than for wall-logs. The larger cross-section of most logs reduces the potential for splitting the wood, and this is even truer for white pine and similar low-density species. While splitting can occur in dryer logs, it is less common in green logs (at fiber saturation). When the fastener splits the green wood fibers, they initially tighten back around the fastener, but they will be pulled away as the wood dries. The idea that spiking a green log without drilling a lead hole has been supported by experience with log walls that settle, but a lead hole is still recommended for fasteners greater than 3/8-inch in diameter. High-density wood species are quite different, and builders may prefer to bore a lead hole just to make installation easier.

In addition to reducing the energy required to pound the spike or drive the lag screw into place, the lead hole will help guide the fastener without deviation due to knots. With smaller diameter fasteners, hitting a knot can bend the

fastener resulting in an undesirable bearing surface in the upper log.

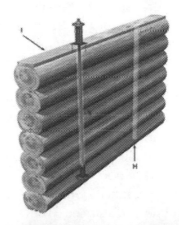

Figure 90: Wall-logs are often connected to one another by proprietary bolting systems, lag screws in pre-bored holes with countersink for head and washer, or log screws that offer self-drilling and countersinking. Sources, respectively: Heritage Log Homes, The Original Lincoln Logs, Ltd., and Real Log Homes.

The edge and end distances and groups of fasteners can also impact the quality of the connection because the fastener is installed too close to the end or edge of the piece of wood or too close to another fastener, resulting in a split in the wood. They are presented as a factor which must be multiplied by the fastener diameter to arrive at the required distance. These requirements (e.g., 10 diameters may be recommended, reduced to 5 diameters if there is a lead hole) are provided to minimize splitting of the wood. Proprietary fasteners are tested for capacity without splitting to determine these distances. The "Z" values are for resistance in pounds to lateral loading both perpendicular and parallel to grain. The "W" values provide the resistance in pounds to withdrawal forces, while the "P" values provide the resistance of the wood to forces that would pull the fastener head through the wood.

Another factor that impacts the connection capacity is the length of the fastener into the piece that is holding it, called the main member. The table below represents commodity fasteners except for the two diameters of the log screws (shown in italics). These two fasteners are proprietary products with specific properties and should not be used without the certainty of capacity provided by an accredited evaluation report (e.g., ICC-ES Evaluation Report completed per Acceptance Criteria AC233). The table shows fastener diameters (dia.) for the various sections of the fastener—threaded, unthreaded shank—the required lead hole and the NDS prescribed/minimum lengths based the log above, called the side member, and the log below, called the main member.

Fasteners	Shank dia. (in.)	Thread dia. (in.)	Lead Hole dia.	Edge Dist.	End Dist.	Thread Length	Length in Main Member	Dowel Bearing (Fyb, psi)	Single shear (lbs.) Z, perp.	Single shear (lbs.) Z, para.	With-drawal, lbs./in.	Pull-Thru, lbs./in.
1/4" spike	0.25	0.25	3/16"	4 x dia.	5 x dia.	NA	6 x dia.	70000	137	200	36	83
5/16" spike	0.3125	0.3125	15/64"	4 x dia.	5 x dia.	NA	6 x dia.	60000	188	290	45	127
3/8" spike	0.375	0.375	9/32"	4 x dia.	5 x dia.	NA	6 x dia.	45000	224	361	54	182
Log Screw	0.19	0.17	NA	8 x dia.	16 x dia.	2"	2 "	190000	230	250	170	73
Log Screw	0.23	0.21	NA	8 x dia.	16 x dia.	3"	3 "	190000	260	280	210	113
1/4" lag	0.25	0.173	NA	8 x dia.	16 x dia.	4-1/2"	4 x dia.	70000	137	200	163	55
5/16' lag	0.3125	0.227	NA	8 x dia.	16 x dia.	4-1/2"	4 x dia.	60000	271	334	193	66
3/8" lag	0.375	0.265	1/16"	4 x dia.	7 x dia.	4-3/4"	4 x dia.	45000	112	180	221	77
7/16" lag	0.4375	0.328	3/32"	4 x dia.	7 x dia.	4-3/4"	4 x dia.	45000	165	276	249	88
1/2" lag	0.5	0.371	7/64"	4 x dia.	7 x dia.	5"	4 x dia.	45000	202	353	275	138
5/8" lag	0.625	0.471	1/8 "	4 x dia.	7 x dia.	5-1/4"	4 x dia.	45000	308	570	325	209
3/4" lag	0.75	0.579	9/64"	4 x dia.	7 x dia.	5-1/2"	4 x dia.	45000	447	861	373	303
1/2" drift pin	0.5	0.5	3/16"	4 x dia.	7 x dia.	NA	6 x dia.	45000			72	NA
3/8" bolt	0.375	0.298	15/64"	4 x dia.	7 x dia.	Full length	Full width / depth	45000	141	228	2511	
1/2" bolt	0.5	0.406	15/32"	4 x dia.	7 x dia.			45000	242	423	4661	
5/8" bolt	0.625	0.514	13/32"	4 x dia.	7 x dia.			45000	366	6/8	7470	
3/4" bolt	0.75	0.627	17/32"	4 x dia.	7 x dia.			45000	525	1009	11115	
7/8" bolt	0.875	0.739	21/32"	4 x dia.	7 x dia.			45000	700	1402	15441	
1" bolt	1	0.847	25/32"	4 x dia.	7 x dia.			45000	892	1842	20284	

based on Eastern Softwoods wood species group, 0.35 unseasoned specific gravity

Bolt withdrawal capacity is based on a bolt tensile strength of 36kpsi with nut and washer sized accordingly.

Figure 91: The table above is provided to example of the different aspects of connection design. Refer to the AF&PA NDS (National Design Specification for Wood Construction) or ICC Evaluation Service, Inc. evaluation reports for actual connection capacities. Source: Author.

Fastener Spacing

The diagrams below indicate some important factors in connection design that apply to log building. The illustration on the left shows how log screws, lag screws, and spikes must be spaced so that they do not generate splitting in the wood. End distances are used to space the fasteners from the ends of the logs (butt joint), but it is also the distance that should be followed as the minimum distance between fasteners. The illustrations show the "S_{end}" end distance at a wall opening (e.g., window or door opening) or butt joint. At the ends of the logs abutting the opening, a column of fasteners is designed to create a solid section at the edge of the opening.

In accordance with the NDS, the end distance (S_{end}) for a 3/8" lag screw would be 3". This would mean that the minimum distance between butt joints in consecutive log courses would be 9" with 6" to either side to next fastener in log directly above and below a butt joint.

A note on butt joint location: Where logs are not full length (corner to corner), butt joints are impossible to avoid. It is generally advised in the log building industry to offset butt joints by 12-24 inches. The fastener spacing illustration would indicate that the offset must be a minimum of $3*S_{end}$. Unless absolutely necessary, it is not industry practice to allow a butt joint to occur directly under a window (window sill log). This sill log typically extends beyond the opening on each side at least as much as the header log. Butt joints under the sill log are limited as they would be elsewhere in the wall.

sufficient to seal over the fastener head so that moisture is not able to sit in that small cavity.

If a log wall is intended to experience settling, a different set of criteria must be addressed. First, the head of the fastener must be set further into the log so that it will not be holding up the log above as the predicted amount settling occurs. The fastener should also be

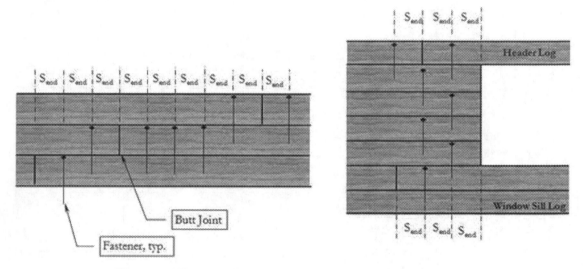

Figure 92: Fastener Spacing Requirements. Source: Author.

Fasteners and Settling

Although settling will be discussed later (see *Accommodating Settling*), it must be noted that the installation of fasteners can play a role in how a wall settles. The log through which the fastener is installed needs to be able to move while the fastener holds it in place to the log below.

If a wall is designed and produced with dry material in such a way that it is not supposed to experience differential shrinkage over a number of courses, then the only concern is to install the fastener so that the head of the fastener is at or below the log surface in which it is installed. Typically, a counter-bore is required to recess the fastener head into the wood surface. A bead of caulk is typically

installed as close to vertical as possible, so that the log will not bear on it as settling occurs. To further facilitate movement along the fastener, the lead hole should be pre-bored to the shank diameter or possibly the major thread diameter where lag screws are used (to minimize the chance of the wood bearing on the threads). It is possible that separation between courses can be built in and maintained if lag screw threads are held in both logs.

It is also important to recognize the potential contribution of the fastener to insure that the log is held tight while resisting the compression force of the sealant between courses. A liquid sealant will provide little resistance, even as denser butyl tape. Once the log is set and fastened, the seal is set. However, polyurethane gaskets can be quite dense and present a significant level of compression recovery force—it wants to expand back to its original shape and needs continuous pressure to hold it to the designed joint tolerance. When this is the case, the fastening schedule should be examined to see if the structural fastening schedule will also provide the holding force to sufficiently compress the gasket.

Fasteners and Structural Considerations

Again, structural considerations are discussed later (*Structural Provisions*), but the selection and installation of fasteners is a key element of how log structures perform. In smaller structures, the joinery itself can be made to transfer the applicable loads to the foundation/ ground. However, this is seldom the case today and connections are an important part of log building.

Oversized lead holes are common for through bolt connections, where all-thread is passed through multiple courses and couplers are used to connect the rod segments. Commonly, the coupling is a much larger diameter than the bolt, so settling concerns are limited to the coupling. The structural impact of this is that the lead hole that accommodates the coupling is far too big for the bolt, and it allows a fraction of an inch of movement before it begins to bear lateral loading onto the wood. For this reason, bolting is typically used as a compression/ tension connector, with dowel-type fasteners (e.g., spikes, lags) added between.

Testing of log wall shear panels has been limited, but the reports to date indicate that the ideal log wall shear panel would consist of a section at a corner or between openings where a threaded rod or cabled tension connection is at each end with multiple dowel-type fasteners between courses to resist shear/racking loads. It should be noted that gravity loads play a role in performance, but friction is not a

factor in engineering the fastening schedule. Compression is seldom the issue, as the logs typically provide sufficient bearing from one course to the next to resist the most extreme loads.

Fire-Resistance Ratings [54]

In 1977, one of the key issues bringing the Charter members of the Log Homes Council (LHC) together was the call for fire-resistance ratings for log walls. The demand at the time was to prove that a log wall could be used as the common wall between a garage and the living area. Homeowners were becoming aggravated that they had invested in the log wall that they wanted, but the building official wouldn't give them a Certificate of Occupancy until they installed 5/8" Type "X" gypsum from the concrete foundation to the bottom side of the sheathing.

The devastating 1991 Oakland Hills Fire in California that resulted in incredible structure loss spurred an effort to create a model building code for construction in rural environments where fire fighting resources were not immediately available. In the development of the code, it was established that exterior walls needed to have a one-hour fire resistance rating. However, the requirement for a one-hour rated wall raised a significant threat to the log home industry that builds primarily in rural areas.

The result of the model code action was the ICC Urban-Wildland Interface Code (IUWIC). It covers construction, but also includes guidance for alternative site development when local fire fighting services are not readily available. Examples include keeping potential fuels (vegetation) a safe distance from the structure, having a water supply available when fire fighters arrive, and providing appropriate access to the building (road width, etc.).

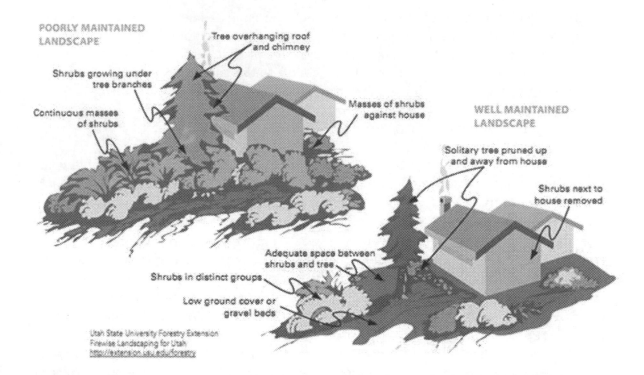

Figure 93: Proper maintenance of the property around a structure may save it in the case of a wildfire. Source: Forest Extension of Utah State University publication "Firewise Landscaping for Utah." [55]

Beyond the reduction of potential fuel around the structure, this approach improves durability as airflow around the building helps dry wood surfaces. Dry log surfaces reduce chances for decay. These methods also help limit exposure and attraction of insects to the log wall.

While fire protection measures as outlined by the IUWIC are a bit beyond the scope of this discussion, the 2012 edition of ICC400 does bring to bear an interesting point. The Standard was revised to include a requirement for roof overhangs for the purpose of protection of the log wall from direct precipitation and from backsplash where roof runoff hits a horizontal surface that is near the bottom log (sill or bottom plate log). This is a good revision intended to reduce maintenance issues and enhance durability and truly applies to any house with exposed wood materials. However, it is a proven fact that roof overhangs collect the smoke and hot gases of a wildfire.

The following are some recommendations that would be helpful in minimizing loss during a fire in rural areas where wildfire can be a hazard. The following points are identified in The Journal of Light Construction online article, "Surviving Wildfire" in which author, Ted Cushman, integrates notes from his interview with Stephen Quarles. Quarles was contracted by the California State Fire Marshal to educate the public on the topic.[56]

- ROOFING: Use a Class A roofing product such as asphalt composition shingles, cement tile, or clay tile. Interesting to note is that many metal roofing products require additional fire-resistant underlayment or cementitious sheathing for a Class A rating. It is important that gaps between roofing layers must be sealed so that embers cannot be blown between the layers.
- VENTS: Apply a 1/4-inch metal wire mess screen to all exterior vents unless the

vents have been designed and tested to resist the intrusion of both flame and embers. When a 100-foot defensible space is provided, common approaches to continuous soffit-ridge venting is typically allowed.

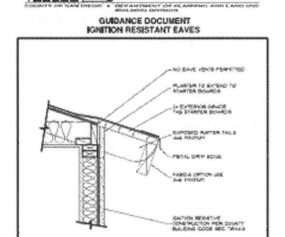

Figure 94: Ignition Resistant Heavy Timber Eave approved for San Diego County, CA. Source: County of San Diego, Department of Planning and Land Use, http://www.co.san-diego.ca.us/dplu/ docs/DPLU198.pdf

o It is common practice to build continuous soffit vents in roof overhangs so that warm air convectively moves over the insulation layer to remove any moisture and exits at a ridge vent. However, this practice correlates to major losses in wildfires. Options to offset the potential of hot gases exploding in the roof include roof vents, gable vents, or a protected fascia inlet. The fascia inlet would have metal screen and would have a drip edge applied below it to deflect heat and combustion gases that rise from under the overhang.

- OVERHANGS: San Diego County, California, has adopted a very stringent series of requirements for ignition resistant eave construction. It is recommended that readers at the fascia must be 3x6 or larger, whereas most log builders use a combination of 1x over 2x to build the fascia (depending on depth of framing).
  o Note that the exterior wall finish is noted as ignition resistive construction per County Building Code Sec. 704A.3 and is shown as cementitious (plaster board) extending to the bottom of the roof decking.
- WINDOWS: Double glazed windows provide superior performance in fast-moving, extreme fire conditions over single glazed. Specifying tempered glass is even better.
- DECKS: Decks are viewed much like overhangs, as they trap fire and heat underneath while providing a landing zone for fire brands. Heavy timber construction with 2x or thicker decking is good, but ignition-resistant protection under a deck is recommended. It could be argued that patio landscapes are the best bet
- LANDSCAPING: This topic is best covered by "Firewise Landscaping for Utah." The authors reflect on the adjustment from the cabin nestled in the forest to firewise landscaping as being analogous to extensive green lawns and thirsty annuals to water-wise landscaping.
- WALLS: A minimum fire-resistance rating of 1-hour for exterior walls is established in the IUWIC. The following discusses how to determine that for log walls.

Prescribed Option

Some of the tests performed by LHC members and other research (e.g., on glued laminated beams) were used to support a LHC proposition that a log wall with a 4" minimum dimension at its narrowest width met the one-hour rating requirement. To support its argument, the LHC documented its argument in a white paper, *Fire Performance of Log Walls*.

Ultimately, the ICC Wildland-Urban Interface Code (now the International Wildland-Urban Interface Code, IWUIC) was published in 1997 and included an exemption of the one-hour fire-resistance rating for exterior walls for log walls that have a 6" minimum dimension at its narrowest width. This continues in ICC400 as the prescriptive option for the fire-resistance rating of a log wall.

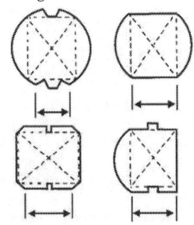

Figure 95: A log wall is recognized as one-hour fire-resistance rated if the minimum horizontal dimension is 6" or greater. Source: Log Homes Council Log Grading Program Training and Operations Manual.

Tested Option

In the 1990's, testing was pursued by a limited number of log home companies. They made the significant investment in ASTM E119, *Standard Test Methods for Fire Tests of Building Construction and Materials* to establish a recognized fire-resistance rating. Prior tests had been performed, but the many box-type tests were actually not in accordance with a standard test method, and therefore these test reports were not accepted by authorities having jurisdiction to permit construction.

Testing offers another important option when it comes to establishing the fire-resistance rating

of a log wall or a log joinery sealant system. The primary test applied to wall assemblies is ASTM E119. This testing is performed at accredited labs to perform the test and facilities to do so. This is not frequently done because the cost per test is quite high ($12,500 or thereabouts in the current market). The result is a report that establishes the fire-resistance rating of a specific assembly. In most cases, larger logs than the tested assembly would be expected to perform at or better than the test data, but changes in fastening or sealing system may possibly nullify any comparison. Using a sealant system to protect the joinery of round log systems is a real option, but the components of the sealant system are specific and cannot be varied without additional testing to verify.

Figure 96: Full-scale testing as reported for a specific proprietary chinking application and as shown being performed on the milled log. Source: Left-Sashco, www.sashco.com; Right-Honka Log Homes, www.honka.com.

Calculated Option

The calculation method is defined in the NDS Ch. 16. It establishes the fire-resistance rating based on char rate and the structural capacity of remaining wood. Another American Wood Council document, DCA 2—*Design of Fire-Resistive Exposed Wood Members*, provides guidelines for the calculation of fire resistance rating for a given timber beam size, in minutes, equal to

"Minutes of Fire Resistance Rating = 2.54 Zb [4-(b/d)]."

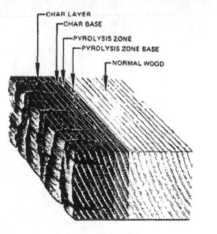

Given: b = W_L	d = H_L	Z	Minutes
1.5	1.5	1.3	15
3.5	3.5	1.3	35
5.5	5.5	1.3	55
6	6	1.3	60
7.25	7.25	1.3	72
7.7	7.5	1.3	76

Install fasteners within the rated char depth – 1.8" for 1-hr.

CHAR LAYER
CHAR BASE
PYROLYSIS ZONE
PYROLYSIS ZONE BASE
NORMAL WOOD

Figure 97: Minutes of Fire Resistance Rating = 2.54 Zb [4-(b/d)]; degradation zones in a wood section. Source: Left-Author, Right-R.H. White.

Note that the illustrations above show how wood chars and protects the wood beneath it from fire. However, the charred wood in now non-structural. This means that the effective fastening schedule may be reduced by a factor that represents the number of fasteners that may be installed in a potential char region. In other words, the fire rating of the wall is not only a function of remaining wood to support the structure, but the number of remaining fasteners in it. One method of insuring this is to install fasteners on alternate sides of the log, with spacing set equal to the maximum distance between fasteners along one side. The alternate side fastening would be at the midpoint of these, so as to halve the fastener spacing along the wall.

Quantifying the Components of Settling

Sections 304 and 305 combine to promote an effective air tight assembly as has been documented in many blower door tests and thermal imaging inspections. The successful performance of log structures is critical to the on-going viability of the handcrafter or manufacturer that provides the log materials package and the builder who assembles them. These are log home professionals who care about the end result. [57]

Section 304 offers a variety of choices. It begins with the overall prescriptive default—if you don't want to worry about moisture content or any other aspect of how the wall performs, the builder must provide a minimum of 6% settling allowance applied to the involved height. A quick example of involved height would be a settling allowance over a door. Using the prescriptive default, 6% of 82 inches is 4.92", so a 5" allowance between the bottom of the header log and the top of the door buck/frame would be required.

The next option offered in Section 304 is to qualify the log building system by calculating total settling, which is defined as the total change in height due to slumping, compaction, and radial shrinkage. Within each subsection describing theses potential areas for change in height, there is a prescriptive path and a calculation path. It is possible that all three factors need to be considered for a scribe-fit building system, while other types of log walls may be able to set one or two of the three factors at zero change.

Calculating Fire-Resistance Ratings

NDS: Minutes of Fire Resistance Rating = 2.54 Zb [4-(b/d)].

Given:	Z=1.3	b = W_L	d = H_L	Sample Case 2.54Z	Sample Case Minutes	Your Product	
	required for thermal barrier	1.5	1.5	3.302	15	W_L =	in.
		3.5	3.5	3.302	35	H_L =	in.
		5.5	5.5	3.302	55	[4-(b/d)] =	
		6	6	3.302	60	3.302b =	
		7.25	7.25	3.302	72		
		7.7	7.5	3.302	76	FRR =	minutes

Figure 98: Log Fire-Resistance Rating Worksheet. Source: Author.

It is also possible that the producer of the log building system has taken the steps necessary to market a log wall that does not settle. This has been taken into account in the standard by requiring that the calculations for total settling (as noted above) cannot result in a change of more than 5% of the involved height (e.g., 1/2 inch for an 8-foot wall).

If none of the above represents the experience of the log home producer, two more avenues are offered to demonstrate that experience. The first is testing by a certified laboratory for a specific wall assembly. The second is to perform a field survey (by an independent third party) of the company's delivered and built product.

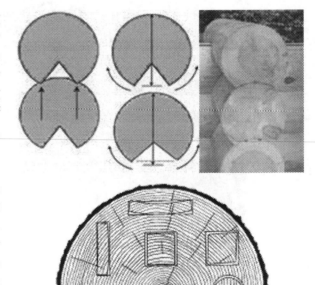

Figure 99: Components of Settling: Slumping, Compaction, and Shrinkage. Sources: Author; Hiawatha Log Homes, www.hiawatha.com; Wood Handbook, respectively.

ICC400 identifies three aspects of log design and construction that may contribute to the overall settling of log walls. Slumping refers to the change in effective stack height when the wood seasons and the notch in the log opens as tangential shrinkage occurs. Compaction occurs when the load above is concentrated along the bearing points (far left). The coped joinery in the photo above illustrates full bearing which would not be expected to exhibit compaction. Shrinkage is the natural dimensional change in wood as it seasons (dries). This is largely a function of radial shrinkage rates (which vary with wood species).

more detailed analysis. This is conservative in most cases and requires significant allowance for settling over doors and windows. This is a good option for handcrafted wall systems because much of the settling will occur shortly after the structure is made weather tight. In other words, the settling allowance is required for proper assembly, the extent of movement after the house has been completed will be considerably less.

Engineering Option: Establish settling performance by engineering analysis. Based entirely on analysis of shrinkage rates, bearing areas, and joint design geometry, an engineered approach avoids prescriptive minimum requirements.

Δ_S	Estimated settling due to shrinkage	Ref. 2.52	in./course	0	-0.102	-0.087	-0.081	-0.076
Δ_C	Estimated settling due to compaction	Ref. 2.53	in./course	NA	NA	NA	NA	NA
Δ_{SL}	Estimated settling due to slumping	Ref. 2.54	in./course	NA	NA	NA	NA	NA
Δ_T	Estimated total settling for typical wall		in./%	0"/0%	1.44"/1.4%	1.19"/1.2%	1.13"/1.1%	1.06"/1.1%

Figure 100: TimberLogic's *Log Wall Performance Estimator* defines the settling allowance on the summary page. This is the result for the milled profile shown in *Figure 79*. Source: Author.

Compliance Options

Prescriptive Option 1—Estimate settling at 6% of involved wall height. If a notched groove is employed in a green log, the designer may choose the first prescriptive option of applying a 6% rate of settling to save time in

Testing Option: Establish settling performance by testing. This option is seldom used, but it can demonstrate the extent of possible impacts from long term environmental change on a given log profile and wood species.

Figure 101: Performing the only known testing for settling using a detailed test protocol and accelerated seasoning using a kiln. Source: Ed Burke, PhD, Wood Science Associates, Missoula, MT.

<u>Field Survey Option</u>: This option establishes extents of settling by field survey. This option requires an independent third-party to document change of a new structure, recording identical measurements of the log wall annually for five years. There is no ASTM standard for this method, and the size of the sample has not been specified. It would be reasonable to assume that at least 3 homes would be surveyed in any one climate zone. The control is the theoretical conditions of the log wall system when first produced and the wall height when the design conditions are applied.

Calculated Option

ICC400 provides a calculation method that incorporates more prescriptive components of settling. Employing the calculation procedure is probably the most often used because components that don't apply can be ignored. The equation to be calculated seems simple: Δt (total settling) $= \Delta_{SL} + \Delta_C + \Delta s$.

Prescribed Slumping (Δ_{SL})

Slumping is understood, but hard to otherwise quantify. A certain allowance for slumping comes from the experience of handcrafters who acknowledge the reduction in wall height as loads are placed on the walls and the logs season in place. Slumping is a function of moisture content and the tangential shrinkage rate. As the log seasons (dries), the cope along the bottom of the log widens. When the cope/notch is deeper than the radius of the log below it, the bearing point is on the edges of the cope on the log beneath. The log will continue to settle down until sufficient area within the cope bears on the supporting log beneath it. Settling is halted by the bearing capacity, but the action itself is a function of the cope design, the moisture content of the wood and properties of the wood species.

Use 1.5% of involved log wall height as prescriptive allowance for tangential shrinkage during seasoning and loss of height as a notch widens. Drying stress is relieved by notch, which opens wider, becomes shallower, and loses stack height. This is a specific application and does not apply to all log joinery methods, hence slumping would not apply (=0).

Also note that when $MC_D = MC_S$, no effects of seasoning would be expected and slumping would not contribute to settling.

Compaction (Δc)

Compaction is a measurable element of settling and is provided with two compliance options.

Prescribed Option

If this is the only element producing settling, it could be considered to be the third prescriptive option, but in reality it is only one of the components.

Use 2% of involved log wall height as prescriptive allowance for compression at bearing points. If adequate bearing across flat or coped surface supports imposed load, set Δ_c equal to "0" as compaction would not apply. Notch and cope systems often compress at bearing points, and use of this prescriptive option offers a simple and easily applied approach.

Calculated Option

The bearing width is a sum of the contact points between the lower log and the next log above it. To eliminate compaction, the required bearing width is determined by summing all loads (in plf, pounds per lineal foot, divided by 12 to convert to inches) on the log divided by the allowable design value for compression perpendicular to grain (in psi, pounds per square inch). Remember that all live and dead loads supported by the log wall must be summed, and since the sill log or bottom plate log supports everything, it is the design (a.k.a., worst case) condition.

Assuming a wood species is used that has a 300psi compression perpendicular to grain stress value, one inch of bearing width is capable of supporting 3,600 pounds per lineal foot. Most residential designs do not put that much load on the log wall, so this case illustrates why many milled log joinery styles provide sufficient bearing width to support loading without compaction, hence compaction would equal "0".

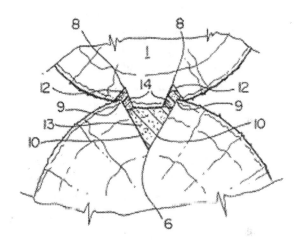

Figure 102: In 1989, Lloyd Beckedorf of Canada patented this design. How would this be expected to perform? Source: U.S. Patent #4,951,435.

Shrinkage (Δs)

Shrinkage is a natural function of wood as it dries. The living tree moves and stores water in cells and cell walls. The elongated cells become even thinner as the water moves out of the cell walls as the wood dries. This explains why shrinkage along the length of a piece of wood is relatively insignificant, while shrinkage across the grain is significant. This dimensional change is the issue being quantified.

It is easy to understand that shrinkage rates and distortion varies between species, but it is hard to understand that within a single tree there are changes in density, specific gravity and grain orientation. All of these factors explain why shrinkage is assumed to be extreme even though a specific building may never experience it. Logs behave differently, with individual trees within a large population can be quite different. Therefore, we rely on extensive testing and statistical analysis to determine shrinkage rates, just as we have established design stress values and other properties of wood.

Shrinkage rates change with the orientation of wood grain around knots and where cross grain occurs. Longitudinal shrinkage (axial, along the pith) is typically very small (1/16" in 16 ft.), but this can become greater when cross grain and large knots occur near the end of the log, creating a radial shrinkage effect. Milling factors also impact wood properties and estimated performance because a log that contains the heart/pith of the tree will behave differently than one that does not. These many variables of working with large cross-sections of wood are controlled by using the options described below. How would you answer the question, "Does a 12-inch diameter log wall shrink the same or less than an 8-inch milled log?" The answer comes by looking at the log as a component of the wall.

Prescribed Options

Settling is one of the few areas of log compliance that has so many options. That is further compounded by the multiple sub-options in each area. For shrinkage, there are actually three prescriptive options that will provide relatively accurate results, but they may be more conservative than a calculated option. Ranked roughly by extent of effort/information needed to demonstrate compliance, they are:

Prescriptive Option 4—Use 3% of involved log wall height. This means that an 8-foot height to the bottom of floor decking would require that interior partition walls and any vertical plumbing or duct runs allow for nearly 3-inches of settling at the ceiling line.

Prescriptive Option 5—Use 1% shrinkage for each 4% difference between MC_D and MC_S. Obviously, if the design moisture content is equal to the in-service or equilibrium moisture content, this option can be used to show that settling due to shrinkage equals "0". Realistically, this option also tells us that settling will be insignificant if the difference between design and equilibrium moisture is less than 4%. It would also be wise to add a 1/2" settling allowance as applicable to insure proper performance.

Prescriptive Option 6—Refer to Table 304.2(4) to select a rate based on Climate Zone, change in moisture content, and specific gravity. Not reproduced here, the table was proposed for inclusion in the standard more to educate readers that these elements affect how a log wall can be expected to perform. However, it is a more detailed option for compliance that takes less time than calculating the settling amount for each involved height.

Calculated Option

Estimate Settling

		Sample Case	Your Product

Options for assessing the components of settling:

Option 1 — 6% settling; Option 2a – ΔS$_L$ — 1.5% slumping

Involved Height (in.)	in.	Option 1 6% settling	Option 2a ΔS$_L$ 1.5% slumping	Your Product in.	6%	1.5%
to bottom of egress window	18	1.125-in.	0.375-in.			
to bottom of kitchen window	42	2.625-in.	0.75-in.			
to bottom of header	82	5-in.	1.25-in.			
to bottom of girder	90	5.5-in.	1.375-in.			
to top of wall	108	6.5-in.	1.625-in.			

Involved Height (in.)	in.	Option 2b = ΔC 2% compaction	2%
to bottom of egress window	18	0.375-in.	
to bottom of kitchen window	42	0.875-in.	
to bottom of header	82	1.75-in.	Is the bearing capacity of the wall-log ≥ the applicable load?
to bottom of girder	90	1.875-in.	
to top of wall	108	2.25-in.	

ΔC=0 when the total vertical load on the bottom log is ≤ bearing capacity from above

	Capacity	Design Value	Sect. Prop.	Capacity
	lbs./in.			lbs.

F$_C$^, compression perp. (psi) **350**   B$_{LP}$, in.=   bearing area   **3**   **1,050**

Involved Height (in.)	in.	Option 2c = ΔS 3% shrinkage	3%
to bottom of egress window	18	0.625-in.	
to bottom of kitchen window	42	1.375-in.	
to bottom of header	82	2.5-in.	
to bottom of girder	90	2.75-in.	
to top of wall	108	3.25-in.	

Calculate Shrinkage

$$\Delta s = [H_L \times (MC_D - MC_S)]/[(MC_{FSP} \times 100/S - MC_{FSP}) + MC_D]$$

MC$_{FSP}$ **30%**   MC$_D$ **30%**   MC$_S$ **12%**

	MC$_{FSP}$	MC$_D$	MC$_S$

from Table 304.2(2) Shrinkage Coefficients, Radial:

H$_L$	26.3	
S	3.7	

for Eastern w. pine   ΔS per log course =   0.625-in.

Remember that MC is a %, so the value is actually x/100, or 0.xx

Total Estimated Settling

Involved Height (in.)	in.	Option 2 = 2a+2b+2c Total	2a+2b+2c
to bottom of egress window	18	0.75-in.	
to bottom of kitchen window	42	1.625-in.	
to bottom of header	82	3-in.	
to bottom of girder	90	3.25-in.	
to top of wall	108	3.875-in.	

Figure 103: Settling Allowance Worksheet. Source: Author.

Non-settling Wall Systems

A log wall system is determined to be **non-settling** when Δt ≤ 0.5% of the involved height to a maximum of 1/2". This is very important as the experience of some log home builders can point to homes that have not exhibited settling affects although the above criteria would predict it to occur. In this case, it would be assumed that slumping will not occur, that compaction is not an issue, that shrinkage is controlled by seasoning the log to within 4% of the equilibrium moisture content of its built environment and that all internal structures are built without accommodation for settling as noted in the next section. Accepting that this is a possibility, the designer and builder would be wise to insure that the joinery between logs will properly respond to changes in individual logs.

Settling is eliminated when

- Mechanical bearing devices fix log placement; and
- The joinery/cope design protects the seal and allows movement; or
- $MC_D ≤ MC_S$ (slumping=0, shrinkage=0) and
- Bearing of log surfaces ≥ required bearing (compaction=0).

Accommodating Settling

Given the quantified amount of settling per the paths described above, several details of log wall construction must be examined. Allowances for the change in wall height must be addressed by the techniques that have been successfully used by log builders for many years. It is imperative to recognize that the first step is to correctly estimate the amount of settling due to the moisture content of the log, the type of joinery, and the climate in which the wall is built.

Accommodating settling will keep windows and doors from binding, will allow joints to stay tight to maintain an effective seal, and will allow structural beams to stay level (keeping ceiling materials tight to the log wall).

Settling Gap

Settling gaps are provided to absorb vertical movement. This is no more than a slip joint provided over rigid assemblies built in the log wall or below ceilings that occur within the height of the log wall. Over wall openings for window or door installation, the settling space is made by providing a space between the bottom of the header log and the top of the rough frame, then protecting the gap from the exterior by flashing and is sealed with insulation. A similar approach applies to the gap provided at the bottom of the logs that pass over the fireplace mantel. Where ceilings are expected to come down, Interior partitions are built with a double top plate. The upper top plate is attached to the ceiling and has the trim attached to it. The lower top plate has the wall finish applied and slides under the fixed trim to conceal settling.

Where vertical elements penetrate the roof, counter-flashing must be properly installed. Flexible plumbing lines and heating ducts are also required to account for change in wall height.

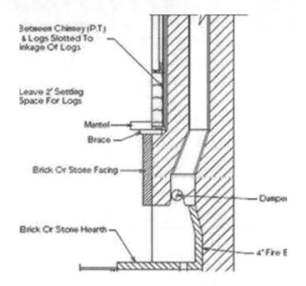

Figure 104: Settling Gaps: Over wall openings, above fireplace mantle. Source: Left-Real Log Homes, www.realloghomes.com; Right-Appalachian Log Structures, Inc., www. applog.com.

Sliding Joints

Vertical elements attached to log walls use slotted holes to allow for settling. This condition includes intersecting interior partitions, stiffener posts, window and door side bucks, upper kitchen wall cabinets, etc.

Figure 105: Examples of sliding joints Source: The Original Lincoln Logs, Ltd., www. lincolnlogs.com

Note that when posts are let into the log wall, the depth and width of the notch is important so that the log movement does not affect the finish of the post (or wall finish where an interior partition wall ends at the log wall. Normally, the depth of the notch is 1/4 to 1/2" deeper than the interior horizontal joint.

Figure 106: Where posts let into the log wall, notches are typically installed deeper than the profile. Source: Heritage Log Homes.

Settling Devices

Settling devices are installed to allow adjustment at post/column point loads. These devices are used to level floors after settling, and they will be used to bring ridge beams down to level.

Figure 107: Log walls stay tight when settling gaps over wall openings, sliding joints, and settling devices are employed. Source: Hiawatha Log Homes, www.hiawatha.com.

The industry has gradually evolved in this area. Where dead loads are not significant and settling is accommodated solely for leveling purposes, it has been common to use wood shims that can be removed as the log wall settles. Another method of allowing movement in a point load scenario is to design for it by holding the critical connection and allowing a less critical bearing point to slide. This has been done with stair assemblies and porch roofs. Where loads are more significant, such as an interior bearing point supporting a roof load, engineered solutions have been used by most log home builders. Those solutions would be sent to a steel fabricator to make the plates and assemble the parts.

With wood shrinkage gaining more attention in platform framed structures, a new variety of settling devices have evolved. These are especially attractive for log walls where through-bolting is necessary to resist lateral loads (see Lateral Load Resistance for more information). Here, the device is intended to be used with hold-down connectors or tension tie connectors with threaded rods or threaded anchor bolts. The same devices developed for framed shear wall connectors can be beneficial for log shear walls.

Shrinkage compensating devices have been covered by ICC Evaluation Service, LLC (ICC-ES) Acceptance Criteria AC316 since June 2005. AC316 has been revised and reapproved seven times since its original approval, with changes including updating to current editions of codes and test standards. This document is particularly useful in that it defines types of devices, proof loads, peak loads, travel distances, and more. The requirements for testing are outlined as is standard for all Acceptance Criteria.

The significance of AC316 is that it was created in response to a specific proponent, but has been open to public comment and discussion similar to the ICC Code Development Process. As additional companies approach ICC-ES for product evaluation, the AC may be updated to account for new and different proprietary approaches to solving the problem of wood shrinkage.

Thermal Envelope

As with other code references, ICC400 relies on ICC's International Energy Conservation Code (IECC) to establish the design conditions for log structures. Through the 2012 edition, the IECC presents a prescriptive path that is focused on steady-state R-values for rated insulation products with associated U-Factors for entire assemblies. Unless insulation is added to the log wall, log walls should only be evaluated by IECC's prescriptive table for mass wall U-Factors. Log walls are analogous to continuous insulation.

When written, ICC400 used existing code references (the 2003 IECC) to generate the process for compliance. With green building and other above-code programs developing, a path was generated for the performance path that complies with the latest versions of the IECC. The effort here was to identify the fact that wood species vary in how they conduct heat (e.g., R-value) due to differences in specific gravity (a function of species and moisture content). With the advent of the DOE climate zone map and associated equilibrium moisture contents, there was an impact on both settling allowance and thermal values. Due to the reference of ICC400 to the 2003 IECC, the section relates to the process as described earlier. With the publication of the 2006 IECC (after the work on ICC400 had concluded the public comment period), the log standard was no longer synchronized with the IECC. This was a resolved in the 2012 update of ICC400.

Just like our skin, the thermal envelope is supposed to provide a barrier and act like a vessel. Perhaps this is the link that explains why our boat building ancestors also built log homes. The goal is to keep what's out out, and what's in in.

Weather Protection

ICC400 addresses protection of air infiltration and vapor transfer in Section 305.1. This section focuses on joint design and sealant application rather than air and vapor barriers. With the tightening of air infiltration rates in the IECC, this section takes on new importance. **This is the second of two mandatory requirements in the standard**. An obvious key to log wall performance is to keep weather out and shed water.

Detailed requirements are not provided. It was determined by the IS-LOG Committee that there are many too many products and methods available to seal log joinery, and it was beyond the scope of ICC400 to specify them. Suffice it to say, it behooves log walls to be both air and water tight. Water entering the log wall by capillary action and/or wind driven is not desirable, and the industry strives to minimize it. For a detailed discussion of the aspects of joint design and sealants, the Log Homes Council document, *"Prevention of Air & Water Infiltration"* can be downloaded from www.loghomes.org.[58] This document was created through a consensus effort of Associate Members of the Log Homes Council that produce sealants and related products for log building.

Figure 108: Several methods are used to seal butt joints—wood dowels set in caulk, PVC splines set in kerfs (shown), intricate scarf cuts, or log joinery similar to interlocking corners. Source: The Original Lincoln Logs Ltd., www. lincolnlogs.com

Sealing methods at joinery and settling considerations are key responses to the normal differential changes in wood. Movement in log walls is accounted for in the design of joinery systems and will not be compromised over time (as when framing members change dimension, e.g., no nail pops in drywall).

Figure 109: Several companies recommend caulking the exteriors of corners and other joints as an additional preventative measure. This is also a common practice by maintenance contractors where separation between log courses has occurred. Source: Southland Log Homes, www.southlandloghomes.com

Air Barrier Requirements

Air infiltration was identified as the culprit for energy consumption decades ago, but the rush to R-value overwhelmed this concern. It has been established that perhaps the superior air tight construction, rather than thermal mass, is really why log home owners repeatedly testify as to their warmth, comfort and low energy cost. Compared to their frame wall contemporaries, energy savings of 30% or more would make sense.

Looking a little more carefully, if holes in the building envelope account for 30% of the cost of heating a home, how much of that can be attributed to the log wall? Considering the attention to weatherization techniques for the past several decades, the latest energy standards are attacking points of leakage that don't apply to log walls. Duct systems, doors and windows, and fireplace construction are being tightened. Ceiling penetrations such as bath vents and recessed lights are being addressed by minimizing them or providing special installations to insure air tightness. Of the major problems identified repeatedly over the years, the only ones that apply solely to walls are vent penetrations (e.g., range, dryer), wall outlets and the seal at the sole plate. While some builders notch the log wall for electrical boxes, this practice does not generate an air leakage concern as vent penetrations. Where possible, vents can be exhausted through the rim joist rather than pass through the log wall. And the seal of the bottom log to the sill or subfloor is no less important than any other joint in the wall.

ICC400 addresses methods to quantify and accommodate differential settling in log walls as solid wood timbers are laid horizontally on one-another. Properly implemented, these methods have proven effective as witnessed by ENERGY STAR 5-Star+ certifications. The key to attaining <3 ACH50 is in the details of connecting the log walls together as well as to the roof and the supporting floor/foundation.

Figure 110: The use of gaskets can seal between log courses and at butt joints and corners. Source: Robert Orth, Detailed Design Services.

While the log home industry has become experienced in designing and building for settlement at all joints and settling allowances, there are different approaches to how this can be achieved. Experience with properly selected gaskets has shown that the use of the correct gasket at the time of construction is preferred. If, for some reason, an air leak is discovered after the home is built, the best solution is likely to be a liquid sealant (caulk) over a backer rod. Either way, the gasket/seal must be designed for movement and properly installed.

ASHRAE published the Advanced Energy Design Guides to help commercial buildings achieve 30% and 50% energy savings over ANSI/ASHRAE/IESNA Standard 90.1-1999. In these guides, direction is provided regarding air-barrier systems. This can be summarized as follows:

Advanced Energy Design Guide	Application to Log Walls
Continuous, with all joints made airtight.	Logs provide a continuous barrier. Horizontal and vertical joinery is to be designed and constructed to be air and water tight.
Capable of withstanding positive and negative combined design wind, fan and stack pressures on the envelope without damage or displacement. (The system should transfer the load to the structure. It should not displace adjacent materials under full load.)	Log walls are required to withstand wind forces. They are the structure and the thermal barrier in one.
Durable or maintainable.	Wood is the strongest building material for its weight. The combination of cells and lignin has been equated to reinforcing in concrete.
Joined in an airtight and flexible manner to the air-barrier material of adjacent assemblies, allowing for the relative movement of these assemblies and components due to thermal and moisture variations, creep, and structural deflection.	A key to log wall design and construction is the joinery and the seal between the wall, floor and roof. Log joinery accounts for all features of movement that can be expected, including pressurization by wind.
Materials used should have an air permeability not to exceed 0.004 cfm/ft2 under a pressure differential of 0.3 in. water (1.57 psf) (0.02 L/s*m2 at 75 Pa) when tested in accordance with ASTM E 2178.	While a variety of materials are used to seal log joinery, closed cell gaskets with good recovery rates are preferred. This specification may be associated with higher cost and the need for increased fastening pull-down to achieve the design compression at which the gasket specifications can be checked against the air permeability requirements.

In response to ASHRAE's Design Guide for where connections need to be sealed, it may be equally beneficial to view the ENERGY STAR® Checklist.[59]

ENERGY STAR Checklist Item	Application to Log Walls
5.2.1 All sill plates adjacent to conditioned space sealed to foundation or sub-floor with caulk. Foam gasket also placed beneath sill plate if resting atop concrete or masonry and adjacent to conditioned space.	**NOTE to 5.2.1:** This requirement should be applied to the sill log or bottom plate log to the supporting surface. Often, log home companies use a seal here that is similar to the seal between log courses.
5.2.2 At the top of walls adjoining unconditioned spaces, continuous top plates or sealed blocking using caulk, foam, or equivalent material.	**NOTE to 5.2.2:** This is probably the biggest area of attention in log building.
5.2.3 Sheetrock sealed to top plate at all attic / wall interfaces using caulk, foam, or equivalent material. Either apply sealant directly between sheetrock and top plate or to the seam between the two from the attic above. Construction adhesive shall not be used.	**NOTE to 5.2.3:** Since sheetrock or other interior wall board is not applied to the log wall, this does not apply. However, frame walls are often a part of a custom log home design, and this would be appropriate there.
5.2.4 Rough opening around windows & exterior doors sealed with caulk or foam.	**NOTE to 5.2.4**: *Gaskets and sealed trim solutions are more often used in log openings because the rough opening must allow for movement along the involved height (see Sliding Joints).*
5.2.5 Marriage joints between modular home modules at all exterior boundary conditions fully sealed with gasket and foam.	**NOTE to 5.2.5:** While not a common approach, there are companies building modular homes using solid wood walls.
5.2.6 All seams between Structural Insulated Panels (SIPs) foamed and / or taped per manufacturer's instructions.	**NOTE to 5.2.6:** Log walls are continuous insulation just as SIPs, but with a lower rated R-value. The two recommended joint designs are dry seal (gasket) and wet seal (internal using pliable material, exterior where designed for maintenance checks).
5.2.7 In multifamily buildings, the gap between the drywall shaft wall (i.e. common wall) and the structural framing between units fully sealed at all exterior boundaries.	**NOTE to 5.2.7:** Log buildings can be used in multifamily applications as well.

Thermal Transfer and Dew Points

The dew point is the temperature at which moisture condenses from vapor into water. Ambient vapor will result in condensation on colder surfaces, as is commonly seen on bathroom windows after a hot shower (when the fan is not used). Eliminating the passage of vapor through the wall is essential for frame construction because the vapor gets cooler as it moves through the assembly toward the colder surfaces, and at some point it condenses. If the dew point is reached inside the wall assembly, materials can become damaged by mold, mildew and fungi. In colder climates, a vapor barrier is typically installed to the warm side of the assembly to keep water vapor from entering the wall cavity.

The dew point issue changes when dealing with different wall technologies. If a wall assembly does not allow air or water to pass through it, the surface will be the point of condensation when the surface temperature reaches the dew point. When a log home is in use, the warm indoor temperature will keep the interior wall surface warm and vapor migration into the wood totally depends on the moisture content of the wood and the indoor relative humidity. Moisture in the wood will move to the dryer and warmer surface

In 2001, Karagiozis, Kunzel and Holm presented research on a hygrothermal model as a result of international collaboration between Oak Ridge National Laboratory (ORNL, USA) and the Fraunhofer Institute in Bauphysics (Germany).[60] The work resulted in the WUFI-ORNL/IBP hygrothermal design tool. Their analysis and the WUFI tool responds to the dynamic variables of hygroscopic behavior in building envelopes rather than the static analysis of glaser or dew point methods.

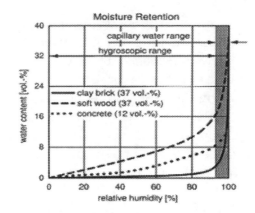

Figure 2 Moisture retention curve for three typical building materials. Shaded area is the part the capillary water range determined with pressure plate apparatus.

Figure 111: Research for the WUFI tool looked at sorption isotherms for three materials often used for mass walls.

Further work in this area was performed by Stéphane Hameury as reported in the Doctoral Thesis of 2006, "The Hygrothermal Inertia of Massive Timber Constructions."[61] Hameury studied the moisture baffle value of wood:

> The results obtained pinpoint the highly synergetic effects between the indoor moisture loads, the ventilation rate, the outdoor climate and the moisture interactions with the structure. The outcomes also show that the Moisture Buffering Capacity of a heavy timber structure is appreciable. The structure is able to even out substantially the day-to-day indoor relative humidity fluctuations for a certain range of ventilation rate.

Hameury's studies substantiate properties of large timbers that were previously not documented. It is encouraging to see the benefit of examining the performance of large timbers versus the 2x2 clear wood samples common to ASTM testing of wood properties. While research that has found that 1-inch of solid wood is sufficient to contain the heat/moisture equilibrium within the piece, Hameury's work offers further evidence that would explain how it is an effective vapor control. As such, no frost will be detected on the interior surface. More importantly, the dynamic interaction of vapor between the wood and the air does not provide an environment conducive to the growth of fungi, mold and mildew.

So the question may be to ask if it is possible to establish a model of temperature gradients across a log profile at a constant interior temperature and varying exterior surface. Ferguson and Turner[62] describes one approach at explaining how timbers react to temperature:

> Drying is a process which involves heat and mass transfer both inside the porous material, where a phase change in moisture occurs from the liquid to the gaseous state, and in the external boundary layer of the convected hot dry air, which heats the porous medium. The equations which govern this process consist of three tightly coupled, highly non-linear partial differential equations for the unknown system variables of moisture content, temperature and pressure. Due to the inherently complex boundary conditions and intricate physical geometries in any practical drying problem, an analytical solution is not possible. In order to obtain a transient drying solution it is necessary to resort to a numerical technique. The numerical solution techniques which were employed in this research were the finite element method and the control volume method. The transient numerical results were compared and contrasted for two timber drying problems, first, at a dry bulb temperature of 50°C, and secondly, at 80°C, both cases being below the boiling point of water.

When an enclosed environment has high humidity, cold surfaces collect condensation. If the winter temperatures of a cold climate zone were sufficient to drive through the thermal envelope, the interior surface would be colder than the indoor temperature and humidity would condense on the cold surface. This can be seen on glazing, and condensation collecting on the window sill can be a major issue. It is not common to log walls which retain a warm surface temperature reflecting the conditioned environment.

Water Management

The need to control the flow of water over and around a building is not news. It starts with precipitation draining off the roof, meaning that overhangs should be long enough and with a drip edge so that water drips to the ground without contacting the log wall. Green building standards credit roof overhangs, porches, insets, or other techniques as methods to protect window and door sills from precipitation.

The approach of using the roof to protect the wall surfaces and sill areas extends to lower roofs, decks, or horizontal surfaces so that water draining off the roof doesn't splash back onto those areas. Rather than applying the minimum clearance from finish grade to top of foundation, it is recommended that the stem wall is raised above grade sufficient to produce an 18 inch clearance to the bottom of the sill log or 24 inches to the bottom of the bottom plate log. Even with soils treatments to keep them away, this distance will be beneficial to controlling termites and carpenter ants.

Draining water down and away affects finish grading and foundations as well. Beyond employing a gutter and downspout system that moves roof drainage well away from the foundation. It is standard practice to collect and remove water from the footing by providing a water barrier along the foundation stem wall, free-draining backfill, to course gravel covering exterior perimeter drains. Interior drains are becoming more popular for additional moisture control. Minimizing water along the foundation is aided by positive sloping of finish grade away from the top of the foundation (1" in 10 feet minimum, more is better). And maintaining several feet between plantings and the foundation will be beneficial, allowing air to flow around the building to evaporate moisture as well as keeping insects further away.

A separate film overlapped at seams works for frame walls, but these are not appropriate for log walls where the wall provides the interior and exterior finish as well as structure and thermal envelope. The exterior wall drainage plane is provided by the logs and the exterior treatments applied to promote water runoff. The quality of the exterior treatment can easily be tested every spring by spraying a fine mist of water on the log surfaces—if the water beads are good and disappearance into the wood is bad. Typically, the walls that receive the most wear from sun, wind and rain will require more frequent retreatment.

Wall Openings

Wall openings are an area that requires attention, but are less of an issue than may be expected. Forming openings for installation of windows, doors, fireplaces or arches all follow the same basic techniques. With the clear wall (solid log) area confirmed, the joinery around wall openings is the next point to examine. As previously noted, settling must be accommodated above the opening and at the sides. Columns of fasteners or through bolting helps the log ends at the opening work together. The next most important element is to look at how the water running down the wall surface will interact at the opening. This discussion is being simplified because of the variety of log wall styles, sizes, etc., but the window needs to be installed with some form of drip edge above the opening so that water stays to the outside. This detail needs to include flashing that does now allow water to get behind any trim application (e.g., apply the flashing in a kerf cut in the log so that it actually bends over the top of the trim head). Next is the trim application at the sides of the opening so that wind pressures cannot force air/water between log ends, buck, or jamb. Sometimes this trim is fastened at the outer extent of the log profile, which often means that a scallop effect must be sealed behind the trim. Sometimes this trim is installed in an area of the log ends which has been routed to receive it and allow the trim face to be nearly flush with the log profile. Assuming that wind can force water in unwanted places, the last step in protecting the opening is to apply a drainage pan beneath the sill of the buck (or on the subfloor for a door) and wrapping up the side and between the jamb and buck. To reinforce the importance of this pan, it is highly recommended that no butt joints be allowed under it, nor under the sides of the buck. Insuring that any potential water penetration will be moved to the exterior by flashing and sealing techniques will insure durability.

Assembly Inspection Points

Most experts in log building would agree that setting the first course of logs is one of the most critical points of assembly. Perhaps one of the inspections by a building official would be as the foundation/subfloor is checked and the first couple of log courses are set. The next reference point is at the top of the windows/doors, then at the top of the wall. After the first log course is properly set and sealed to the supporting structure, the method of setting consecutive log courses is redundant to the top of the log wall with alignment, sealing the horizontal joinery, keeping butt joints and corners tight and holding them in place with fasteners. After the logs are fastened down, additional steps are used to seal butt joints and corners before setting the next course. It is a recommended practice to continuing to check the wall for plumb using a 6' carpenter's level at least every three feet of wall height.

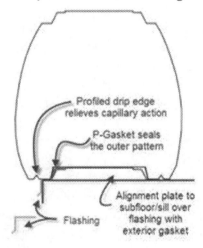

Figure 112: Using a profiled alignment plate on the subfloor or sill makes it easier to properly locate the first log, seal the joint and flash the seam. Flashing must at least cover the edge of the subfloor deck, but if log siding is installed, it should carry down below the top of the foundation. Source: Author

The log-corner interface is a difficult area to seal, but it is done properly on a regular basis. Corners should be designed to drain to the outside so that moisture does not collect in the tails. There is truth to the idea that the corners of a log structure provide significant strength. Corners (and log wall intersections) are used to conceal and align joints, but the intersection stiffens the wall assembly. Whether the courses are aligned or half-lapped (e.g., dovetail, saddle notch, interlocking), effective corners can be built, connected and sealed.

Figure 113 Examples of corners: Dovetail, butt and pass, saddle/interlock. Sources: Southland Log Homes, www.southlandloghomes.com and Hiawatha Log Homes, www.hiawatha.com.

Energy Conservation Compliance Options

Consistent with the approach for developing other sections of the standard, ICC400 provides options for demonstrating compliance of a log structure with the IECC. A log home can demonstrate compliance with the prescriptive tables in the IECC or may use the UA Tradeoff method described in the IECC. The IECC also allows for use of an energy compliance program to analyze the proposed design and elements of the thermal envelope. As noted earlier (Completing a REScheck Analysis), one of the more readily accepted programs is REScheck®, which has been modified to match information provided by ICC400-2007. Also as provided in the IECC, a log home can use the performance path to demonstrate compliance under IECC's requirements for "Simulated Performance Alternative." This last approach, similar to practices used to achieve an ENERGY STAR rating, is highly recommended to clearly demonstrate the benefit of log building and to build a record of such performance.

ICC400-2012 offers an exception to the IECC path by providing a prescriptive table for log wall U-Factors and by providing a prescriptive thermal envelope requirement for all climate zones. The latter table is based on work done in Vermont to update Vermont's Residential Building Energy Standard. It was expanded to include the other climate zones by following the proposed code changes to the 2012 IECC. The intention was to strive to exceed the requirements of the IECC in glazing as a trade off that allowed the 5" minimum average log wall thickness. For the most part, the goal was achieved. As occurred with the overlapping development of ICC400 and prior IECC editions, it is noted that there are two instances where that goal was not met when the standard and the code were published: 1.) Climate Zone 5 shows glazing U-Factor better than the 2009 IECC, but equal to the 2012 edition; and 2.) Climate Zone 6 shows wood frame wall insulation equal to the 2009 IECC but not the 2012. While meeting or exceeding the 2009 IECC in all areas, the ICC400 requirements also include increases in slab R-value and depth and add a column for heated slab foundations.

Establishing Thermal Properties of Logs/Log Walls

The development of options for establishing thermal properties began with existing codes and standards that have established the resistance to heat flow of building materials and assemblies. This section addresses thermal performance as measured by R-value (for thermal resistance = 1/U-Factor), or more correctly, the thermal conductive heat flow as reflected by the U-Factor. According to FPL's Wood Handbook[63],

> "The thermal conductivity of wood is affected by a number of basic factors: density, moisture content, extractive content, grain direction, structural irregularities such as checks and knots, fibril angle, and temperature. Thermal conductivity increases as density, moisture content, temperature, or extractive content of the wood increases. Thermal conductivity is nearly the same in the radial and tangential directions. However, conductivity along the grain has been reported as greater than conductivity across the grain by a factor of 1.5 to 2.8, with an average of about 1.8."

It has been repeatedly observed that there is a linear relationship of thermal conductivity of solid wood as a function of density and moisture content.[64] Further, the research defines the thermal properties of solid wood, paraphrased as follows:

> "The thermal conductivity of solid wood increases with density (or specific gravity), MC, and temperature. A number of other factors also play a role, such as extractive content and the

number of checks and knots in the wood. Extractives are substances in wood, not an integral part of the cellular structure, that can be removed by solution in hot or cold water, ether, benzene, or other solvents that do not react chemically with wood components.

A check is a lengthwise separation of the wood that usually extends across the rings of annual growth and commonly results from stresses set up in wood during seasoning. Wood is an anisotropic material, and conductivity along the grain (longitudinal) is between 1.5 to 2.8 times the conductivity across the grain (radial). While test data for density and moisture content are consistent and substantial, the variation in measurement temperature in the data was not sufficient to confidently establish the effect of temperature over a wide range of temperatures."

ICC400 takes the first step toward acknowledging that wood has a poor record as an insulation product. It provides methods to quantify conductance properties of wood which vary with the specific gravity. The R-value of wood is widely recognized as R-1.25 per inch of thickness for softwoods and R-0.91 for hardwoods. Given variation in wood species and moisture content, there is actually a range from R-0.8 for dense woods to R-1.4 per inch of wood thickness.

The thermal value for a log wall is based on its average width (area of the log cross-section divided by the stack height) rather than its nominal width. This can be significant since the shape can produce a reduction factor of 0.77

(e.g., traditional Swedish cope or scribe-fit log systems) to 0.88 (e.g., D-shape milled logs) to 0.95 (e.g., rectangular dovetail systems) from the nominal callout. ICC400 indicates a minimum average width of 5 inches in Table 305.3.1, which would represent all profile logs milled from a 6-inch sawn cant and 7-inch round logs.

Figure 114: Clear Wall—Focus on joinery and seal, average wall thickness

To legitimize existing log homes without need for adding insulation to the log wall will require more work however. As discussed in the *LOG BUILDING*, log walls have been built with similar sizes of logs for many decades/ centuries because of economic factors tied to the ability and to gather the raw material, form the piece, transport, handle and install the logs. When the most economical nominal wall-log width is milled into its final profile, the average width can be as narrow as 5-inches. East of the Mississippi River, this width of log wall is prevalent and has performed.

It must also be recognized that the log wall is not the only element of the building that affects energy efficiency. In fact, the percentage of heat lost through exterior walls can be very small in the overall scheme of things. With new construction or renovation/remodeling, the focus on thermal performance must start with air tightness. Next focus moves to roof insulation, then foundation insulation, the window glazing. It is very likely that the majority of energy cost reductions can be realized in these areas without adding insulation to the log wall.

Comparing Wall Technologies

For thermal performance, there is an understanding of what the goals are but the options that were sufficient for structural purposes have many pros and cons on the thermal front. Frame walls require management of framing cavities and air/moisture barriers, with many pieces installed in different steps, possibly by different trades. Concrete/masonry walls provide thermal mass, but readily conduct heat and must have additional materials applied to enhance resistance to conductivity. And the discussion needs to be tempered by the fact that rated insulation R-values are not the true measure of assembly (wall) performance which relies on the proper installation of external water screens, vapor barriers, and insulation to minimize degradation (e.g., sagging).

Mass walls have a distinct advantage over other wall technologies. They are equivalent to **solid/rigid continuous insulation** because the wall has the same thermal property across the entire opaque assembly area. They are airtight in the opaque wall areas and do not permit internal convection currents to degrade the thermal value as it moves air and vapor within the assembly as they can in the cavities of frame wall construction. The thermal performance of a mass wall does not degrade from sagging insulation, damaged vapor barriers, or failure of external water screens.

Log walls are unique from masonry/concrete mass walls in that the thermal mass benefit exists at a lower heat capacity (e.g., 5 Btu/ft$^{2\cdot0}$F vs. 6 as stated in ICC400-2007 and IECC-2004). Log walls provide a **warm wall** surface through the effects of thermal mass rather than by adding insulation (super insulating keeps the surface temperature of the wall closer to the interior temperature of the building, preventing condensation and proliferation of mold).

Despite criticisms leveled at log wall construction, this wall technology is **suitable** for the thermal envelope in all climate zones. It provides a **durable** component for the life of the structure and maintain an **air/water seal** at all joints, and provides an effective barrier to air and moisture via its **cell structure** (radial direction as normally found in a wall).

Prescribed Option

The prescriptive ICC400-2007 Table 305.3.1 *R-Value of Log Wall (R$_o$) by Average Width and Specific Gravity* is beneficial to those log builders/log home companies who produce homes nationwide and do not wish to spend time calculating thermal performance for each climate zone. This table was created using ASHRAE's 12% equilibrium moisture content standard for wood exposed to the outside. It expands the range of wood species/densities beyond those available in the ASHRAE standards. Note that average width = area of the log profile divided by its stack height.

The thickened line in the R-Value table was used to denote those logs that qualified under the 2003 IECC ruling as having thermal mass. In the 2006, that qualification was removed as log walls joined other mass wall technologies in a single group with its own column in the prescriptive tables of the IECC.

Given the misapplication of R-value requirements in wall assemblies, it is important to compare log walls on the basis of overall assembly (a.k.a., clear wall or opaque wall). Log walls are analogous to continuous insulation, with consistent thermal properties across the entire wall. Rated insulation R-values are not the true measure of the wall performance—they must be reduced by framing factors.

The key point here is to recognize that the rated insulation levels presented in IECC Table 402.1 are not applicable to the log wall. For log walls, it would be appropriate to modify the IECC to eliminate mass walls from the Prescriptive R-Value table in the IECC. A footnote would be required that would refer the reader to the Prescriptive U-Factor table for wall assemblies, where the Mass Wall provision would be maintained. This will force readers of the code to compare mass walls uniquely rather than try to apply rated insulation values to a wall with integrated mass and insulation such as a log wall.

R-Value of Log Wall by Average Width and Specific Gravity

Average Width

Specific Gravity (SG)	5 in.	6 in.	7 in.	8 in.	9 in.	10 in.	12 in.	14 in.	16 in.
0.29	8.98	10.61	12.23	13.86	15.48	17.11	20.36	23.61	26.86
0.3	8.76	10.35	11.93	13.51	15.1	16.68	19.84	23.01	26.17
0.31	8.56	10.1	11.64	13.19	14.73	16.27	19.35	22.44	25.52
0.32	8.37	9.87	11.37	12.87	14.38	15.88	18.89	21.89	24.9
0.33	8.18	9.65	11.11	12.58	14.04	15.51	18.44	21.38	24.31
0.34	8	9.44	10.87	12.3	13.73	15.16	18.02	20.88	23.75
0.35	7.84	9.23	10.63	12.03	13.43	14.82	17.62	20.41	23.21
0.36	7.68	9.04	10.41	11.77	13.14	14.5	17.24	19.97	22.7
0.38	7.38	8.68	9.99	11.3	12.6	13.91	16.52	19.13	21.74
0.39	7.24	8.52	9.79	11.07	12.35	13.63	16.18	18.74	21.29
0.41	6.98	8.2	9.43	10.65	11.88	13.1	15.55	18	20.45
0.42	6.85	8.05	9.25	10.45	11.66	12.86	15.26	17.66	20.06
0.44	6.62	7.77	8.93	10.08	11.24	12.39	14.7	17.01	19.32
0.47	6.3	7.4	8.49	9.58	10.67	11.76	13.94	16.12	18.3
0.5	6.02	7.05	8.09	9.12	10.16	11.19	13.26	15.33	17.4
0.51	5.93	6.95	7.97	8.98	10	11.02	13.05	15.08	17.11
0.52	5.85	6.85	7.85	8.85	9.85	10.84	12.84	14.84	16.84
0.53	5.77	6.75	7.73	8.71	9.7	10.68	12.65	14.61	16.58
0.54	5.69	6.65	7.62	8.59	9.55	10.52	12.45	14.39	16.32
0.55	5.61	6.56	7.51	8.46	9.41	10.37	12.27	14.17	16.08
0.59	5.32	6.22	7.11	8.01	8.9	9.8	11.58	13.37	15.16
0.6	5.26	6.14	7.02	7.9	8.78	9.66	11.43	13.19	14.95
0.7	4.69	5.46	6.23	6.99	7.76	8.53	10.07	11.6	13.14

Figure 115: Steady-state R-Values of opaque log wall (calculated at 12% MCs; R-Values include inside and outside air films)

Another option is to refer readers to ICC400-2012, which includes the following U-Factor table for log walls when the Service Moisture Content is 12%. Because the R-Value Prescriptive Table for Mass Walls represents the level of insulation added to the mass wall, it is pertinent to generate a U-Factor version to replace ICC400's Table 305.3.1. The following table is a more accurate representation of a log wall and is comparable to the required mass wall U-Factors in the current IECC prescriptive tables. When assembly U-factors are the point of comparison, it is easier to see that the differential between the log wall and prescriptive code minimum is not as drastic.

U-Factor of Log Wall (Uw) by Average Width (WL) and Specific Gravity

Specific Gravity (Gu)	Average Width															
	5 in.	5.5 in.	6 in.	7 in.	7.5 in.	8 in.	9 in.	9.5 in.	10 in.	11 in.	12 in.	13 in.	14 in.	15 in.	16 in.	18 in.
0.29	0.115	0.106	0.098	0.085	0.079	0.075	0.067	0.064	0.061	0.055	0.051	0.047	0.044	0.041	0.039	0.034
0.30	0.118	0.108	0.100	0.087	0.082	0.077	0.069	0.065	0.062	0.057	0.052	0.048	0.045	0.042	0.040	0.035
0.31	0.121	0.111	0.103	0.089	0.084	0.079	0.071	0.067	0.064	0.058	0.054	0.050	0.046	0.043	0.041	0.036
0.32	0.124	0.114	0.105	0.091	0.086	0.081	0.072	0.069	0.066	0.060	0.055	0.051	0.048	0.045	0.042	0.037
0.33	0.127	0.117	0.108	0.094	0.088	0.083	0.074	0.071	0.067	0.061	0.057	0.052	0.049	0.046	0.043	0.038
0.34	0.130	0.119	0.110	0.096	0.090	0.085	0.076	0.072	0.069	0.063	0.058	0.054	0.050	0.047	0.044	0.039
0.35	0.133	0.122	0.113	0.098	0.092	0.087	0.078	0.074	0.071	0.064	0.059	0.055	0.051	0.048	0.045	0.040
0.36	0.136	0.125	0.116	0.100	0.094	0.089	0.080	0.076	0.072	0.066	0.061	0.056	0.052	0.049	0.046	0.041
0.37	0.139	0.128	0.118	0.103	0.096	0.091	0.081	0.077	0.074	0.068	0.062	0.058	0.054	0.050	0.047	0.042
0.38	0.142	0.130	0.121	0.105	0.099	0.093	0.083	0.079	0.076	0.069	0.064	0.059	0.055	0.051	0.048	0.043
0.39	0.145	0.133	0.123	0.107	0.101	0.095	0.085	0.081	0.077	0.071	0.065	0.060	0.056	0.053	0.049	0.044
0.40	0.148	0.136	0.126	0.109	0.103	0.097	0.087	0.083	0.079	0.072	0.066	0.062	0.057	0.054	0.051	0.045
0.41	0.151	0.139	0.128	0.112	0.105	0.099	0.089	0.084	0.080	0.074	0.068	0.063	0.059	0.055	0.052	0.046
0.42	0.154	0.141	0.131	0.114	0.107	0.101	0.091	0.086	0.082	0.075	0.069	0.064	0.060	0.056	0.053	0.047
0.43	0.157	0.144	0.133	0.116	0.109	0.103	0.092	0.088	0.084	0.077	0.071	0.066	0.061	0.057	0.054	0.048
0.45	0.162	0.149	0.138	0.121	0.113	0.107	0.096	0.091	0.087	0.080	0.074	0.068	0.064	0.060	0.056	0.050
0.46	0.165	0.152	0.141	0.123	0.116	0.109	0.098	0.093	0.089	0.081	0.075	0.070	0.065	0.061	0.057	0.051
0.47	0.168	0.155	0.143	0.125	0.118	0.111	0.100	0.095	0.090	0.083	0.076	0.071	0.066	0.062	0.058	0.052
0.48	0.171	0.157	0.146	0.127	0.120	0.113	0.102	0.097	0.092	0.084	0.078	0.072	0.067	0.063	0.059	0.053
0.49	0.174	0.160	0.148	0.130	0.122	0.115	0.103	0.098	0.094	0.086	0.079	0.074	0.069	0.064	0.060	0.054
0.51	0.180	0.165	0.153	0.134	0.126	0.119	0.107	0.102	0.097	0.089	0.082	0.076	0.071	0.067	0.063	0.056
0.53	0.185	0.171	0.158	0.139	0.130	0.123	0.111	0.105	0.101	0.092	0.085	0.079	0.074	0.069	0.065	0.058
0.54	0.188	0.173	0.161	0.141	0.132	0.125	0.112	0.107	0.102	0.094	0.086	0.080	0.075	0.070	0.066	0.059
0.55	0.191	0.176	0.163	0.143	0.135	0.127	0.114	0.109	0.104	0.095	0.088	0.082	0.076	0.071	0.067	0.060
0.56	0.194	0.179	0.166	0.145	0.137	0.129	0.116	0.111	0.106	0.097	0.089	0.083	0.077	0.073	0.068	0.061
0.57	0.197	0.181	0.168	0.147	0.139	0.131	0.118	0.112	0.107	0.098	0.091	0.084	0.079	0.074	0.069	0.062
0.62	0.210	0.195	0.181	0.158	0.149	0.141	0.127	0.121	0.116	0.106	0.098	0.091	0.085	0.080	0.075	0.067
0.70	0.233	0.215	0.200	0.176	0.166	0.157	0.142	0.135	0.129	0.118	0.110	0.102	0.095	0.089	0.084	0.075

Figure 116: Log Wall U-Factors Wall (calculated at 12% MCs; U-Factors include inside and outside air films).

The use of the table above is beneficial for completing the UA Alternative approach to energy code compliance, but the values are tabulated at 12% service moisture content when there is a range of service moisture content across North America. These values provide a good estimation, and the designer must adjust for the conditions at the site. Site conditions further adjust climate zone data, such as an open site where wind continually acts on wall surfaces and drifts snow. Just like roof framing capacity needs to be adjusted for the loads of snow drifts, designers should consider the drying effects of wind.

With so many factors affecting our design assumptions, prescriptive requirements save considerable time in the design and construction process. For this simple reason, the prescriptive path has remained in the IECC. The debate about prescriptive standards for the thermal envelope has run for a long time, and as performance requirements become more elevated, the education of the designer and the builder are becoming more important. A combination of certified training (e.g., NAHB's Certified Green Professional or AIA's LEED AP) with performance testing may be the best answer.

The best answer is not always the "best" answer though. Let's think about the inventory of existing log homes and the level of knowledge available to correctly evaluate that inventory. For this reason, ICC400-2012 includes a new prescriptive table, 305.3.1.2. This table was created so that the industry can remain viable for new construction, but the table should also be applicable to renovations and remodels of existing log homes. This will help reduce the trauma of log home owners who need to sell. They will not have uninformed "experts" commanding that they add insulation to their log wall. Instead, log home owners can upgrade their home by addressing roof, glazing, and foundation components

and know that their well-maintained log wall works. In fact, insulating the floor perimeter at the foundation can have a bigger impact on saving energy than one would think.

Tested Option

Similar to other performance options in the standard, ICC400 allows for testing to establish R-values (e.g., ORNL Whole Wall Program). An important element of this research notes that ASTM test specification C177 *Standard Test Method for Steady-State Thermal Transmission Properties by Means of the Guarded Hot Plate* has been most often used in the determination of thermal conductivity of wood and wood products. An optional approach using calibrated heat flow meters is described in ASTM test specification C518, *Standard Test Method for Steady-state Thermal Transmission Properties by Means of the Heat Flow Meter*.

Two primary ASTM test standards define the process of evaluating thermal performance of building materials/assemblies, C1363 and C518. ASTM defines the significance of the use of C1363 as follows:

> "A need exists for accurate data on heat transfer through insulated structures at representative test conditions. The data are needed to judge compliance with specifications and regulations, for design guidance, for research evaluations of the effect of changes in materials or constructions, and for verification of, or use in, simulation models. Other ASTM standards such as Test Methods C177 and C518 provide data on homogeneous specimens bounded by temperature controlled flat impervious plates. The hot box test method is more suitable for providing such data

for large building elements, usually of a built-up or composite nature, which are exposed to temperature-controlled air on both sides."

Changes made to the ASTM Standards have eliminated the dynamic aspects of the whole wall testing. This benefits R-value ratings since these are static measures. Dynamic testing has distinct benefits to thermal mass.

Calculating U-Factor

The thermal properties worksheet shows how the R-value table values were generated for ICC400 Table 305.3.1. This is the method to calculate an R-Value/U-Factor for a specific equilibrium moisture content and specific gravity. The calculations in ICC400 provide alternative values in accordance with ASTM Standards that establish the wood properties used to calculate thermal value of a given species, density, and moisture content. These calculations have been verified by labs performing the ASTM Hot Plate Tests with test data matching calculated results. The variability between the two is easily explained by the known variability of wood.

It was previously noted that the REScheck® program includes the option of selecting log walls. This is important because the code requirement will be based on the mass wall U-Factor to calculate UA. The proposed design UA is then compared to the mass wall UA. This becomes more complicated in REScheck when one tries to use the calculated log wall as per the following thermal properties worksheet. The direction in REScheck would be to enter

the wall as "Other wall." This will allow the user to enter the gross area of the wall as before, but now the U-Factor can be entered. This will be compared to a typical frame wall with a significantly lower overall U-Factor requirement than a log wall in many climate zones.

There is no straightforward way to remedy the mass wall difference when entering the U-Factor in "Other wall." It is suggested that the gross wall area be entered as "Log" and the log thickness and wood species changed until the nearly equivalent (not lower) U-Factor appears in REScheck to that calculated on the worksheet. Notes in the REScheck report should refer to "an attached U-Factor worksheet for the log wall." It is always recommended that supporting documentation be submitted with a REScheck for "Other wall" or when the log wall specification in REScheck does not match that of the actual log wall.

Calculate thermal properties

				Sample Case	Your Product
Calculate conductive value k = Gx[B+Cx(MC$_S$)]+A				**k**	

*Wood Handbook Equation 3-7 constants for k in Btu·in/(h·ft2·F):					
A=	0.129	MC$_S$, ASHRAE	12%	G=	0.37063	0.750

		Sample Case	Your Product
MC$_S$, ASHRAE	12%	G=	0.37063	0.750
MC$_S$, Dry	10%	G=	0.37307	0.733
MC$_S$, Moist	13%	G=	0.36942	0.758
MC$_S$, Warm-Humid	14%	G=	0.36821	0.767
MC$_S$, Marine	15%	G=	0.36702	0.775

*Wood Handbook Equation 3-7 constants for k in Btu·in/(h·ft2·F):
A= 0.129
B= 1.34
C= 0.028

Do not divide MC$_S$ by 100.

Convert to R/inch = 1/k

			Sample Case	Your Product
MC$_S$, ASHRAE	12%	k=	0.750	1.333
MC$_S$, Dry	10%	k=	0.733	1.364
MC$_S$, Moist	13%	k=	0.758	1.319
MC$_S$, Warm-Humid	14%	k=	0.767	1.304
MC$_S$, Marine	15%	k=	0.775	1.290

Convert to U-Factor: 1 / Sum(R-Values for log + inside and outside air films)

Air Film R-values
inside 0.68
outside 0.25

			Sample Case	Your Product
MC$_S$, ASHRAE	12%		10.267	0.089
MC$_S$, Dry	10%		10.505	0.087
MC$_S$, Moist	13%	R per W$_L$=	10.159	0.090
MC$_S$, Warm-Humid	14%		10.040	0.091
MC$_S$, Marine	15%		9.936	0.092

Figure 117: Thermal Properties Worksheet (refer to Figure 84: Log Density Worksheet to see how G was calculated)

Thermal Mass

Like all mass wall construction, log walls absorb and store heat from the environment—ambient temperature and solar gain—then radiate the heat back into the building when the inside temperature is colder than the wall. Management of the energy performance of a log structure therefore involves consideration for thermal mass and radiant heat that is dramatically different than that used for conventional (framed wall) construction.

DOE contributes an interesting statement on log walls in their discussion of the R-Value of Wood on their EERE website, http://www.energysavers.gov/your_home/designing_remodeling/index.cfm/mytopic=10180.

"Logs act like "thermal batteries" and can, under the right circumstances, store heat during the day and gradually release it at night. This generally increases the apparent R-value of a log by 0.1 per inch of thickness in mild, sunny climates that have a substantial temperature swing from day to night. Such climates generally exist in the Earth's temperate zones between the 15th and 40th parallels."

The EERE website also lists factors that effect the efficiency of using thermal mass in buildings as:

- Building configuration, type of building structure, amount of thermal mass in building
- Solar orientation and window area
- Internal heat sources, how much of the time during the day a room is used

- Climate—Daily and seasonal outside temperature/humidity fluctuations
- Steady-state wall R-value, and
- Wall configuration—when insulation is added to a mass wall, thermal mass exposed to the interior side of the wall is most thermally effective.

DOE's statement has been reinforced by laboratory testing, finding that the thermal mass benefit of log wall constructions becomes diminished in cold climates. Test data has demonstrated that the lag time benefit of thermal mass is lost when the outside temperatures remain cold rather than provide the swing of day and night conditions (e.g., the outdoor environment varies from warmer to colder compared to the indoor temperature). However, there is a question of how the lab testing is prepared, performed and recorded. Even when installed in test frames by experienced log builders, lab tests have shown that leaks around the perimeter of the wall assembly are a challenge. Door buck sealing techniques help at each end, with the seal between the buck and the test frame being the same as for other wall technologies. The quality of the whole wall thermal test can be qualified by first pressurizing one side, effectively creating an air infiltration test.

A mass wall does not conceal issues the way a frame wall does, and there will not be hidden incidents of mold and mildew. Due to the ease of working directly on the log wall, repairs do not involve the same level of deconstruction and material waste of frame walls.

Energy Code Compliance

The thermal mass component of energy code compliance can be satisfied using one of the following three options.

Prescriptive Option—Referring to the IECC (2006-2012 editions), all log walls have thermal mass. No further evaluation is required.

Testing Option—Perform testing in accordance with ASTM C976.

Calculated Option—A calculated path is provided solely for the convenience of engineers who need the formulas to complete computer modeling/simulations. The equation for determining heat capacity is HC = wc, where "w" is the log density converted to square feet and "c" is the specific heat based on moisture content and temperature. The result is in Btu/$ft^2x^\circ F$ [kJ/(m²xK)].

The evaluation of log walls for thermal mass in ICC400-2007 correlates directly to the 2003 IECC. The effect provided by solid wood as a mass wall has been part of the IECC and ASHRAE standards since mid-1980 In 2003, the IECC had three tables (insulation on the outside of the mass wall, insulation on the inside of the mass wall, and mass walls with integral mass and insulation, a.k.a. log) requiring an involved process for implementing those tables in heat loss calculations. In the 2006 IECC code development process, the evaluation of mass walls was simplified by adding a section for all mass wall technologies and generating a mass wall column in both prescriptive tables (R-Value and U-Factor).

Therefore, analysis is no longer necessary to qualify log walls for thermal mass. This is a benefit to low density wood species with lower heat transmission rates. However, the tabulated minimum U-factors benefit mass wall technologies are not clear in how they are to be applied. Adding a rated insulation product to the outside is easily understood and is a common approach to insulating foundation walls. The question is how to apply the prescribed minimum R-Value to the integrated insulation and mass as in solid wood walls.

The interpretation heard in the field is that insulation has to be added to the log wall. This interpretation would have one believe that solid wood walls are required to have the same level of insulation as concrete or block walls. A more appropriate response would be that the R-Value for the wall assembly should compare to that rated insulation value. To leap over this debate, the preferred approach is to move the discussion to the *Equivalent U-Factor* table.

In cold climate zones (7-8), thermal mass is not recognized in the IECC, and the prescriptive *Equivalent U-Factors* for mass walls are the same as for frame walls. A marginal benefit is given for mass walls in Climate Zone 6. A difference between solid wood and other mass wall technologies may exist, but the argument must first be made at the ASHRAE committee level before submitting a code change proposal.

Solar Gain Effect

Solid wood, like other mass walls, provide a unique opportunity for solar gain. Most thermal mass design is focused on the solar gain of internal mass. From Trombe wall design to sunrooms to internal heat sinks, the benefit of internal mass is well documented. Maximizing the use of log walls as interior bearing walls will bring additional storage and tempering benefit.

With a log wall, the mass is exposed to both the interior and the exterior. It's integrated mass and insulation allows a similar response to both environments. But the criticism of mass walls is that the mass effect is only beneficial when the outside temperatures do not stay extremely cold for a long period of time. One theory of why log walls perform even in cold climates is that the external solar gain effectively counteracts heat transmission loss. Thus, **log walls do provide a thermal mass benefit in cold climates**.

The daytime heat from solar gain on the exterior of the log wall and night cooling would act on heat transmission losses in a similar manner to temperature swing such as seen in warmer climates. Surface temperatures of the wood elevate dramatically, offsetting and limiting the expected thermal conduction through the solid wood wall. This has been supported by observations from testing by Sashco Sealants[65] (to test their exterior finishes). Supporting documentation for Sashco's *Start-Right Log Home Finishing System* notes how log walls get hotter than regular wood applications:

> "The upper curvatures of round logs get much hotter in direct sunlight than conventional vertical wood elements (like flat siding, window trim, vertical logs, etc.) that get the same exposure to the sun. Flat siding reflects away much of the sun's heat, the tops of logs don't . . . Recent actual temperature measurements [2003] taken by Sashco personnel with an infrared thermometer in Denver, CO on typical August and December afternoons, when the sun was shining brightly and directly on south-facing walls . . . the higher temperature and heat causing far more stress and damage to the log's upper curvature stain and wood than to the stain and wood of the vertical siding and trim."

Temperature Readings	August	December
Mid-afternoon	93°F	42°F
Vertical surfaces	127°F	115°F
Upper log surfaces	166°F	143°F

Tracy Hansen of StormBusters Inc. provided the following thermographic images of his house at 8,000 feet of elevation in Wyoming. Hanson's business has been building, maintaining, and auditing log homes in the Rocky Mountain region for many years. It was overcast on the day he captured these images, providing solar gain in diffuse sunlight. It was 45°F outside and 65°F inside the house. This series of thermal images provides additional support to the theory that solar gain during continuously cold temperatures is a contributor to the thermal performance of log walls.

Figure 118: Thermographic study of solar gain on the exterior of a log wall on a cloudy day at 8,000-ft. elevation in WY. Where shaded from solar exposure, walls match the outside

temperature (45-degF) although the indoor temperature was 65-degF. Solar gain on logs and roof both measure 70-degF or more. Source: Tracy Hansen, StormBusters, Inc.

STRUCTURAL PROVISIONS

A chapter on structural requirements is no less important than any of the preceding chapters of ICC400. AF&PA's *Wood Frame Construction Manual (WFCM)* was used a model for this section of the standard.[66] An exceptional resource for any builder, the WFCM is also referenced in the IRC and IBC. For log structures, the engineered provisions were developed to ensure that a load path is maintained for the structure, including connections and resistance of both gravity and lateral loads.

The structural elements of the I-codes demonstrate that certain criteria can be used to meet 80% of North America. The other 20% involves special wind, seismic or snow load provisions. The experience of the log home industry has shown successes in even the most dramatic load conditions, allowing easy adoption of industry standard practices as the minimum prescriptive requirements. Therefore, when conditions and loads exceed the following criteria, engineering analysis is required to be submitted with plans for a permit.

In reviewing the load maps of the IRC or IBC (ICC's International Residential and Building

Codes, respectively), the following loads are found to be the base case across the majority of North America. With successful experience of log structures in these vast areas, the following load conditions can be applied without engineering analysis:

- o   40-psf floor live load
- o   70-psf ground snow load
- o   >90 mph wind speed, exp. C
- o   Seismic design category >B

Log structures bring a slightly different set of standard design practices that may be applied successfully under the above load conditions. These practices are enhanced by adding the particular approach of the WFCM.

- o   3 stories or 33-ft. average grade to average roof elevation
- o   Floor-to-floor story height of 10-ft.
- o   Building dimension (length or width) greater than 80 feet
- o   Building aspect ratio (L: W) < 1:4 or >4:1.
- o   Joist/rafter spacing of 48" o/c
- o   4-ft. roof overhangs; 12:12 pitch

Figure 119: All designers, builders and building officials should be familiar with AF&PA's Wood Frame Construction Manual. An excellent resource for wood structures, it is referenced in the I-Codes.

Log Framing

When the design conditions are beyond the extents listed above, they trigger the need for engineering analysis. The size of structural members, their spacing and overhang length (cantilevers) are the common elements that differentiate log structures from light wood framing systems. Log floor or roof framing at 48" on center is often limited to this maximum by the capacity of the decking spanning that distance. Most 2x tongue and groove decking products satisfy the design conditions. Using a wider spacing or building in a heavier snow load area would be triggers to examine the ability of the decking to support the load, then the ability of the log framing to carry the imposed loads to their bearing points.

Log framing varies from region to region due to the availability of structural timber. In the Northwest forests of the U.S. and Canada, the availability of long length fir and pine logs with little sweep make the 26-foot single/simple span very much a reality. Elsewhere, the available resource may require a shorter joist span and intermediate support (e.g., a bearing wall or posted girder). Often, sawn timbers are used that match the stack height of the log (e.g., the log profile in Figure 79 has a 7-3/8" stack height while the joists shown in Figure 121 are 8" or less in height) so that minimal notching is required to provide a good mortise and tenon connection.

Nominal Size			End Bearing	Max. Notch over Bearing	Spacing	Grade 1	
						40#LL	30#LL
4x8			1-1/2"	1-3/4 "	24" o/c	13 ft - 1 in	13 ft - 10 in
	Eastern Softwoods (ESW)		1-1/2"	1-3/4 "	32" o/c	11 ft - 10 in	12 ft - 7 in
Actual	Header / Wall		1-1/2"	1-3/4 "	36" o/c	11 ft - 5 in	12 ft - 1 in
3 1/2	x	7 1/8	1-1/2"	1-11/16"	48" o/c	10 ft - 4 in	11 ft - 0 in
6x8			1-1/2"	1-3/4 "	24" o/c	15 ft - 2 in	16 ft - 1 in
	Eastern Softwoods (ESW)		1-1/2"	1-3/4 "	32" o/c	13 ft - 7 in	14 ft - 8 in
Actual	Header / Wall		1-1/2"	1-3/4 "	36" o/c	12 ft - 9 in	14 ft - 1 in
5 1/2	x	7 1/8	1-1/2"	1-3/4 "	48" o/c	11 ft - 1 in	12 ft - 3 in
8x8			1-1/2"	1-3/4 "	24" o/c	16 ft - 10 in	17 ft - 10 in
	Eastern Softwoods (ESW)		1-1/2"	1-3/4 "	32" o/c	15 ft - 4 in	16 ft - 3 in
Actual	Header / Wall		1-1/2"	1-3/4 "	36" o/c	14 ft - 9 in	15 ft - 7 in
7 1/2	x	7 1/8	1-1/2"	1-3/4 "	48" o/c	12 ft - 11 in	14 ft - 2 in
9" dia.			1-1/2"	1-13/16"	24" o/c	16 ft - 0 in	16 ft - 0 in
	Eastern Softwoods (ESW)		1-1/2"	1-13/16"	32" o/c	15 ft - 5 in	16 ft - 0 in
Actual	Header / Wall		1-1/2"	1-13/16"	36" o/c	14 ft - 10 in	15 ft - 8 in
9	" actual dia.	7 1/4	1-1/2"	1-13/16"	48" o/c	12 ft - 11 in	14 ft - 3 in
10" dia.			1-1/2"	2 "	24" o/c	16 ft - 0 in	16 ft - 0 in
	Eastern Softwoods (ESW)		1-1/2"	2 "	32" o/c	16 ft - 0 in	16 ft - 0 in
Actual	Header / Wall		1-1/2"	2 "	36" o/c	16 ft - 0 in	16 ft - 0 in
10	" actual dia.	8	1-1/2"	2 "	48" o/c	15 ft - 0 in	16 ft - 0 in
8 SRTB			1-1/2"	2 "	24" o/c	14 ft - 6 in	15 ft - 4 in
	Eastern Softwoods (ESW)		1-1/2"	2 "	32" o/c	13 ft - 2 in	13 ft - 11 in
Actual	#1 SRTB / #2 SRTB		1-1/2"	2 "	36" o/c	12 ft - 8 in	13 ft - 5 in
8		dia.	1-1/2"	2 "	48" o/c	11 ft - 6 in	12 ft - 2 in
10 SRTB			1-1/2"	2-1/2 "	24" o/c	19 ft - 6 in	20 ft - 8 in
	Eastern Softwoods (ESW)		1-1/2"	2-1/2 "	32" o/c	17 ft - 9 in	18 ft - 10 in
Actual	#1 SRTB / #2 SRTB		1-1/2"	2-1/2 "	36" o/c	17 ft - 1 in	18 ft - 1 in
10		dia.	1-1/2"	2-1/2 "	48" o/c	15 ft - 6 in	16 ft - 5 in
12 SRTB			1-1/2"	3 "	24" o/c	24 ft - 11 in	26 ft - 5 in
	Eastern Softwoods (ESW)		1-1/2"	3 "	32" o/c	22 ft - 7 in	24 ft - 0 in
Actual	#1 SRTB / #2 SRTB		1-1/2"	3 "	36" o/c	21 ft - 9 in	23 ft - 1 in
12		dia.	1-1/2"	3 "	48" o/c	19 ft - 9 in	20 ft - 11 in

Figure 120: This joist span table is from TimberLogic's *Span Table Report*. It shows the variability in allowable single span may affect design.

Note the 9" dia. and 10" dia. Joists have a maximum length of 16-feet. These are logs milled to a uniform diameter and are often limited by available length—here, limited to the 16-feet. The SRTB log joists are often available up to 40-feet. When cut to the shorter length required for a joist, the cutoff may be used as a post or porch rafter. The two allowable span columns are for the better of the two grades listed in the far left column, for the live loads (LL) specified (40 pound for main living areas and 30 pound for sleeping areas, per the IRC).

The calculations for this table include a dead load (weight of construction) of 15 pounds per square foot (psf) and deflection criteria of l/360 (designed for stiffness by limiting deflection to one inch over a 30-foot span).

The relationship of log size, wood species, grade, and load conditions is very similar for roof rafter spans as it is for joists. In ICC400, the line for prescriptive approval is set at 70 pounds per square foot of ground snow loading (70 psf SL=LL). Using the same timber sizes, grade and species, one can readily see the impact of snow loads above 70 psf. This impact will affect support throughout the structure to insure that loads from the roof are properly carried to the foundation (a.k.a., load path, this is always a fundamental design consideration).

overhang to be 84" (7-feet) because this more closely represented one third of the maximum allowable simple rafter span of 26'. Again, one can see from the example that these spans and overhangs represent the larger sawn round timbers.

Nominal Size		End Bearing	Max. Notch over Bearing	Spacing	15 psf Dead Load			
					70#LL	70# LL	50#LL	20#LL
4x8		1-1/2"	1-3/4 "	24" o/c	12 ft - 0 in	12 ft - 0 in	13 ft - 5 in	18 ft - 3 in
	Eastern Softwoods (ESW)	1-1/2"	1-11/16"	32" o/c	10 ft - 3 in	10 ft - 3 in	11 ft - 10 in	16 ft - 4 in
Actual	Header	1-1/2"	1-1/2 "	36" o/c	9 ft - 8 in	9 ft - 8 in	11 ft - 1 in	15 ft - 5 in
3 1/2 x 7 1/8		1-1/2"	1-1/8 "	48" o/c	8 ft - 5 in	8 ft - 5 in	9 ft - 8 in	13 ft - 4 in
6x8		1-1/2"	1-3/4 "	24" o/c	12 ft - 9 in	12 ft - 9 in	14 ft - 7 in	20 ft - 3 in
	Eastern Softwoods (ESW)	1-1/2"	1-3/4 "	32" o/c	11 ft - 0 in	11 ft - 0 in	12 ft - 7 in	17 ft - 6 in
Actual	Header	1-1/2"	1-3/4 "	36" o/c	10 ft - 4 in	10 ft - 4 in	11 ft - 11 in	16 ft - 6 in
5 1/2 x 7 1/8		1-1/2"	1-3/4 "	48" o/c	9 ft - 0 in	9 ft - 0 in	10 ft - 4 in	14 ft - 3 in
8x8		1-1/2"	1-3/4 "	24" o/c	14 ft - 10 in	14 ft - 10 in	17 ft - 0 in	23 ft - 6 in
	Eastern Softwoods (ESW)	1-1/2"	1-3/4 "	32" o/c	12 ft - 10 in	12 ft - 10 in	14 ft - 9 in	20 ft - 5 in
Actual	Header	1-1/2"	1-3/4 "	36" o/c	12 ft - 1 in	12 ft - 1 in	13 ft - 11 in	19 ft - 3 in
7 1/2 x 7 1/8		1-1/2"	1-3/4 "	48" o/c	10 ft - 6 in	10 ft - 6 in	12 ft - 0 in	16 ft - 8 in
9" dia.		1-1/2"	1-13/16"	24" o/c	14 ft - 10 in	14 ft - 10 in	16 ft - 0 in	16 ft - 0 in
	Eastern Softwoods (ESW)	1-1/2"	1-13/16"	32" o/c	12 ft - 10 in	12 ft - 10 in	14 ft - 9 in	16 ft - 0 in
Actual	Header	1-1/2"	1-13/16"	36" o/c	12 ft - 1 in	12 ft - 1 in	13 ft - 11 in	16 ft - 0 in
9 " actual dia. 7 1/4		1-1/2"	1-13/16"	48" o/c	10 ft - 6 in	10 ft - 6 in	12 ft - 0 in	16 ft - 0 in
10" dia.		1-1/2"	2 "	24" o/c	16 ft - 0 in	16 ft - 0 in	16 ft - 0 in	16 ft - 0 in
	Eastern Softwoods (ESW)	1-1/2"	2 "	32" o/c	14 ft - 11 in	14 ft - 11 in	16 ft - 0 in	16 ft - 0 in
Actual	Header	1-1/2"	2 "	36" o/c	14 ft - 1 in	14 ft - 1 in	16 ft - 0 in	16 ft - 0 in
10 " actual dia. 8		1-1/2"	2 "	48" o/c	12 ft - 2 in	12 ft - 2 in	14 ft - 0 in	16 ft - 0 in
8 SRTB		1-1/2"	2 "	24" o/c	13 ft - 3 in	13 ft - 3 in	14 ft - 10 in	20 ft - 3 in
	Eastern Softwoods (ESW)	1-1/2"	2 "	32" o/c	11 ft - 7 in	11 ft - 7 in	13 ft - 4 in	18 ft - 4 in
Actual	#1 SRTB	1-1/2"	2 "	36" o/c	10 ft - 11 in	10 ft - 11 in	12 ft - 7 in	17 ft - 5 in
8 dia.		1-1/2"	2 "	48" o/c	9 ft - 6 in	9 ft - 6 in	10 ft - 10 in	15 ft - 1 in
10 SRTB		1-1/2"	2-1/2 "	24" o/c	17 ft - 11 in	17 ft - 11 in	20 ft - 0 in	27 ft - 3 in
	Eastern Softwoods (ESW)	1-1/2"	2-1/2 "	32" o/c	16 ft - 3 in	16 ft - 3 in	18 ft - 2 in	24 ft - 9 in
Actual	#1 SRTB	1-1/2"	2-1/2 "	36" o/c	15 ft - 4 in	15 ft - 4 in	17 ft - 6 in	23 ft - 10 in
10 dia.		1-1/2"	2-1/2 "	48" o/c	13 ft - 3 in	13 ft - 3 in	15 ft - 2 in	21 ft - 1 in
12 SRTB		1-1/2"	3 "	24" o/c	22 ft - 10 in	22 ft - 10 in	25 ft - 6 in	34 ft - 9 in
	Eastern Softwoods (ESW)	1-1/2"	3 "	32" o/c	20 ft - 9 in	20 ft - 9 in	23 ft - 2 in	31 ft - 7 in
Actual	#1 SRTB	1-1/2"	3 "	36" o/c	19 ft - 11 in	19 ft - 11 in	22 ft - 4 in	30 ft - 4 in
12 dia.		1-1/2"	3 "	48" o/c	17 ft - 5 in	17 ft - 5 in	20 ft - 0 in	27 ft - 7 in

Figure 121: Like joists, log rafters are permitted to have a simple span of 26-feet. TimberLogic's *Span Table Report* again illustrates the impact of smaller framing members and changes in load conditions (with 1/240 deflection criteria). These are simple spans (not including overhang) represent the horizontal dimension rather than the rafter length, taking into account a pitch of 3:12 or greater.

Further analysis has demonstrated that standard overhang rules of thumb have not impacted the rafter size in the majority of cases. ICC400-2007 recognized that most log homes have longer overhangs and accommodated that by setting the maximum overhang length to 48" or 1/3 of the maximum allowable span in the table above. In the 2012 update of ICC400, a revision was approved allowing the maximum

Other limitations on roof and floor framing are outlined in ICC400 such as diaphragm aspect ratios, openings (e.g., stair wells), cantilevers, and elements of load path design. These are adapted from the same considerations used for light wood framing and have proven reliability. In typical log home design and construction, these elements are typically not an issue until high lateral loads are encountered, and those conditions will require engineering review anyway.

Log Walls

ICC400 includes prescriptive requirements for the log wall that allow log walls to be designed without the need for an engineering review. The key limitations are a maximum unsupported wall height of 20-feet, a maximum log shear wall segment aspect ratio of 1:1 (e.g., if the log wall is 8-feet tall, the shortest shear wall segment will be 8-feet long), and must resist vertical and horizontal loads.

Vertical loading on a log wall has never been the big concern. Where log profiles provide little bearing area, the compression of the logs helps seal the joinery and where the log profiles provide a bearing area the vertical loads are uniformly carried down to the floor/foundation. Walls with bottom plate logs will require sufficient solid blocking in the floor below the log wall. Typically, the foundation wall or a massive beam is used to support log walls.

Over openings in the wall, log builders and designers typically provide a minimum of one solid log that bears on either side of the opening. On shorter openings, the load capacity of the log header will be based on shear value (Fv). As the span over the opening gets longer, the load capacity becomes limited by bending strength (Fb). In either case, the header must extend beyond the opening and over supporting log courses with sufficient length to provide the sufficient bearing area without compression. What typically controls the bearing length, though, is the number of fasteners and relation to other fasteners above and below the header. This distance, at a minimum, will be twice the fastener end distance so that at least one fastener can be installed there (see Mechanical Connections & Fasteners).

Lateral Load Resistance

Probably the single biggest issue facing engineering evaluation of log structures is the resistance to lateral loading such as seismic or high wind conditions. Though ICC400 does not provide distinct direction on log wall design to resist lateral loads, guidance is available from other sources.

Many studies have looked at log walls fastening to resist loads, but the results are typically the same. The connection of the log wall to the foundation is key to resisting seismic loading, and the recommended practice is to extend anchor bolts up through the first course of the log wall. When lateral loads are extreme or where shear panel length is too short to install the number of fasteners required, the anchor bolts may be extended up the entire height of the log wall. The through bolts (another option is steel cable) provide handle significant tension loads. The downside of through bolting is the oversized holes bored in the logs to allow construction. Without direct bearing of the tension rod in the hole, the logs are allowed to slip before the rod interacts with the wood. To remedy the log-to-log shear in combination with the tension rod, dowel-type fasteners (lag screws, spikes, or proprietary threaded log fasteners) should be used. The capacity of the log profile to provide suitable bearing will resolve the compressive load at the ends of the shear panel.

Without further guidance by code or standard, log homes are designed to resist lateral loading using conventional framing wisdom. The principles do apply to some degree, but the engineering community has little flexibility to modify the current standards unless they have specific testing or research that gives them a foundation for their opinions. Papers and research available today would indicate that log walls perform in a manner similar to reinforced concrete, yet the governing bodies that maintain the codes and standards have not been convinced. [67] Therefore, structural engineers are still put in the position of analyzing the resistance of each log course to resist the entire load on the shear wall, and the application of the R-factor (not for energy as in R-value, but for seismic resistance) is a matter of opinion relative to a fastening schedule. For example, it is known that through-bolts and cable systems are optimal for resisting the tension loads at the corners and openings, and that a pattern of dowel-type fasteners along each log course is effective to resist shear.

> Leichti, et.al.—"Wall performance is strongly influenced by the coefficient of friction and the normal forces developed by thru-rods. Thus, maintaining the thru-rod tension will enhance building system performance under seismic loads. Changing the wall aspect from 1:1 to 2:1 decreased the post-slip stiffness and increased overall wall displacement more than any other attribute. High aspect ratio walls may require additional stiffening. Additional thru-rods are often included in construction details for doors and windows and are important to minimizing the effect of wall perforations. Thru-rod hole size affects overall wall displacement. Minimizing the hole diameter minimizes slip displacement potential."

> Haney—"An analysis of log joinery leads to a unique model that deals with lateral loading. Friction plays a role in this model, as well as the ability of the structure to act as an interconnected whole. In many structures, wind loads are usually a concern only for the roof and the top several courses of logs. Seismic loads require that all logs in the building be adequately secured to the foundation so that uplift is prevented. Once uplift is eliminated, then friction and interlocking joinery work to an advantage. This model should let designers and builders move away from having to create a shear wall with logs by using steel drifts, lag screws, pegs, and the like."

> Popovski performed tests on handcrafted walls at the labs of Forintek Canada Corp. for the ILBA, concluding that handcrafted log walls possess unique lateral load resistance characteristics and lateral load transfer mechanisms, markedly different from the characteristics of conventional wood-frame systems. Higher vertical loading offset uplift loading in all models.

Log shear walls have been tested, with the following article from *Wood Homes Industry News* in their Oct. 8, 2007 e-newsletter:

> Edgewood is participating in a number of tests, including not only Washington State but also the universities of Idaho and Montana, all evaluating the shear performance, and similar stability tests, of its log walls and lag screw connections.

> The WSU study utilized log lengths and lag screw connections at sizes and spacing most commonly used in the log-building industry. Separate tests were conducted to evaluate the performance of log shear walls verses the

performance of light frame shear walls (stick frame homes) in active seismic and high wind regions.

In both tests, log shear walls demonstrated higher shear strength than light frame shear walls. In particular, Edgewood Log Structures' method of log fastening, which consists of lag screw connections, performed better than industry standards. Additionally, log shear wall R factor, a measure of over-strength and ductility, was found to be equivalent to that of concrete shear walls, Edgewood said in a release.

"It can be justified that higher R-factors could be applied to the walls tested in this study because the walls were allowed to exhibit a rocking behavior," said Drew Graham, who conducted the study for Washington State.

"We are excited to be a part of this testing," said Brian Schafer, president of Edgewood Log Structures. "The company has donated time and materials to further the research efforts by Washington State University, so it is gratifying to see the positive results of this study."

The following draws on the experience of a Missoula, MT engineering firm with considerable experience in the design of log structures for seismic conditions, Beaudette Consulting Engineers, Inc. (www.bceweb.com, 406-721-7315). In an undated statement (likely from 2005), the following is their justification for the response modification coefficient ("R") they used in their analysis:

Traditional horizontally stacked log walls are directly categorized as bearing wall systems. Under the 1997 Uniform Building Code (UBC), an R value of 5.5 is designated for wood structural panel walls and 4.5 for all other light framed walls. This directly compares to an R of 4.5 for both concrete and steel shear walls also classified as bearing walls. We therefore also consider pinned log shear walls to have an R of 4.5.

The 2003 International Building Code has established an R of 7 for light frame walls with shear panels (wood or sheet steel). But the IBC establishes an R of 2.5 for light framed walls with shear panels—all other materials. BCE has established usage of an R of 4.0 or 4.5 (depending on the engineer) based on the following:

While the values of R are largely based on engineering judgment of the performance of the various materials and systems in past earthquakes, the response modification factor (R) is based on a period dependent strength factor, a period dependent ductility factor and a redundancy factor. A pinned log wall collects and distributes lateral forces similar to a wood sheathed shear wall element. Energy dissipation (dampening) is considered to be very similar to sheathed wood shear walls. The elastic behavior of the pinned wall imitates the light frame shear panel walls. Further, a regularly spaced pinned log has considerable system redundancy.

The combination of the above noted factors allows justification for a seismic response modification coefficient for regularly spaced pinned log walls to be equal to that of the wood sheathed wall panel. The tighter spaced, small diameter log walls (pins or fasteners at 12" to 18" o/c) could have a higher R values (R = 5.5 or 6.0). While a typically spaced large diameter log wall (large steel pins from 24" to 48" o/c max) can conservatively have an R of 4.0 to 4.5. Log walls systems which rely on through rods at openings and corners only, should have a low R value of 2.5. BCE does not design log walls systems without regularly spaced pins (max 48" o/c), therefore we have established an 2003 IBC Response Modification Coefficient R of 4.0 or 4.5. The 4.0 to 4.5 values is used for tighter pinned spaced log walls also.

A Sample Analysis

The TimberLogic approach in the *Log Wall Performance Estimator* is to recognize that log walls are bearing walls that act as part of the Lateral Force Resisting System (LFRS). This sample approach was developed in partnership with Alex Charvat, P.E., Alexander Structures LLC.

Sidewall Span

Sidewalls resist lateral loads placed perpendicular to them with the horizontal members acting as a beam over a single span, simply supported with reaction points at shear wall locations. Log shear walls resist loads parallel to them, or in line with the logs. It is assumed that the maximum allowable log wall span equals that of an individual log acting as a beam, with maximum deflection set at l/360. Neither wind loading on the roof or dead load resisting an overturning force is accounted for in the analysis, producing a conservative response. Neither friction nor horizontal joinery connecting the consecutive logs is considered to add to the evaluation of the LFRS.

Wind Loads (WL) are calculated on basis of Exposure B, mean roof height = 20-ft, and wind speeds noted below.

Wind	85	90	100	110	120	130	140	150	mph
Design WL	11.26	12.62	15.58	18.85	22.43	26.34	30.53	35.06	psf
WL * H_L	7	8	10	12	14	16	19	21	plf, log
Log Grade	Maximum Allowable Sidewall Span (Lw, max. per Log Grade) per Wind Load								
Beam	75	70	62	57	53	49	45	43	ft
Header	68	64	57	52	48	45	41	39	ft
Wall	55	51	46	42	39	36	33	32	ft
Utility	46	43	38	35	32	30	28	26	ft

Figure 122: TimberLogic's *Log Wall Performance Estimator*: Maximum Allowable Log Wall Length (Lw) as limited by wind loading (see Figure 79 for log profile info).

Based on the above and the following analysis of log shear walls due to wind loads (following), it is reasonable to conclude that the seismic response modification coefficient is at least equal to the highest value given to any wood assembly by codes and standards (R=4.5).

After checking the capacity of the log profile to resist lateral loads, the fastening schedule is checked. Fastener lateral design values (Z) for single shear are used to resist the horizontal lateral load; C_D x $Z_{perpendicular}$ for sidewalls. Required fastener spacing is the minimum of standard fastener spacing (e.g., 30" on center), withdrawal capacity, or shear resistance. Using a 3/8" diameter lag screw that is 12" long at 30" on center will produce more than enough resistance to support the spans (L_w) and allow the wall to act as a single unit. This schedule does not include any consideration for fasteners added at butt joints or other locations.

Shear Walls

With the above wall spans verified to resist direct lateral loads, the next step is to examine the shear wall fastening schedule. The shear wall is assumed to be the perpendicular log wall at each end of the wall span (a.k.a., end walls). Continuous log courses above (header) and below (sill) wall openings act as boundary elements (drag struts) to distribute the horizontal shear force to shear elements within the wall. In multiple course headers/sills, the fastening schedule shall be determined by the horizontal shear so that log courses act collectively.

If the log wall is of full log wall span without any openings ($L_s = L_w$), the standard fastening schedule is again proven to be sufficient. As the shear panel segment becomes shorter (even less than the 1:1 aspect ratio of height to length required by ICC400), we see the spacing between fasteners shorten. This fastening schedule will not allow the logs to slide or displace horizontally, also known as racking.

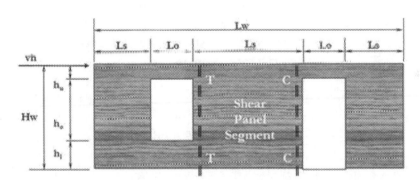

Figure 123: Log Shear Wall: The shear segment can be a solid wall from end to end, the panel from the corner to an opening, or a full height section of log between openings.

Wall Height = Log stack	7-3/16"	x log courses	14	= wall height (Hw) of	100.625 in.	or 8'-4.625" (8.385-ft)

Wind	85	90	100	110	120	130	140	150	mph
Lw, max.	55 ft.	51 ft.	46 ft.	42 ft.	39 ft.	36 ft.	33 ft.	32 ft.	

3/8" lag fasteners with washer 1.5 in. dia. w/hole dia. of 0.5 in.

Ls = Lw	30	30	30	30	30	30	30	30	in o/c
16.77 ft	30	30	30	30	30	30	30	30	in o/c
8.39 ft	30	30	30	30	30	30	30	30	in o/c
6.71 ft	30	30	30	30	26	26	26	26	in o/c
4.19 ft	25	25	25	25	16	16	16	16	in o/c
2.8 ft	16	16	16	16	11	11	11	11	in o/c
2.1 ft	12	12	12	12	8	8	8	8	in o/c

Figure 124: Based on the log wall spans for a Wall Grade wall-log, fastener spacing in the shear wall are established based on the load (vh) and the length of the shear segment (Ls).

The shear walls must also resist the uplift/ overturning action of the load applied on it by the sidewalls. So, the shear segment must also resist compression and tension and be able to resist those overturning loads from both ends of the wall. In <u>Figure 124</u>, this is noted by the T (tension) and C (compression). If the load comes from the other side, the labels of C and T would be reversed. The compressive force at the corners of a wall opening is resisted by the perpendicular to grain bearing capacity of the header/sill log. This is typically not a controlling element of the shear segment, and a short length of log is sufficient. Tension loads are another story and rely on the withdrawal capacity of the fastener. When the standard fastener cannot resist the overturning load, the common response is to connect the ends of the shear segment with through bolts or tension rods. Note that gable end wall area above the log header is not used to resist shear loads.

In the table below, one can see that a column of fasteners at wall openings will satisfy T_{OT}. Consistent with ICC400's parameters, the column of fasteners reaches its logical limit when the aspect ratio is 1:1. The shear segment besides a wall opening and between the header and sill log courses defines the aspect ratio for that segment. Therefore, the shear wall height is equal to the wall opening height and equal to the length of the shear segment. To maximize the withdrawal capacity of the fastener, the fastener head cannot be allowed to pull through the wood. Therefore, a washer must be sized for placement under the lag head that will equal its withdrawal capacity. In this case, the 3/8" lag screw will require a 1.5" washer with a 1/2" hole. This washer is only required in this application.

When the shear segment becomes shorter, more lag screws are required until the spacing requirements of the fastener no longer fit within the length of the shear panel. The table shows the required bolt diameter and bearing plate (washer) per overturning calculations.

When high wind or seismic loads are applied to a log structure, this analysis can be used to identify an initial fastening schedule. It also shows why engineers require through-bolts in log walls, especially at corners and wall openings. This analysis is not specific to any one design, and it is absolutely advised that an engineer with wood design experience be retained to analyze the lateral force resisting system when conditions exceed the ICC400 parameters.

The number of fasteners refers to quantity repeated at each end of each log in the wall, effectively forming a column

Ls = Lw   Shear Wall fastening controls over Segment fastening at end of wall

Hw : Ls	Ls = Lw	1	1	1	1	1	1	1	1	fasteners
1:2	16.77 ft	1	1	2	2	2	2	2	2	fasteners
1:1	8.39 ft	3	3	3	3	4	4	4	5	fasteners
1.2 : 1	6.71 ft	3	4	4	4	5	5	5	6	fasteners
2:1	4.19 ft	5	5	6	Use bolts	Use bolts	Use bolts	Use bolts	Use bolts	fasteners
3:1	2.8 ft	Use bolts	Use bolts	Use bolts	Use bolts	Use bolts	Use bolts	Use bolts	Use bolts	fasteners
4:1	2.1 ft	Use bolts	Use bolts	Use bolts	Use bolts	Use bolts	Use bolts	Use bolts	Use bolts	fasteners
Through-bolt connections:	4.19 ft	0.625	0.625	0.625	0.625	0.625	0.625	0.625	0.625	bolt dia.
		3.25 sq.in	3.25 sq.in	3.75 sq.in	4 sq.in	4.5 sq.in	4.75 sq.in	5 sq.in	5.75 sq.in	washer
	2.8 ft	0.625	0.625	0.625	0.625	0.625	0.625	0.625	0.625	bolt dia.
36000		3.25 sq.in	3.25 sq.in	3.75 sq.in	4 sq.in	4.5 sq.in	4.75 sq.in	5 sq.in	5.75 sq.in	washer
psi tensile	2.1 ft	0.625	0.625	0.625	0.625	0.625	0.625	0.625	0.625	bolt dia.
strength		6.25 sq.in	6.5 sq.in	7.25 sq.in	8 sq.in	8.75 sq.in	9.5 sq.in	10 sq.in	11.25 sq.in	washer

Bolts are to be ASTM F1554 Grade 36 All Thread Rod or better.

Figure 125: Fastening Schedule for Shear Segments in Endwalls: T_{OT} & C_{OT} (column at each end of Shear Walls)

Pilasters & Interior Shear Walls

In some cases, the log wall requires additional support along its length. Pilasters provide that support, stiffening the log wall by connecting posts to the log wall with lag screws through slotted holes. Often, log producers will specify a system of installing wall stiffeners (pilasters) where interior framed partitions intersect the log wall. Connecting end posts in partition walls may not be required, but they will contribute to the stability of the wall. The connection is typically into the top and bottom log course and at least one intermediate course and is allowed to slip as described in Sliding Joints.

When a pilaster is built into an interior shear wall, the length of the shear panel is defined by double top and bottom plates with sheathing (15/32" minimum nominal thickness, OSB or 3-ply plywood structural panels conforming to standard PS1 or PS2) overlapping both plates top and bottom. The load resisted by the shear wall must be transferred to the foundation. The load path can be achieved by building a foundation wall under the shear panel, by installing a post to a footing beneath the interior end of the shear panel, or installing a beam in the floor under the shear panel suitably sized to carry the point load at the end of the shear panel.

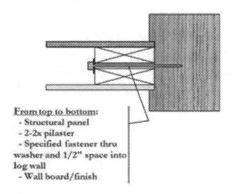

From top to bottom:
- Structural panel
- 2-2x pilaster
- Specified fastener thru washer and 1/2" space into log wall
- Wall board/finish

Figure 126: Intersection of Interior Partitions/ Shear Walls

As a stiffener post, pilasters of solid timbers or glued laminated timbers can also be installed using log screws in slotted holes. Solid blocking to a foundation pilaster is advised to transfer the resulting point load at the base of the pilaster, even if it is only fastened to the log wall.

BEYOND ICC400

Key Details for Construction

Building log structures requires specific knowledge of the construction method employed as outlined in ICC400. That knowledge is applied in the design phase of the building project and is executed in the building phase. As noted in Testimony to Durability log building is a simple form of construction, and therefore means that anyone can participate—*as long as there is an experienced individual providing supervision and quality control*. Construction manuals are provided by all Log Homes Council member companies and are becoming more widely available throughout the industry. An excellent construction manual for handcrafted wall systems was written in 2010 by Dalibor Houdek.[68]

Adherence to these instructions by the builder is very important and is likely tied to any warranty program. Builders who have not built a company's proprietary product before should not ignore the plans and construction manual provided with the materials package. In fact, the builder assumes responsibility for any work that deviates from those directions—analogous to log/lumber grading, a piece that is cut/installed at the site constitutes acceptance as on grade by the builder. This sounds like a simple concept, but many handcrafters have found that it is much wiser to send supervision for the re-assembly of their log structures.

Quality log construction begins with the same principles that drive quality construction using any building method:

- Prepare for the project by involving **appropriate planning**. Green building standards promote bringing in professionals prior to construction to help assess, design and manage site/lot conservation, energy conservation, certified mechanical design, and training of those working on the project.
- Most log home companies have enough guidance from prior experience to reasonably design structurally sound buildings. The key is to compare their base design criteria to the environment in which the structure is to be built. This information is available from many places, most commonly from code references, building departments, etc. In some cases, the load conditions of the building site will exceed the prescriptive measures of ICC400 Chapter 4, and a professional engineer will be required.
- Insure that the structure remains **plumb, square and level construction**—Checking regularly is recommended with key points being at the bearing grade prior to pouring footings, at the top of foundation and adjusted when setting the sill plate, at multiple points along the height of the log wall (course one, course 3, half way up the wall, at the header course, and at top of log wall), and finally, at the roof ridge.
- Provide adequate time, resources and space for proper care, handling and storage of materials.

Figure 127: Setting the bottom plate log is critical. Bottom plate logs are often set against a chalk line to insure proper offset on the subfloor.

Much of the content developed for ICC400 focused on the design and specification of the materials that would be assembled. Using ASTM and AF&PA standards for guidance, these specifications were translated into capacities and other performance criteria. This is the proper approach for a standard of its type, but it fails to provide an inspector who is not proficient on the content of the standard to readily apply its requirements. The details of construction need to be thought through before building begins. This is accomplished by gaining a thorough understanding of the construction documents—primarily the details shown in the plans and/or construction manual.

As with all methods of construction today, new approaches are being employed to achieve better building energy performance, and log walls are no different. Third-party inspections (HERS raters, ENERGY STAR verifiers, etc.) have demonstrated areas where log builders can improve their work. Examples can be established to assist building officials, accredited Green Building Program Verifiers, and HERS raters in their inspections, but the plans and construction manuals are the best place to document methods for consistent construction performance.

Log building performance should require inspections of the elements of log walls that truly impact air infiltration. The solid wood will resist air flow, and the joinery between logs provides a air and water tight seal when built in compliance with ICC400. The wood and joinery are critical elements that log designers and producers have established to protect their business interests—good performance builds a good business. However, some areas of construction are beyond their control and site inspection is required.

The ridge area of vaulted ceilings (typical of all timber frame roofs);

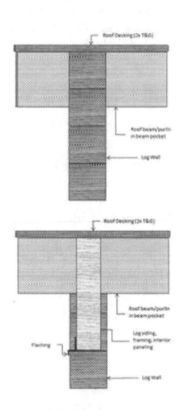

Figure 128: Roof to Wall Connection @ Endwall (Rake)

The joint between the top plate log and the roof is often a culprit where air infiltration is concerned. Focus on seal of rafter to top plate log, seal and insulation above log wall and between rafters to bottom of ceiling/decking.

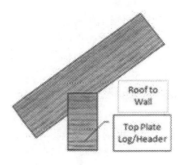

Figure 129: Roof to Wall Connection @ Sidewall (Eave)

All wall penetrations (e.g., by vents, electrical installations or protrusion of logs through the both frame walls and log walls) of the exterior wall must be properly addressed by gaskets and/or sealants.

The connections between the floor and a bottom plate log, or the foundation and the sill log can be very effectively sealed using gaskets. Focus on seal of log to sill plate, and sill plate to foundation; similar for slab foundations. Focus on seal of log to subfloor, subfloor to sill plate, and sill plate to foundation, insulation at floor perimeter.

The connection of the log with contiguous frame wall assemblies (e.g., dormers, gable ends, extensions, etc.) need to provide air and water seal, but it also must have flashing to insure that water cascading down the surface of the wall continues down the face of the log wall rather than being able to wick into this joint. Where upper walls (e.g., dormers, gable end walls) bear over the log wall, focus on the seal with flashing and gasket between the dissimilar wall types. Above these walls, seal to the bottom of the roof deck.

Good performance of a log wall during a blower door test requires attention to detail in the design of the joinery, execution of that design in production and final assembly. Insure that proper assembly includes attention to structural considerations, such as fastening schedules, lateral bracing, continuous load path, etc. Verifiers should focus on partition pilasters that support log walls; interior shear walls require additional consideration in floor framing; settling allowance/slip joint at top of partition to 2nd floor deck or ceiling. Proper roof design requires that outward thrust (a natural element of a triangle-like gable roof) not be permitted to push out the tops of the log walls. Adding structural beams to support upper ends of the roof are one approach. Using wall ties or collar ties with proper mechanical fastening (connection design) also responds to this condition. This latter condition is often satisfied by incorporating a timber truss.

Log Additions

Building log additions to an existing structure requires the contractor to follow all of the normal processes with one exception: The connection of the log walls to the existing structure must be designed to allow differential settling. This principle applies regardless of the construction of the existing house. If the existing house is a log wall that has been in use for several years, it is likely that movement will be limited, but it would be recommended that any frame addition still have a slip joint where the walls intersect. This also alludes to the idea that aligning addition walls with existing exterior walls will require careful assessment of the structure and construction of the alignment. This is why most additions are offset from the existing parallel exterior wall by about 2-feet.

Assessing the existing structure is essential before tying in another structure. A building audit will help align floor elevations, but it may be a good idea to intentionally design steps between to eliminate issues relating to changes in floor height. The same idea is recommended at the roof, where aligning fascia and ridge lines is next to impossible. Dropping or raising the addition roof (or adding it perpendicular to

the existing roof line) leaves management of settlement to the flashing detail between new and old.

Sound Transmission

Sound transmission is an element of a structure's occupancy that is related to comfort and tranquility, and it has nothing to do with life or fire safety or even energy conservation. It is very much related to the design of the structure, the finishes and textures integrated into it, and the location relative to external sources of noise. However, it is worthy of mention as a property of materials and construction.

Airborne sound is effectively reflected by the mass and shape of the log wall. It is dampened by soft materials. It passes through openings in assemblies just like air, and the features that improve a home's thermal performance will also help improve its ambient noise level. This concept is expanded in the Log Homes Council Technical Note on the topic:[69]

As with most building topics, quality construction is the best prevention for noise leaks. While landscaping techniques (earth berms; tall, dense foliage) can be barriers to outside noise, construction decisions are likely to have a larger impact.

- *Seal or insulate all gaps prior to applying finish trim.*
- *Double glazed windows are quieter than single glazed.*
- *Use weatherstripped, solid core doors.*
- *Appropriate design and installation of plumbing lines will reduce vibrations and noise.*
- *In multi-family construction, avoid penetrations of the party wall (e.g. flush-mounted*

fixtures or medicine cabinets) and be sure to seal around and insulate behind electrical boxes.

Sound transmission class (STC) ratings are used to evaluate products and assemblies to help designers control sound. It is unknown at this time if any company has tested their log profile for an STC rating. However, sound controls used in conventional construction will similarly benefit log homes. As noted for energy conservation, seal all electrical penetrations through interior partitions to minimize air or noise moving to another space in the house. Another technique often used for sound control is to insulate bathroom walls, stair walls, etc., where there is a desire to isolate the sounds from those spaces.

Balanced Ventilation

An interesting development in high performance design and construction is the use of materials that provide great thermal value but also off-gas for a couple of heating/cooling cycles. Experience in log building has shown that a similar event happens. Rather than releasing chemicals into the indoor environment, log walls may release moisture into the house as heating systems are put into use and the moisture is drawn from the logs into the dryer interior atmosphere. The owner/builder sees the impact as condensation forms on cooler surfaces, most often on windows.

In log construction, it is advisable to allow wall openings to be open during the first few days on colder days when the interior is heated. This simple venting approach is appropriate for unseasoned log components. Operating exhaust vents (bath fans) that are vented to the exterior and opening windows on lower levels will enhance the flow of moisture laden air to the outside. This same ventilation helps to control chemical pollutants that are undesirable byproducts of otherwise beneficial products.

INDUSTRY'S CHALLENGE

Without a doubt, the single biggest obstacle for the log wall is an appropriate comparison to the requirements for exterior walls in the IECC. Without further empirical evidence to support greater thermal resistance, a prescriptive path response (meeting a minimum insulation requirement) will not succeed, and the performance path will be the industry's only hope. What is the next step for the log home industry? The single over-riding conclusion is that many of the issues facing the log home industry continue from political action during a time when the log home industry can barely raise its voice.

Objective 1: Encourage others to read this book. Send it to everyone that can help—consumers, building officials, mortgage lenders, utilities, state legislatures. Perhaps the facts and analysis provided here can be used to counter the bad information, misperceptions, and biased opinions of those seeking a bigger share of the homebuilding market. There truly is tremendous room for many wall technologies which will gain acceptance based on their individual merits. Let it remain to be a choice for those who dream of a log home.

Objective 2: Embrace and promote the performance path. Speakers at DOE's Energy Codes 2011 (July, Salt Lake City) confirmed that the minimum requirements for the thermal envelope (roof, walls, floor/foundation, and fenestration) have nearly reached their "optimum" levels. Optimum means that the requirements have reached the level where economic viability and actual performance have reached their peak and further increases produce marginal benefit at greater cost.

Objective 3: Maintain acceptance of the 5" minimum average thickness. In the section "Applying the IECC to Log Walls", it was demonstrated that the overall UA calculations can demonstrate compliance of smaller log width than expected. The prescriptive codes would have us think that the log width will need to jump up to 11 or 12 inches. However, UA alternatives show otherwise. For many climate zones, log walls should be entered as "**Log (W_L): 5-inch average thickness minimum per ICC400**" with a 7-inch average width used in colder climates (2009 IECC), depending on the specific gravity of the wood. Even with the more restrictive requirements of the 2012 IECC, an 8-inch white pine log satisfies Climate Zones 6-8. Moving from prescriptive (minimum) requirements to the UA Alternative might show an advantage by using an average log width of 7-1/2" to 8-7/16" in the very cold climates is far more palatable than applying prescriptive interpretations. It is clear that rated thermal transmission value for the wall will remain to be a focal point.

It is also clear that energy codes of the future may no longer look only at the thermal envelope, performance of distribution systems, or controls that reduce power demand when spaces are not in use. Mechanical efficiency will again become a question and alternative energy sources will be integrated to reach net zero. Build to above code standards and pay attention to the details. Log structures will perform!

Objective 4: Raise a unified voice based on a platform for the future. The facts are that log structures **do** meet the ICC life safety codes and standards. They are the epitome of sustainable—environmentally friendly and durable. The platform should be based on some simple resolutions:

- Work toward the vision of building technology of the future

- Adopt and promote ICC400 as the "Log Home Code"
- Educate others on the benefits of log wall construction
- Focus log builders on all of the above.

THE BUILDINGS TECHNOLOGY VISION

It is clear that the goal for building more energy efficient buildings remains targeted on net-zero building energy consumption by 2030. It is equally clear that the log building industry (like all of the building industry) needs to demonstrate that it is willing to be responsible for the performance of its products.

Returning to the NIST report cited in the Scope, part of the resolution comes from the thermal envelope, some from internal systems, some from alternative energy, and some from using building materials, products and systems.

Buildings Technology Research and Development Vision

Enable designs of new buildings and retrofits of existing building that over the life cycle:

- Produce as much energy as they consume (net-zero energy) and significantly reduce GHGs.
- Double the service life of building materials, products, and systems and minimize life cycle impacts.
- Halve the use of domestic water (e.g., to 50 gal/day/person or less), maximize water recycling and rainwater harvesting, and minimize storm water runoff.
- Achieve breakthrough improvements in indoor occupant health, productivity, and comfort.

- Log walls do not produce energy, so it is appropriate to **support the integration**

of geothermal, wind and solar technologies that would help a log building function "off the grid."

- Implementing energy-generation that does not burn fossil fuels is not the only way to **reduce Green House Gases (GHG)**. It is also the use of materials that reduce the use of fossil fuels throughout the process of expediting raw materials, producing the product, delivering the product and assembling it into a useable form. Wood is the target of other building material industries because it does just that, and far better.

- It could be argued that all properly-maintained building materials, products, and systems can **double the currently acknowledged service life of 60 years**. However, it could just as easily be argued that the only ancient structures that still exist today are built of solid wall construction that can be maintained and repaired easily from either the interior or exterior surface. Like log walls, all of these wall systems rely on sealed joinery, sacrificial outside layers or surface design that promotes water runoff. The witnessed longevity of log homes is testimony to doubling the service life.

- A primary objective of the log home industry must be to **establish data for life cycle assessment (LCA) of log walls** over other methods of wall construction with to demonstrate environmental benefits. LCA will demonstrate the benefits of building with log due to carbon sequestration, low embodied energy, and much lower levels of pollutants released to the environment.

- Managing **water resources** is no different for log homes than any other construction method. The issues of water conservation, recycling, and collection are beyond the scope of this project. Support for these principles as presented in **ICC700 National Green Building Standard** would respond to this. Without doubt, the service life of the building benefits from the proper management of water moving off the roof and away from the foundation.

- Log home owners have testified to **Indoor occupant health, productivity and comfort**. They note their homes are healthy, warm and calming. Limited air infiltration and balanced ventilation strategies provide the direct health benefit. As noted by Dave Fell in his article "More Wood = Less Stress".[70] Fell notes, ". . . the presence of wood indoors reduces stress and promotes better long-term health." Citing a study at the University of British Columbia, Fell correlates their findings to the evidence-based design movement in health care.

Looking Ahead

Conserving energy via the thermal envelope is seen as the #1 priority to all advocates of net-zero concepts. While those advocates would insulate to extreme levels, nearly suitable of survival beyond Earth's atmosphere, are these levels of insulation also socially responsible? Doesn't the incremental benefit have to be relative to the marginal gain? Rather than point to insulation levels as the selling point, **demonstrate the superior performance by completing energy audits** by certified raters as compliant with certified HERS programs.

Another approach for evaluating a building's energy performance has been suggested by several. The idea is to set a base performance level with the 2006 IECC requirements to establish a Btu per square foot rate. From that base case, cut the Btu total by 50% and set that as the energy consumption goal for heating, cooling, and domestic hot water supply. With the thermal envelope and solar orientation optimized, where else can designers go for savings . . .

- Locate mechanicals central to the design to shorten distribution runs to the farthest points.
- Cut hot water heat loss by insulating pipes, stacking plumbing to shorten supply lines, and manage distribution to reduce the number of cups of water that have to be run through the pipes to get the water temperature desired.
- Design to maximize passive solar and air flow benefits. Internal mass generally helps temper the indoor environment, and stores solar gain. Natural ventilation and shading methods can minimize mechanical cooling demand.
- Rooms with large window areas and cathedral ceilings need to be specifically designed to minimize the perception of cold spots. Conduction and convection are both at play, with window treatments becoming a low-cost option that saves a lot of energy.
- Design to maximize energy efficient natural lighting—Using good glass has always been part of the log home energy package. If glazing area is less than 15% of the wall area and the glass has a U-Factor of 0.30 or less, solar orientation will not contribute greatly.

ICC400 AS THE LOG BUILDING CODE

The log home industry is adjusting where it can. Many log home companies are adjusting their thinking to insure that they can pass a demanding air infiltration requirement (a maximum of 3 air changes per hour under 50 Pascals of pressure generated by a blower door under specific test standards, a.k.a <3ACH50). Some companies are considering changes to the log profiles they have been producing for many years but are limited by their resource and/or process. Prescriptive code

interpretations may call for 11-inch or 12-inch log walls, but this is certainly not economically viable for many potential buyers. Greater wall thickness impacts harvest yield and material handling at the mill and on the building site. To avoid these issues, the industry is looking at performance simulations with blower door testing. For log home enthusiasts, it may be critical to make sure that everyone recognizes the benefits that they have enjoyed for years.

To maintain the viability of a unique and traditional alternative wall system that has performed successfully for centuries, recognize ICC400 *Standard on the Design and Construction of Log Structures* as the **"log building code."** Establish ICC400 as the single reference for the proper design, construction and evaluation of log structures. It calls for

- Log grading per accredited program
- Fire rating based on least width
- Appropriate settling allowance
- Weather-tight joinery design and seal
- Thermal value based on **minimum average log width.**
  The minimum average width established in ICC400 (TABLE 305.3.1) is 5-inches and REScheck® version 3.7 Release 1 was modified in coordination with the standard. With this precedent set, it is easy to adopt a 5-inch as the essential minimum average log width for code development purposes.
- Structural capacity matched to design loads
- Load paths follow to foundation.

Log structures should be evaluated only as stipulated in the ICC400 standard and not on the basis of specifications established for other materials or methods of construction as published in the I-Codes. The I-Codes set the design conditions and minimum requirements for building elements that are beyond the scope of the standard.

Perhaps a Federal mandate is necessary? Federal legislation should demonstrate a respect for our national heritage by acknowledging that solid wood walls perform differently than the insulated cavity wall construction that has been the focus of the IECC. By providing support for log structures, the Federal government would not only support the social benefit of maintaining a place for traditional construction that is part of our national heritage, but it would also support free choice and maintain the economic welfare of those involved or supporting the industry.

PROMOTE THE BENEFITS

Establishing ICC400 as the foundation for education will help the public, design professionals, building inspectors and administrators and others appreciate the benefits of log wall construction. One way to raise awareness and educate readers about log components and building systems is to step into "*The Product Transparency Movement.*"[71]

As described in the article, a Product Category Rule (PCR) provides the guidance to complete a Life-Cycle Assessment (LCA) which gets summarized in an Environmental Product Declaration (EPD). The wood industry has the benefit of already being incorporated into the U.S. Life Cycle Inventory Database, and log homes can start from there. But the disclosures listed in the article provide an excellent basis for building a product label/disclosure form for log component producers and the associated products used by them.

Environmental Disclosure

The following is a proposed outline and discussion for a disclosure statement for log structures. Does this have to appear on a specific product label? No. This information should be documented in one place, yes, but that location can be in the construction manual, in the assembly drawings, or the architectural plans. In the modular home approval process, the certified package includes all of this information. Some log home producers may need to tweak their presentations to support this approach, but most have the process already in place to implement this disclosure.

The goal here is to make this a more important piece of the documentation supplied with every log package. Make certain the building official gets a copy and understands it. Make certain the home owner knows what it means now and when they are preparing for resale of the home. Use this to promote the benefits of log structures in every way possible. Provide comparisons to other forms of construction for appraisers so they can appreciate the benefits of log building.

The following table can be developed by any log company to promote its products, or it can hire a third-party to provide an objective review and complete the necessary documentation.

Category	Information to Disclose
General Information	Company information such as the name, address, and contact information; list of services, years in business, number of homes shipped, and other marketing information can be included here.
Content	Describe the products included in the materials package. Each component produced via a different process needs to be described separately.
	Don't expect standard practices to be the only source—such as a loading list that is sent along with the Bill of Lading or a list of purchased materials as part of the contract. Integrate these into a coordinated presentation.
	A recommended practice is to provide a copy of Material Safety Data Sheets (MSDS) for materials manufactured by others. Many companies send materials that are needed for assembly but that are manufactured by others (e.g., fasteners, caulk, and gasket). If environmental impact information is available, it should be included as well. In a typical log package, these materials comprise a small percentage and are not a critical impact. Include an MSDS for sawdust.
	Other pass through type materials may include windows, exterior doors, decking and roofing materials. This is typically called a weather-tight shell. Some companies offer complete materials packages which can include trim, interior partition framing and finishes, interior doors, cabinets and more.
Process	Detail the process involved in producing the log components and other materials used to complete the log structure. Include all steps in the process to create an assessment of energy and resources used.
	Using the US Life Cycle Database, the embodied energy of raw materials used by the log component producer can be estimated. Whether raw logs, peeled logs, or cants are purchased, the database provides
	Beyond raw materials, the log producer should work with an accredited auditing firm or CPA that can certify annual records of the company to establish the elements of the process used to produce the components.
	The process carries forward from receipt of raw materials to loading the truck for shipment and includes all overhead operations.

Category	Information to Disclose
Design & Capacity	Identifying the fact that the structure is designed to comply with ICC400 is not sufficient. For full disclosure, a full evaluation of the log components should be included. TimberLogic Reports, the worksheets found in this book, or other documentation should clearly define the structural capacity of the log components, the fire-resistance and thermal rating of the log wall, estimated allowance for settling,
	Design documents should utilize the log grading program by identifying where higher grade logs are to be used. For example, the sill/bottom plate log may want to be a header grade because of the connections to the foundation. A higher grade log will remain true to its original placement. Lower grade logs can be used within the opaque sections of the wall, since they are uniformly supported. Then higher grade logs can be used for header and top plate logs to carry loads over wall openings while supporting roof and upper floor structures.
	Just as log grades are identified, the fastening schedule is equally important. Even assuming that an experienced log builder is assembling the log package, the documentation needs to clearly note the type and frequency of connections. Standard fastening patterns will likely govern most of construction, but special attention needs to be given to sill/bottom plate log to foundation, shear panel connections, corners and butt joints, connection of header logs over openings, and the column of fasteners either side of openings.
Delivery	The process of delivery to the building site prior to actual construction is the next step that needs to be assessed. Again, using an accredited auditing firm to verify reported numbers, the cost of shipment to the building site is converted into life cycle assessment factors. Loaded miles may be used as the comparison with averages for fuel use, maintenance, etc. of equipment. The assessment can be simplified by taking the total energy added by shipping and dividing by the volume of components on the average truck.
Assembly	Accounting for the energy consumed in the assembly of the log structure is the next step. This section focuses on materials and methods that are used on the building site to complete the log structure.
	A list of tools required for assembly, recommendations for crew size and powered equipment will provide a glimpse at the extent of energy that will be required to assemble the log structure.

Category	Information to Disclose
Recyclability / End of Use	As previously noted, adding solid wood to a landfill is counterproductive—the wood does not decompose as one would expect. At worst, log cutoffs and other waste from the construction process should be recycled for fuel purposes. Precut or preassembled (handcrafted) systems manage the majority of cutoffs at the production facility.
	When the structure is to be replaced, careful examination of the structure can identify the pieces that can be reused or remanufactured for use in another building. Assuming the roof has been maintained, roof and upper floor framing members are likely to be in good condition for reuse. Wall components are also likely candidates for reuse, but a closer inspection is advised. It should be remembered that the grade of the log component is accepted when the piece is installed. When it is removed for reuse, it is assumed that the original grade is void and the piece will be graded again before put into another structural use.
	The key to the log structure is the extent of materials that can be readily disassembled and reused in comparison to other forms of construction. The concrete industry explains that old concrete can be reconstituted and reused. The gypsum industry also prides its ability to recycle removed product, as long as the material can be kept dry. Do other construction materials offer similarly low impact reuse of its products?
	No log producer will be able to predict how long any given structure will survive, and the potential reuse depends on many variables. The potential for reuse is great however. Instead, most log producers focus on appropriate care and maintenance of the wall logs, recognizing that it is the key for unlimited durability.
Care & Maintenance	Each company that produces log components will have their own philosophy about the elements of their material packages. Some find that it is advantageous to include wood finish products while others only recommend suppliers of wood finishes. The key is that the wood surfaces exposed to the outside environment need to be protected.
	At a minimum, documentation should describe minimal inspection and maintenance instructions. Each log building system has particular aspects that need to be considered, so a broad generalization of maintenance and inspection is inappropriate. The only known aspect is that neglect of the wood will likely lead to expensive repairs at some point.
	Maintenance of the grounds and vegetation around the structure are also relevant to the durability of the log structure. This topic should be included in the documentation.
Energy Efficiency Certificates	The REScheck® program provides a print option for the energy label that is supposed to be posted permanently on or near the electrical panel. It describes what was done in the thermal envelope to comply with the energy code at the time of construction (and insulation inspection).

Category	Information to Disclose
Certifications	Product certifications should be listed to cover the properties claimed by the company. This documentation should list the name of the accredited grading agency that certifies the company's grading activities. If moisture content is certified by the grading agency, this should be described.
	Treatment certifications may be provided by the grading agency or by another accredited inspection agency. Self-certification should be described in the contents section only. Treatments that could be listed here would include preservative treatments via dip process, pressurized systems, or heat sterilization.
	Resource certifications relating to forest management and sustainability should be listed.
	Manufacturer certifications for quality assurance may be listed here as well.
Estimate Your Carbon Footprint	**Step 1:** Incoming Materials: Determine the amount of wood received for production of log components.
	The following is derived from information presented in Environmental Building News, published by BuildingGreen Inc.
	Step 2: *Divide the company's annual electricity use (assuming one operating location), in kilowatt-hours, by twelve to get an average monthly use. Enter your company's zip code on EPA's Power Profiler website* (http://www.epa.gov/cleanenergy/energy-and-you/how-clean.html), select the utility providing power to the company, and then click on "My Emissions" to enter the company's monthly electricity use and note the annual carbon emissions from electricity.
	Estimate the carbon emissions from any fuels burned onsite—Find the average carbon content of various fuels and a factor to account for the energy it takes to get the fuel to your operating location in the Greenhouse Gas Protocol (http://www.ghgprotocol.org/calculation-tools/all-tools). To convert fuel from other units (for example, natural gas usage in therms but not cubic feet), a handy converter is available at http://www.eia.gov/kids/energy.cfm?page=about_energy_conversion_calculator-basics.
	Sum the carbon from the prior steps. To get the carbon footprint for log components, divide annual carbon estimate by the annual volume of log shipped (e.g., lineal feet or board feet) to find the pounds of CO_2 per lineal foot.

Ecological Benchmarks

Log walls, when properly built in accordance with the provisions of ICC 400 *Standard on the Design and Construction of Log Structures*, compare favorably to other technologies used to build exterior walls.

Benchmark	Wall Type					
	Solid Wood	**Wood Frame**	**Steel Frame**	**SIP**	**ICF**	**Concrete/CMU**
Insulation	Integrated insulation and mass, allowing solar gain on exterior. Effective for heat, sound, and electrical insulation. Continuous full length of log wall.	Cavity insulation provides approx. 80% of wall	Cavity insulation provides approx. 80% of wall	Foam core with framing around openings, splines at seams; insulation provides approx. 91% of roof panels and 86% of walls	Continuous foam insulation forms contain concrete. No gain from thermal mass gain on either interior or exterior	Continuous foam insulation on exterior limits heat loss while exposure to interior can temper indoor climate.
Insulation Stability	As logs acclimate to the building climate, R-value increases	Wind-washing occurs as unconditioned air is allowed to move within air-permeable cavity insulations, such as fiberglass, cellulose and board-stock insulations		Thermal drift (aging) is the phenomenon by which R-value decreases as foam plastic insulation material ages		Mass wall systems are monolithic and seams can be controlled
Drainage Plane	Profile design sheds moisture when properly maintained with an exterior finish	Siding design sheds cascading water; interior drainage plane / rainscreen requires weep holes for moisture drainage and ventilation appropriate for drying air flow.			Stucco or similar coatings over foam provide rainscreen.	
Indoor Air Quality (IAQ)	Wood fragrance, moderation of relative humidity	With proper vapor and air barrier construction, wall assemblies will not affect IAQ		Early release of gas propellants used to create it; may have unpleasant lingering odors		Moderation of relative humidity
Fire Rating	3/4" solid wood meets thermal barrier	Type V construction per code.		Thermal barrier is required between foam plastic and interior spaces.		None

Benchmark	Wall Type					
	Solid Wood	Wood Frame	Steel Frame	SIP	ICF	Concrete/CMU
Renewable	100% wood, logs can be reclaimed & remanufactured	20% framing, sheathing	sheathing	sheathing	none	Produced from a finite supply of raw materials, intense heat to produce increases embodied energy, but less fossil fuel is now being used. The cement mixture uses a broad range of manufacturing by-products that diverts it from landfills.
Embodied Energy	A natural, renewable resource, least of all structural building materials.	Embodied energy varies with insulation and siding products used.		Embodied energy varies with siding applications and thickness of foam used.		
Waste Management	All byproducts are usable; no land fill	Wood can be reused, remanufac-tured, or used for fuel.	Steel framing can be recycled.	Extremely limited resources for recycling foam.		
Carbon Storage	100% in use	Wood framing, sheathing, siding	Wood sheathing, siding	Wood skins/ sheathing	None	None
Products of Petroleum	Gaskets	Vinyl siding, air/vapor barrier, drainage plane, gaskets		Vinyl siding	Insulation	none

*Based on test where the impact of a 2x4 wood stud traveling at up to 100 mph strikes the wall. Concrete and frame wall results from the Wind Engineering Research Center, Texas Tech University. Log wall results from

A Tradition of Care & Conservation

There are certain well-documented and thoroughly studied properties of wood that must be included in the discussion of solid wood walls. In the previous chapters, that vast body of work has been referenced and explained to identify the several factors of nature that all log building traditionalists already honor:

- Understand the behavior of wood and use grading techniques to predict performance
- Prepare for the environmental conditions of use. Where high humidity exists, prepare the site to promote air flow around the building. Where ground water, snow pack, or termites are a factor, raise the building and promote movement of water away from the structure.
- The forest is a community that needs care. Utilizing small diameter trees is actually a benefit to the forest, strengthening the forest community. Removing dead-stand timber reduces the fuel load of a potential forest fire.

- AND ONE NEW ONE—From the world of building science, the entire building industry is learning how to adapt the motto, "Build it tight, ventilate it right." Log builders like other building trades must pay attention to the details of their work in order to demonstrate performance. Then, recommending mechanical ventilation (e.g., heat recovery ventilation or energy recovery ventilation) becomes a good idea to maintain good indoor air quality.

of integral insulation value and mass would be better served by using dynamic measurements rather than steady-state measurements.

The science of building materials today does not provide sufficient answers to the testimony of home owners who know that their log homes are energy efficient. The secret may be that testing based on small samples is not the answer. Finding the funding to evaluate larger cross-sections of wood is necessary.

MODIFY PERCEPTIONS

Room for Research?

Focusing on the very cold climate zones, what is the dynamic that answers the remaining unknowns? Why are log wall surface temperatures in a heated home always warm to the touch? Is thermal mass really the answer? Solid wood walls allow moisture to migrate from the wood to the ambient air and vice-versa to produce a comfortable environment. Is this an area of study that will generate better understanding?

The question lives on: What is it about wood mass that it does not behave as predicted by ASTM testing to rate insulation products would suggest?

Perhaps revisiting ASTM testing is the right idea. Wood species have been thoroughly tested to establish heat transfer through a one-inch thickness. Perhaps the better test is a 5-inch thick sample of heart-center wood so that the direction of the heat transfer is radial. Perhaps the grain pattern and knots of a larger timber will generate a different dynamic.

Perhaps the dynamic evaluation methods offered in older, non-renewed ASTM test standards for measuring wall performance should be revived from the archives so that better evaluation is available. The true benefit

Refute Misinformation

Referencing DOE's EERE website one last time, it is important to reinforce a couple of points relating to building durable log structures. The website (http://www.energysavers.gov/your_home/designing_remodeling/index.cfm/mytopic=10190) again mixes inappropriate and incorrect bias with a recommendation that the log home industry would support.

> "Since trees absorb large amounts of water as they grow, the tree cells are also able to absorb water very readily after the wood has dried. For this reason, a log home is very hydroscopic—it can absorb water quickly. This promotes wood rot and insect infestation.
>
> It is strongly recommended that you protect the logs from any contact with any water or moisture. One moisture control method is to use only waterproofed and insecticide-treated logs. Reapply these treatments every few years for the life of the house.
>
> Generous roof overhangs, properly sized gutters and downspouts, and drainage plains around the house are also critical for moisture control."

The first statement sounds dramatic, but it is very misleading. Wood does not absorb moisture as fast as a paper towel or sponge. In fact, it only wicks water through end grain at the ends of each log or at knots. The change is not as dramatic as has been seen along the edges of some sheathing products that are exposed to rain. However, it is true that repeated wetting and drying will degrade exposed wood fiber that is not otherwise protected—like any wood siding.

The second statement is also a mix of fact and fiction. Yes, protect exterior wood from water or moisture just as we have for wood products in conventionally framed, sided and trimmed construction. This is not specific to log walls, nor is the recommendation for treatment of a protective exterior stain every few years. However, it is extremely misleading to recommend "only waterproofed and insecticide-treated logs." Does that refer to treatments applied at the point of production? Relatively few log components are available this way, and logs treated with borates during manufacture must have a exterior treatment—allowing water to contact the wood surface will promote leaching of the borate salts out of the wood.

That brings us to the third statement upon which all log building professionals agree. Just as with other forms of construction and as recommended by green building standards, moving water away from the structure is a high priority. In addition, design elements should be used that minimize the potential for water to splash back onto the log surfaces.

Instead of DOE's statement, the benefits of log walls should be remembered:

- Maintenance schedules and expenses are the same as for any natural wood siding on the exterior and paneling on the interior. It is recognized that maintenance is recommended, just like re-pointing a brick wall or cleaning and staining a cedar clapboard siding.
- Recognize the log wall as one that can be repaired without disturbing any other element of the building. The relative ease of repairing a section of log is less costly than remediating mold in a frame wall.

The Naysayers

To many in the building industry, log homes have a reputation for air leaks. This is one of the biggest misnomers about building with logs.

It is not denied that some log walls leak, even so severely that a wind through a joint can blow out a candle. However, several questions have to be asked and answered: 1.) What experience and training did the builder have? 2.) What was the design of the joinery and was settling accommodated? 3.) Were the logs graded? 4.) And what care and maintenance was applied by the occupant. Following good design practices and using experienced log builders, one should expect that log homes will achieve ENERGY STAR® 5-Star+ certifications. To those who have endured a log wall that the wind freely blows through, one should ask what they did to provide appropriate maintenance measures.

Another aspect of this discussion comes from the statistics of buildings demonstrating air leakage. When comparing wall technologies in the built inventory of homes across America, the odds are quite good that the mass wall systems show lower percentages than their contemporary frame wall construction. New construction of all methods and materials require the builder to be competent and detail-oriented.

The most common areas of air infiltration come from elements common to all dwelling construction and are not log home specific. According to research studies in both Canada and the US, a log home will provide equal or better energy efficiency when compared to a stick frame home provided it is designed and built per industry standard.

FINAL THOUGHTS

A few years ago, there were massive wildfires in the southern U.S. Rockies. It was great to hear the report that the Sierra Club was organizing an effort to assist in the effort to extinguish it. This is the type of true conservationism that needs to take place—where the love of the forests and its bounty teams up with the agricultural management of it.

When the oil embargoes of the 1970's heightened our awareness of our energy consumption, passive and active solar technologies expanded. Building performance was identified as an area we could address to reduce consumption of oil. Today, we use many byproducts from oil refining to build structures that conserve more energy. The "peak oil" concept[72] points to diminishing resources of all fossil fuels while noting that hydrogen, biodiesel, and ethanol are not viable alternatives because the level of energy invested into the process is likely to be more than returned by the fuel product. The National Academy of Sciences reported that fossil-fuel emissions produce enough greenhouse gases to contribute to a rise in atmospheric temperatures.

Our society once evolved using wood for fuel as well as shelter. Now we use wood for an amazing array of products. We manage this renewable resource so that lands that had been cleared of all timber now have renewed woodlands which are helping to reduce the single biggest contributor to greenhouse effects, carbon dioxide. We are intolerable of the past contributions of this resource because it cannot replace the economy provided by today's fuels. But what happens when those are gone? We can generate power from wind, tidal, solar and nuclear installations. Perhaps the all-electric house will return and play a bigger role nationwide.

If the climate changes drastically over the next hundred years, what buildings will be best suited to the adjustment? Will homes in Climate Zones 5-8 be built correctly to manage moisture migration in the wall? Log homes will not require modification to perform properly in the changing environment. Remember, we are told the mass wall impact is better in a warm climate than a cold one.

Despite many challenges, solid wood walls continue to be an excellent use of a renewable resource to build shelter for our populace that provides a warm, comfortable, and healthy environment.

Despite many challenges, solid wood walls continue to be an excellent use of a renewable resource to build shelter for our populace that provides a warm, comfortable, and healthy environment.

TABLE OF FIGURES

Reference Endnotes

The following are the endnotes of this document, but they also serve as an excellent collection of resources for further information.

1   Federal Research and Development Agenda for Net-Zero Energy, High Performance Green Buildings, National Science and Technology Council, Committee on Technology, Report of the Subcommittee on Buildings Technology Research and Development, October 2008

2   National Park Service, http://www.nps.gov/history/logcabin/html/restore.html

3   National Park Service, http://www.nps.gov/history/logcabin/html/mc.html

4   Building and Log Construction, United States Patent Office Patent 2,040,110, Carl Tahvonen and Royale A. Wright, Grayling, Mich., assignors to National Log Construction Co., Grayling, Mich., Patented May 12, 1936

5   Rosenfeld, Stuart A. and Swanson, Linda, "Prefabricated Log Homes and Complementary Products in Western Montana—Organization for Economic Cooperation and Development," February 2004, Regional Technology Strategies, 205 Lloyd Street, Suite 210, Carrboro, NC 27510 www.rtsinc.org

6   Rist, Curtis, U.S. Architecture: The Love and Lore of Log Cabins, This Old House magazine, http://www.thisoldhouse.com/toh/article/0, 198634,00.html#

7   Architecture in the Parks: A National Historic Landmark Theme Study, U.S. National Park Service, http://www.nps.gov/history/history/online_books/harrison/index.htm

8   The Northeast Entrance Station of Yellowstone National Park, National Park Service, Architecture in the Parks: A National Historic Landmark Theme Study

9   Log Home Living 2007 Annual Buyer's Guide, Active Interest Media, 425 Lafayette Center Drive, Suite 100, Chantilly, VA 20151

10 Techline GR-1, "Structural Grading of Logs from Small-Diameter Trees", Issued 03/04, Forest Products Laboratory, Engineering Properties of Wood, One Gifford Pinchot Dr., Madison, WI 53726-2398, 608-231-9200, 608-231-9592 (fax), mailroom_forest_products_laboratory@fs.fed.us, www.fpl.fs.fed.us

11 Backus, Perry, Ravalli Republic, Hamilton, MT http://ravallirepublic.com/business/article_5c2a5e44-0035-11e1-ad8f-001cc4c03286.html#ixzz1c4gzykyo, 10-26-11

12 Ritter, Michael A.; Skog, Kenneth E.; Bergman, Richard, *"Science Supporting the Economic and Environmental Benefits of Using Wood and Wood Products in Green Building Construction: The use of wood as a building material can provide substantial economic and environmental benefits to our nation's citizens"*, USDA Forest Service

13 JLCOnline In the News, July 08, 2009, http://www.jlconline.com/cgi-bin/jlconline.

storefront/EN/UserTemplate/82?c=4fda09b24a2e483d129184f3f6e6cd50#Bark

14 Certification Criteria Document CCD 016, Environmental Choice^M Program, First published June 1997, updated March 2005, http://www.terrachoice.com/

15 "Western Lumber: The Original Green Building Product", 0207-1/02-08, Western Wood Products Association, 522 SW Fifth Ave., Suite 500, Portland, Oregon 97204, www.wwpa.org

16 ECO magazine, "Wood—another low carbon footprint solution", adapted excerpt from the A3P (Australian Plantation Products and Paper Industry) Sustainability Action Plan, the development of which is being assisted by Philip Toyne (EcoFutures Ltd), with research and contributions from Michael H Smith and Karlson 'Charlie' Hargroves (The Natural Edge Project). CSIRO PUBLISHING, PO Box 1139, (150 Oxford Street), Collingwood Victoria 3066, Australia

17 Ximenes, F.A. et al., The decomposition of wood products in landfills in Sydney, Australia, Waste Management (2008), doi:10.1016/j.wasman.2007.11.006

18 Heath, Linda S.; Maltby Van; Miner, Reid; Skog, Kenneth E.; and Upton, Brad, "Greenhouse Gas and Carbon Profile of the U.S. Forest Products Industry Value Chain", U.S. Department of Agriculture, Forest Service, Northern Research Station, Durham, New Hampshire, National Council for Air and Stream Improvement, Inc., Raleigh, North Carolina, and U.S. Department of Agriculture, Forest Service, Forest Products Laboratory, Madison, Wisconsin. Received September 10, 2009. Revised manuscript received February 17, 2010. Accepted March 11, 2010.

19 U.S. Forests and Carbon: Some Important Facts, Climate Change Advisor's Office, USDA Forest Service

20 Ritter, Michael A.; Skog, Kenneth E.; Bergman, Richard, "Science Supporting the Economic and Environmental Benefits of Using Wood and Wood Products in Green Building Construction: The use of wood as a building material can provide substantial economic and environmental benefits to our nation's citizens", USDA Forest Service

21 Heath, Linda S.; Maltby Van; Miner, Reid; Skog, Kenneth E.; and Upton, Brad, "Greenhouse Gas and Carbon Profile of the U.S. Forest Products Industry Value Chain", U.S. Department of Agriculture, Forest Service, Northern Research Station, Durham, New Hampshire, National Council for Air and Stream Improvement, Inc., Raleigh, North Carolina, and U.S. Department of Agriculture, Forest Service, Forest Products Laboratory, Madison, Wisconsin. Received September 10, 2009. Revised manuscript received February 17, 2010. Accepted March 11, 2010.

22 Moosehead Cedar Log Homes Verification Letter of a standard materials package, http://www.mclh.net/news-events.html, http://www.mclh.net/PDFs/NAHB-letter.pdf

23 Howard, Bion D.; ed. Pickett, Rob, 2003. "The Energy Performance of Log Homes, Documented Energy-efficiency and Thermal Mass Benefits", Log Homes Council, National Association of Home Builders, Washington, DC

24 Nation's Building News Online for November 24, 2008, http://www.nbnnews.com/NBN/textonly/2008-11-24/Building+Systems/index.html

25 Goodall, Harrison; Freidman, Renee, 1980. "Log Structures: Preservation and Problem-Solving", The American Association for State and Local History, Nashville, TN

26 A. Karagiozis, H. Künzel and A Holm, WUFI-ORNL/IBP—A North American hygrothermal model, Proceedings of Performance of Exterior Envelopes of Whole Buildings VIII, December 2-7, 2001. ASHRAE, Atlanta, US

27 Concrete Homes Technology Brief #7, Portland Cement Association, Skokie, IL www.cement.org

28 References regarding insects and log homes:
- Palmere, Vincent R.; ed. Murray, Barbara, 2002. "LOG TECH NOTE 02-01: Controlling Carpenter Bees". Technical Committee of the Log Homes Council, Building Systems Councils, National Association of Home Builders, Washington, DC.
- Palmere, Vincent R.; ed. Pickett, Rob, 2003. "LOG TECH NOTE 03-02: Termite Prevention and Control". Technical Committee of the Log Homes Council, Building Systems Councils, National Association of Home Builders, Washington, DC.

29 "The Log Homes Council Log Grading Program Rules, Training & Operations Manual, prepared by the Log Grading Committee of the Log Homes Council, Building Systems Councils, National Association of Home Builders, Washington, DC 2010 v. 7-1-10.

30 References regarding maintenance and inspection of log homes:
- Allen, J. Frederick, Director; "Log Home Construction and Maintenance Tips: How to Prevent Decay and Insects," Georgia Forestry Commission, Feb. 2001
- Bomberger, Bruce D., Preservation Brief 26: "The Preservation and Repair of Historic Log Buildings," National Park Service, U.S. Dept. of the Interior, http://www.nps.gov/history/hps/tps/briefs/brief26.htm
- Dunston, Rich, Founder and President Perma-Chink Systems, Inc., Knoxville, TN; "Do it Right the First Time with LifeLine Ultra", product brochure, www.permachink.com.
- "Protecting and Finishing Log Buildings: A Wood Protection Fact Sheet," Forintek Canada Corp., Sept. 2003
- "Home Buyers/Owners Guide to Log Homes." 2003, InspectAPedia.com, http://inspectapedia.com/structure/Log_Home_Guide.htm#bannertop
- International Association of Certified Home Inspectors, 1750 30th Street, Boulder, CO 80301, http://www.nachi.org/inspecting-log-homes.htm
- "The Preservation & Maintenance of Log Structures", 2000, Rev'd. 2003 Technical Committee of the Log Homes Council, National Association of Home Builders, Washington, DC
- Sashco, Inc., "Zero Failures Reference Guide," part of the Zero Failures Seminar for Professional Contractor Training, 2009, Brighton, CO, www.sashco.com.

31 Architecture in the Parks—A National Historic Landmark Theme Study, an On-Line Book from the National Park Service, U.S. Dept. of the Interior; http://www.nps.gov/history/history/online_books/harrison/harrisont.htm

32 Taylor, Z Todd, Pacific Northwest National Laboratory, todd.taylor@pnl.gov, "An

Update on the Status of the IECC/IRC -or- What the RICC Means to Me," presented July 21, 2004 to the National Workshop on State Building Energy Codes.

33 Building Energy Code Resource Guide: Air Leakage Guide, 9/2011, Prepared by DOE Building Energy Codes Program (BECP) for the U.S. Department of Energy under Contract DE-AC05-76RLO 1830

34 Source: http://resourcecenter.pnl.gov/cocoon/morf/ResourceCenter/article//1563

35 Swinton, M.C., "Life Cycle Costing of Log Walls for the National Energy Code for Houses", A-3107.1, National Research Council of Canada, January 5, 1996.

36 Gorman, Thomas M. Ph.D. Associate Professor, University of Idaho, Moscow, ID. "The Thermal Performance of Log Homes Walls," Fall 1995 issue of Wood Design Focus

37 Burch, D.M.; D.F. Krintz; R.S. Spain. 1982. "A Field study of the effect of wall mass on the Heating and cooling loads of residential buildings." Proc. Thermal Mass Effects in Buildings Conference, ORNL, Oak Ridge TN

38 Burch, D.M.; D.F. Krintz; R.S. Spain. 1984. "The Effect of Wall Mass on Winter Heating Loads and Indoor Comfort—An Experimental Study." ASHRAE Transactions. V-90.Pt-1. American Society of Heating, Refrigerating, and Air-conditioning Engineers, Atlanta, GA

39 Burch, D M; K L Davis; S A Malcolm. 1984, "The Effect of Wall Mass on the Summer Space Cooling of Six Test Buildings" ASHRAE Trans. V.90—Pt 2. American Society of Heating, Refrigerating, and Air-conditioning Engineers, Atlanta, GA

40 Burch, D M; W L Johns; T Jacobsen; G N Walton; C P Reeve. 1984, "The Effect of Thermal Mass on Night Temperature Setback Savings," ASHRAE Trans. V.90—Pt 2. American Society of Heating, Refrigerating, and Air-conditioning Engineers, Atlanta, GA

41 Robertson, David K 1984. "Observation and Prediction of the Heating Season Thermal Mass Effect for Eight Test Buildings With and Without Windows." US DOE Thermal Mass Program Phase II. NM ERDI, University of New Mexico Albuquerque, NM.

42 Energy Related Performance Testing of Minnesota Log Homes, June 1990, Minnesota Department of Public Service, Energy Division, Prepared by Stephen R. Klossner, Advanced Certified Thermography, Lakeland Minnesota

43 Bellamy, Larry; Mackenzie, Don, 10/2007, "Simulation analysis of the energy performance and humidity of solid wood and light timber frame homes", Ensys Ltd, 3 Prebblewood Drive, Prebbleton 7604, New Zealand

44 Howard, Bion D., 2001, Building Environmental Science & Technology (www.energybuilder.com), "Log Homes Thermal Mass and Energy Efficiency: Assessment of Energy Efficiency Calculations and Ratings of Log Homes Compared to Other Residential Wall Structural Systems"; contractor report to NAHB Log Homes Council.

45 ENERGY STAR, http://www.energystar.gov/index.cfm?c=new_bldg_design.new_bldg_design_guidance

46 Yost, Harry, October/November 1991, "Log Home Insulation Saves Energy," Mother Earth News magazine, http://www.

motherearthnews.com/do-it-yourself/ log-home-insulation.aspx. *Reprinted from Home Insulation: Do It Yourself & Save As Much As 40% (Storey Communications).*

47 ICC 400-2007 American National Standard, Standard on the Design and Construction of Log Structures, International Code Council 500 New Jersey Avenue, NW, 6th Floor, Washington, D.C. 20001 © 2007

48 Gen. Tech. Rep. FPL-GTR-Wood handbook—Wood as an engineering material; U.S. Department of Agriculture, Forest Service, Forest Products Laboratory, 113 Madison, WI, 1999, 463 p.

49 2004 Log Home Production & Construction Report, Log Home Living Institute Inc., 4125 Lafayette Center Drive, Suite 100, Chantilly, VA 20151

50 Log grading references:
- Burke, Edwin J., Ph.D; Pickett, Rob 2008. "LOG TECH NOTE 08-01: LHC Log Grading Program". Technical & Grading Committees of the Log Homes Council, Building Systems Councils, National Association of Home Builders, Washington, DC.
- Burke, Edwin J. Ph.D., 3/2006. "Visual Stress Grading Logs and Timbers Used in Log Structures,", Forest Products Society STRUCTURE magazine
- Burke, Edwin J. Ph.D., 10/2006. "Making the Grade ENSURING THAT YOUR LOGS PASS THEIR FINAL EXAM". Log Homes Illustrated magazine.

51 Log moisture content references:
- Burke, Edwin J. Ph.D., 3/2007. "Drying Time STABILITY IS THE AIM OF DIFFERENT METHODS", Log Homes Illustrated magazine.
- Burke, Edwin J. Ph.D., 11/2006. "Weighty Matters ALL YOU NEED TO KNOW ABOUT THE WATER IN WOOD", Log Homes Illustrated magazine.

52 Panshin, A.J., and de Zeeuw, Carl; 1980. "Textbook of Wood Technology: Structure, Identification, Properties, and Uses of the Commercial Woods of the United States and Canada", Fourth Edition; McGraw-Hill, Inc., NY, NY.

53 TimberLogic is a collection of analysis tools created by Rob Pickett, RobPickett &Associates, LLC and Alex Charvat, P.E., Alexander Structures, LLC. TimberLogic Reports include the Log Wall Performance Estimator and Span Tables Reports. Each is customized to proprietary building components and systems. www. timberlogic.com.

54 References on fastening wall-logs:
- Charvat, Alex P.E., 5/2008. "HOLD EVERYTHING Fasteners Help Logs Combat Enemy Forces", Log Homes Illustrated magazine.
- Charvat, Alex P.E., 4/2008. "TIGHTEN UP Fasteners Turn Logs Into Walls", Log Homes Illustrated magazine.
- Feb. & Mar. 2004. "LOG FASTENING SOLUTIONS Everything you need to know about the fasteners that hold your logs together", Log Home Design Ideas magazine.
- Moffatt, Bill; Pickett, Rob. 2003. "LOG TECH NOTE 02-02: Fasteners for Log Homes", Technical Committee of the Log Homes Council, Building Systems Councils, National Association of Home Builders, Washington, DC.

55 References on fire resistance:
- Pickett, Rob ed.; 2001, 2002, 2003, 2008. "Fire Performance of Log Walls", Technical Committee of the Log Homes Council, Building Systems Councils,

National Association of Home Builders, Washington, DC.

- Houdek, Dalibor; Bahyl, Vladimer; 8/2001 "Fire Resistance of Handcrafted Log Walls", Journal of Fire Protection Engineering, Society of Fire Protection Engineers
- "Analytical Methods for Determining Fire Resistance of Timber Members", Robert H. White, The SFPE handbook of fire protection engineering. 2d ed., Boston, MA: Society of Fire Protection Engineers: 4-217-4-229; 1995. Chapter 11.

[56] Kuhns, Michael; Daniels, Barbara, "Firewise Landscaping for Utah", Cooperative Extension Service, Utah State University, July 2005, www.forestry.usu.edu

[57] Cushman, Ted., *Surviving Wildfire*, The Journal of Light Construction, April 2008, Hanley-Wood.

[58] Reference on settling in log walls:
- Charvat, Alex P.E., 4/2007. "Honey, I Shrunk the Logs UNDERSTANDING AND DEALING WITH SETTLEMENT", Log Homes Illustrated magazine.

[59] Pickett, Rob ed.; Peebles, Paul; Summons, Wayne; 2004. "Prevention of Air & Water Infiltration", Technical Committee of the Log Homes Council, Building Systems Councils, National Association of Home Builders, Washington, DC.

[60] *ENERGY STAR Qualified Homes, Version 3 (Rev. 04) Inspection Checklists for National Program Requirements*, Effective for homes permitted starting 10/1/2011 Revised 8/29/2011, ENERGY STAR is a joint program of the U.S. Environmental Protection Agency and the U.S. Department of Energy; http://www.energystar.gov/index.cfm?c=bldrs_lenders_raters.nh_v3_guidelines.

[61] A. Karagiozis, H. Künzel and A Holm, WUFI-ORNL/IBP—A North American hygrothermal model, Proceedings of Performance of Exterior Envelopes of Whole Buildings VIII, December 2-7, 2001. ASHRAE, Atlanta, US

[62] Hameury, Stéphane "The Hygrothermal Inertia of Massive Timber Constructions," 2006 Doctoral Thesis, KTH, Royal Institute of Technology, School of Architecture and the Built Environment, Dept. of Civil and Architectural Engineering, Div. of Building Materials, SE-100 44 Stockholm, Sweden

[63] Ferguson, W. J., Turner, I. W., "A comparison of the finite element and control volume numerical solution techniques applied to timber drying problems below the boiling point", International Journal for Numerical Methods in Engineering, Vol. 38, Issue 3, 1995 John Wiley & Sons, Ltd. http://dx.doi.org/10.1002/nme.1620380307

[64] Wood Handbook: Wood as an Engineering Material; 4/2010, United States Department of Agriculture, Forest Service, Forest Products Laboratory, General Technical Report FPL-GTR-190, Madison, WI

[65] DOE / USDA-21697/ 1, ORNL / Sub / 87-21697 / 1—"Thermal Properties of Wood Panel Products Buildings Wood and for Use in Buildings," Anton TenWolde, J. Dobbin McNatt, and Lorraine Krahn; Part of The National Program for Building Thermal Envelope Systems and Materials, Prepared for the U.S. Department of Energy, Conservation and Renewable Energy, Office of Buildings and Community Systems, Building Systems Division, Sept. 1988.

[66] Sashco S-R Graphic #1, Sashco's Start-Right Log Home Finishing System, ©Sashco Inc. 2003

67 Showalter, John P.E.; Pickett, Rob; 3/2006. "ICC Standard on Log Construction," Codes and Standards column, STRUCTURE magazine.

68 Lateral Loading References:
- Leichti, Robert; Scott, Randy; Miller, Thomas, "Lateral Resistance of Log Walls and Foundation Anchorage", Wood Design Focus, Spring 2004.
- Hahney, Tom, "How Log Buildings Resist Lateral Loads", ILBA Log Building News, No. 32, October 2000.
- Popovski, Dr. Marjan, "Testing of Lateral Resistance of Handcrafted Log Walls Phase I and II, Forintek Canada Corp., Vancouver, BC March 2002

69 Houdek, Dalibor, The Illustrated Guide to Log Home Construction, From Log Shell to Finished Home, FPInnovations, 2010 www.fpinnovations.ca

70 Pickett, Rob. 2003, Rev. 2004. "LOG TECH NOTE 03-01: Sound Transmission & Log Walls", Technical Committee of the Log Homes Council, Building Systems Councils, National Association of Home Builders, Washington, DC.

71 Fell, David, March/April issue of Woodworking magazine p.25, www.woodworkingcanada.com.

72 Atlee, Jennifer and Melton, Paula, "The Product Transparency Movement, Peeking Behind the Corporate Veil", Environmental Building News, Volume 21, Number 1, Jan. 2012, a publication of BuildingGreen, Inc. www.buildinggreen.com

73 Grubb, Adam, "Peak Oil Primer", published at http://www.energybulletin.net/primer.php, Energy Bulletin is a program of Post Carbon Institute, a nonprofit organization dedicated to helping the world transition away from fossil fuels and build sustainable, resilient communities.